WITHDRAWN

American Log Buildings

American Log Buildings
An Old World Heritage

Terry G. Jordan

The University of North Carolina Press
Chapel Hill and London

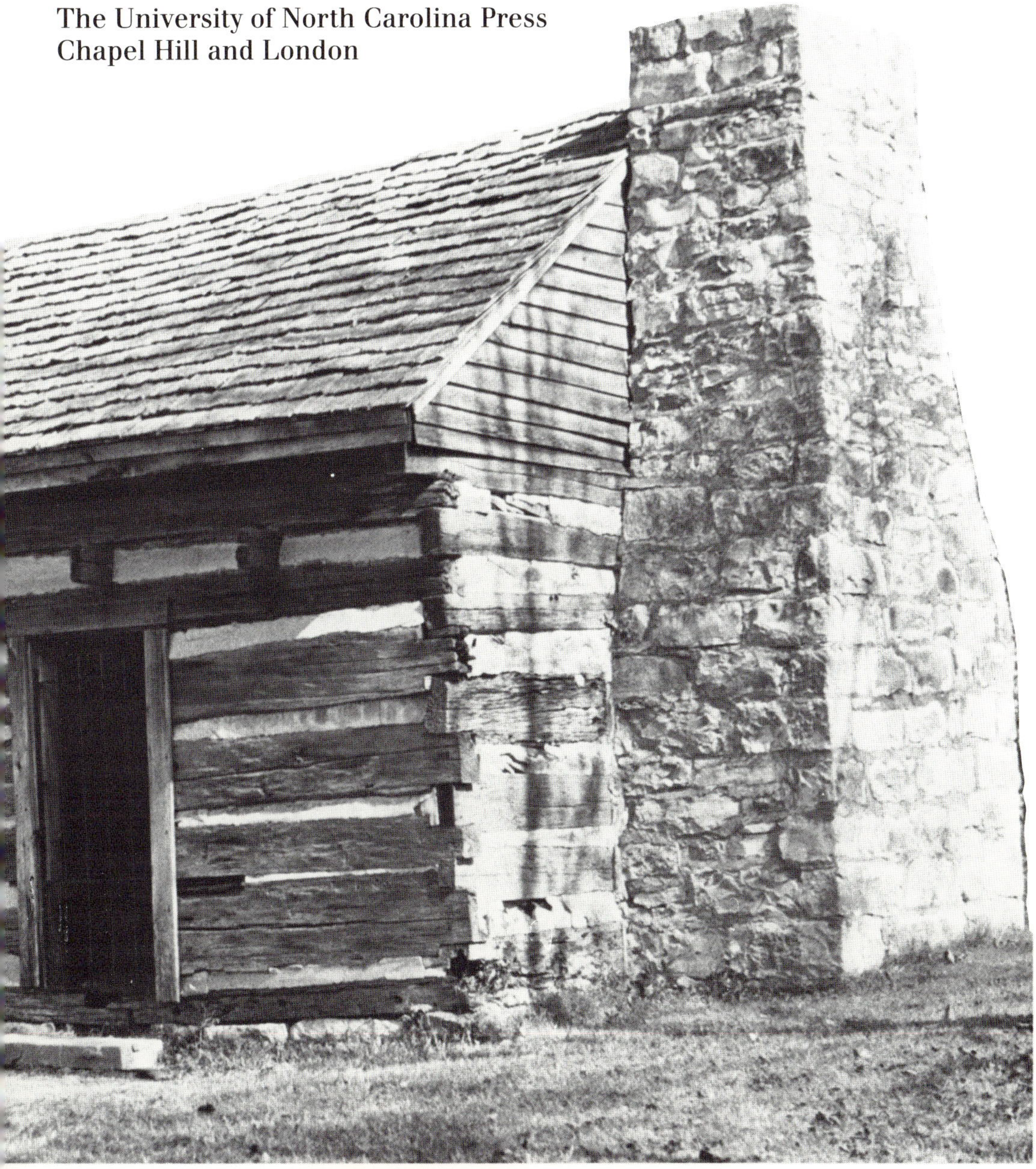

© 1985 The University of North Carolina Press
All rights reserved
Manufactured in the United States of America

Library of Congress Cataloging in
Publication Data

Jordan, Terry G.
  American log buildings.

  Bibliography: p.
  Includes index.
  1. Log buildings—United States. I. Title.
TH4840.J67   694′.2   84-5169
ISBN 0-8078-1617-5

Designed by Naomi P. Slifkin

To Dr. Jean Andrews Smith
and Mr. C. B. Smith, Sr.

Friends, benefactors, patrons

Contents

Preface, ix

One
Log Construction in
American Culture, 3

Two
Midland American Log
Construction, 14

Three
Northern Europe, 41

Four
The Alps and
Southwestern Germany, 86

Five
The German-Slavic
Borderland, 116

Six
Conclusion, 146

Notes, 157

Bibliography, 171

Index, 187

Preface

Log construction and architecture occupy a special place in American pioneer iconography. In common with most elements of traditional culture in the United States, building with notched logs has Old World origins, and my purpose in preparing the present study was to investigate, largely through field research, the European roots of our log architecture and at the same time to seek to identify the processes at work in the evolution of American colonial culture.

The potential source regions for log carpentry lie in central and northern Europe, in the lands bordering the Baltic Sea and in several German-speaking provinces. In four seasons of field research there, I devoted the summer of 1978 to the Alps and southwestern Germany, the mercifully mild winter of 1980–81 to southern Finland and Soviet Karelia, June and July of 1981 to Sweden and Norway, and the summer of 1982 to the German-Slavic borderland in Silesia, Saxony, Bohemia, and Moravia—today divided among Poland, Czechoslovakia, and the German Democratic Republic.

In addition, certain floor-plan types common in American log architecture are believed to be of British origin, introduced in colonial times mainly by English and Scotch-Irish immigrants. Accordingly, I spent an additional field season, the summer of 1974, in Great Britain and Ireland.

During the five field seasons, I inspected hundreds of folk buildings in the European countryside, visited over thirty open-air folk museums containing restored vernacular structures, and used collections in the major ethnographic museums at Prague, Leningrad, Stockholm, and Innsbruck. The European field research was funded by a number of grants, most notably from the National Endowment for the Humanities (number RO-20039-81-1673), covering the period 1 June 1981 through 31 December 1982. Addtional overseas field research grants were provided by the Faculty Research Committee of North Texas State University, Denton, including number 34240 in the summer of 1978, 34241 in 1980–81, and 34232 in the summer of 1982. On a trip supported by an earlier field research grant from that committee on an unrelated topic in 1971, I first learned of the presence of American-like log buildings in the Alps.

Nor was domestic field research lacking. On thirteen different excursions through the eastern and central United States between 1973 and 1983, I inspected vernacular buildings in Louisiana, Oklahoma, Arkansas, Missouri, Iowa, and every state east of the Mississippi except Maine and Florida. These excursions were funded by North Texas State University, the University of Tennessee at Knoxville, the Oklahoma Historical Society, and the Walter Prescott Webb Chair of History and Ideas endowment at the University of Texas, Austin. Funds for data processing, photography, and cartography were also provided from the operating budget of the Webb Chair, with the approval of the dean of the College of Liberal Arts of the University of Texas.

I am indebted to Kaj Long for arranging an unusual midwinter visit to the Seurasaari open-air museum in Helsinki and to Riitta Ailonen, curator, Museovirasto, Finnish National Board of Antiquities and Historical Monuments, for escorting our inspection of that museum. I am also indebted to Dr. Richard H. Hulan of Washington, D.C., for sharing his extensive knowledge concerning the Swedes and Finns in colonial America. Dr. Milan Reban of North Texas State University was most helpful in matters pertaining to the Czech language and culture.

Professor John B. Rehder of the University of Tennessee, Catherine W. Bishir of Raleigh, and T. H. Pearce of Franklinton, North Carolina, accompanied me on field excursions, providing both good company and valuable insights about the log architecture of their regions.

Robert Ensminger of Kutztown State College in Pennsylvania; Claire Conway, secretary of the Schwenkfelder Library Corporation; Francis E. Abernethy of Stephen F. Austin State University; Catherine W. Bishir of the North Carolina State Division of Archives and History; Florence Eney of the Moravian Museums of Bethlehem; the Nordiska Museet of Stockholm all provided permissions to use certain photographs taken by them or copyrighted in their name. To each I am most grateful.

Preliminary versions of three of the chapters in this book appeared in articles in the *Annals of the Association of American Geographers*; the *Geographical Review*, published by the American Geographical Society; and *Pennsylvania Folklife*, published by the Pennsylvania Folklife Society. I am grateful to the editors and directors of those journals and societies for permitting the articles to appear in this book in revised form.

Without the help of these diverse individuals and institutions, the present study would have been impossible or seriously weakened, but any errors of fact or interpretation which might appear in this work are solely my responsibility.

American Log Buildings

One
Log Construction in American Culture

Folk architecture, reflecting the ancestral memories and handiwork of common people, constitutes a highly revealing aspect of culture. Owing nothing to the creative genius and blueprints of professional architects, folk buildings represent tradition, demonstrate diffusion, and offer a key to regionalism.[1] Protected by the highly conservative nature of folk culture, style changes little from one generation to the next, and elements of architectural form often survive the overseas migrations of their builders largely intact. The dimension of variation for folk architecture is largely spatial rather than temporal, and the observant traveler recognizes the role such buildings play in providing a unique character or essence for each province and district. Regardless of their function—dwelling, barn, church, or stable—these traditional structures are vivid expressions of people and place.

August Meitzen, one of the earliest students of vernacular buildings, sensed this potent symbolism, describing the folk dwelling as "the embodiment of a people's soul."[2] Edwin Brumbaugh, concurring, went so far as to say that traditional architecture was a statement of "all that is really worth telling about a people."[3] The present volume represents an attempt to learn from one particular type of folk architecture—log construction—something about the formation and evolution of colonial American culture, about the transplanting, merging, and modification of European ways of life in the New World setting. The study is based in the belief that Meitzen and Brumbaugh were correct, that old buildings do bear worthwhile messages and provide useful insights.

Log buildings became fitting sym-

Figure 1.1. "Honesty, integrity, and self-sufficient simplicity"—pioneer log cabin in northern Texas. (Reproduced from Paddock, *Twentieth Century History and Biographical Record*, vol. 1, pp. 310–11.)

bols of the settlement of America's forested east. In the course of attaining a widespread diffusion, log architecture and its related carpentry tradition became firmly enmeshed in the pioneer lifestyle, society, legend, and politics of the American heartland. With the advent of Jacksonian democracy, birth in a log cabin became desirable and even necessary for aspirants to the presidency.[4] Following the decline of log housing in later times, these humble structures came to represent the romanticized preindustrial age, to epitomize the "honesty, integrity, and self-sufficient simplicity" that we of the city nostalgically associate with the era of initial land colonization (Figure 1.1).[5]

Given the far-flung distribution and iconlike symbolism, it is small wonder that log construction attracted the attention of many students of Americana, in particular cultural geographers, historians, folklorists, and anthropologists.[6] In part, this book constitutes a summary of the major findings of these diverse scholars, but, more important, in describing American log culture and tracing its roots to Europe, it seeks to test several previously held concepts concerning the development of American culture.

Four Concepts

The transferal of European culture to overseas colonial areas has commanded multidisciplinary attention.

From decades of research one can distill four hypotheses which, taken together, purport to explain what happened culturally in the American colonies in the formative period between 1600 and 1775, the period when our national character took shape. These four concepts we can call first effective settlement, colonial cultural simplification, syncretism, and cultural preadaptation.

The doctrine of first effective settlement, proposed in 1973 by cultural geographer Wilbur Zelinsky, holds that "the first group able to establish a viable, self-perpetuating society in an empty land are of crucial significance for the later social and cultural geography of the area," regardless of how small the initial group of settlers may have been.[7] A decade earlier, geographer Fred B. Kniffen had presented the very similar concept of "initial occupance," an expression of his belief that the first postpioneer, permanent settlement imprint in the backcountry sections of the wooded eastern United States was "long lasting, surviving even where a new ethnic stock . . . succeeded the original settlers."[8] We should, then, look to the early successful colonies if we wish to understand the regional cultures of the United States, even if much larger numbers of persons of different ethnic backgrounds arrived later and acquired majority status in the population. For example, New England, in this view, owes more culturally to the relative handful of seventeenth-century English Calvinists than to the masses of Irish, Italian, and French-Canadian Catholics who arrived after 1840.

Geographer R. C. Harris expressed the second concept, colonial cultural simplification, succinctly when he proposed, in 1977, that "Europeans established overseas drastically simplified versions of European society."[9] The same idea earlier found expression in the work of anthropologist George M. Foster, who, referring to Latin America, suggested that colonial cultural forms were less numerous and varied than those of the Iberian homeland.[10] Louis Hartz also found cultures transplanted overseas to be mere fragments of the European model.[11]

The causes of colonial cultural simplification remain in dispute. Harris and Foster argued that, while considerable Old World diversity was implanted in the colonial regions, strong selective frontier pressures acted to reduce the complexity. Hartz, on the other hand, maintained that only selected European cultural elements were transferred overseas, that simplification occurred at the point of departure. He observed that the individual colonial realms received migrants from selected regions during a limited time period. Only spatial and temporal fragments of Europe diffused overseas. One of the few architectural studies to address the issue of simplification was Dell Upton's work on colonial Virginia, and his conclusion supported the Harris-Foster position. "While the first emigrants to Virginia built a wide variety of traditional English house plans," Upton wrote, "a process of social winnowing" reduced the diversity substantially by 1700 and produced the "characteristic Virginia vernacular house forms."[12]

A corollary of the simplification process is a lack of inventiveness by the overseas Europeans. As Zelinsky suggested, the settlement frontier, "despite the stubborn romantic inclination to believe otherwise," cannot in truth "be credited with the origination of any important inventions, material or otherwise."[13] In this view, rather than call forth creative genius to cope with the new setting and the demands of pioneer life, the frontier experience served merely to reduce, through pragmatic selection, the imported European diversity and complexity. Overseas cultures, isolated from mother Europe, lose "the stimulus toward change that the whole provides" and become simplified fossils.[14] This being so, a study of the roots of traditional American culture becomes, necessarily, diffusionist. That is, if innovation provides few, if any, answers in the interpretation of the overseas Europeans, then we must look to Europe itself as the source of the colonial cultures.

The concept of syncretism is closely tied to simplification. Sometimes referred to with the term "melting pot," syncretism represents the belief that American and other colonial cultures result from a blending of several Old World traditions, sometimes further complicated by absorption of selected traits from indigenous peoples. The funerary culture of the American Deep South, for example, has been interpreted as an amalgamation of British, African, and American Indian traits, while the cattle-ranching culture of the Great Plains has been attributed to a blending of Hispanic, British, and African cultures.[15] Syncretism also implies simplification. Few of the European regional cultures thrown together in colonial America had enough practitioners to survive, perhaps causing the numerous local immigrant cultures to collapse into only several.[16] The cultural items most likely to survive such mixing are those known in at least proximate form to two or more of the constituent groups before their merging.

Syncretism, its proponents believe, operates both through acculturation, during which the constituent groups retain ethnic identities while exchanging traits, and through assimilation, in which identities are lost, perhaps most often because of intermarriage, a process possibly more common in the backcountry than on the seaboard. In this view, the American differs from the European in part because a colonial juxtaposition caused, for example, German to be neighbor to Finn, Switzer to Swede, or Dutch to Scotch-Irishman, permitting blendings impossible or unlikely in Europe. If Zelinsky is correct, then the first effective colonizers contribute disproportionately to the mixture.

From biology through anthropology came the concept of cultural preadaptation, also first applied to geography by Zelinsky in his survey study of the United States.[17] As defined by cultural geographer Milton Newton, cultural preadaptation involves a trait or traits possessed before migration by a group that give it "competitive advantage in occupying a new environment."[18] As Zelinsky suggested, the favored traits might have been marginal, relict, latent, or even condemned in the European homeland, but in the colonial setting they proved to be valuable for survival and facilitated a successful occupation.[19] Both Zelinsky and Newton felt that cultural preadaptation helped explain the evolution of early American culture, and Newton suggested that between 1725 and 1775 in the backcountry of the colonies, from southern Pennsylvania to the Georgia Piedmont, a culture was shaped consisting of traits preadapted to successful pioneering.[20]

Preadaptation, without question, has Turnerian overtones. Historian Frederick Jackson Turner first proposed almost a century ago that the frontier experience made Americans out of

Log Construction in American Culture

Europeans, that the process of occupying a new land and wresting it from Indian and wilderness produced a new society and culture.[21] The "competitive advantage" of preadapted traits, in the Turnerian view, derives in the main from their suitability to frontier conditions.

This study attempts to evaluate these four concepts in the light of one particular type of folk architecture and one colonial culture. The particular variety of log construction under study is linked to the Middle Atlantic colonies, especially Pennsylvania. From a presumed hearth area in the Delaware Valley, this style spread with the yeoman farmer frontier and eventually dominated a large wedge of territory broadening to the west from its Pennsylvanian apex, extending as far as the Great Plains (Figure 1.2).[22] Its domain is often referred to as the Midland culture area. On the southern perimeter of this wedge, Midland-inspired log houses stood within sight of the Gulf of Mexico in Texas, while others of similar origin were erected as far north as Iowa, Michigan, and southern Ontario. Eventually, bearers of Midland American construction techniques crossed the Great Plains to implant the tradition in parts of the mountain West and even Mexico.[23]

Omitted from the study will be the distinctive log construction traditions of the Russians in Alaska, the Hispanics in the highlands of the American Southwest and Mexico, the Ukrainians in the Canadian prairie provinces, and the French Canadians in Québec and the western fur trading frontier.[24] Worthy as these traditions are, they possess no relevance to the evolution of colonial culture and architecture in the eastern United States. Nor is attention devoted to the log buildings identified with small parts of colonial New England, since their carpentry differs fundamentally from that of Midland America and clearly reflects another style and origin.[25] Also largely omitted from consideration is the log building tradition of the Upper Midwest, implanted in the late nineteenth and early twentieth centuries by Finns and Scandinavians.[26] These latter-day Fenno-Scandian immigrants came to America two and one-half centuries after their Delaware Valley ethnic kin and derived in the main from different provinces. Their log architecture was more refined and is only marginally comparable with styles prevailing in northern Europe a quarter millennium earlier.

Central to this evaluation of the four concepts is a study of diffusion of log construction from Europe to colonial Midland America, a diffusion that has been the subject of considerable academic controversy over the years. Three different theses of origin have been proposed.

Three Theses of Origin

The potential agents of diffusion include (1) northern Europeans, mainly Swedes and Finns from central Sweden, who colonized the Delaware Valley beginning in the 1630s; (2) German-speaking Moravians and Schwenkfelders, who came to Pennsylvania and several other colonies from the Czech–Polish–East German borderland in the middle of the eighteenth century; and (3) German-speaking Lutherans, Swiss Reformed, and Mennonites, who emigrated from Alpine and Alemannic regions of southern central Europe beginning about 1710 (Figure 1.3). The debate, for the most part, has been between proponents of

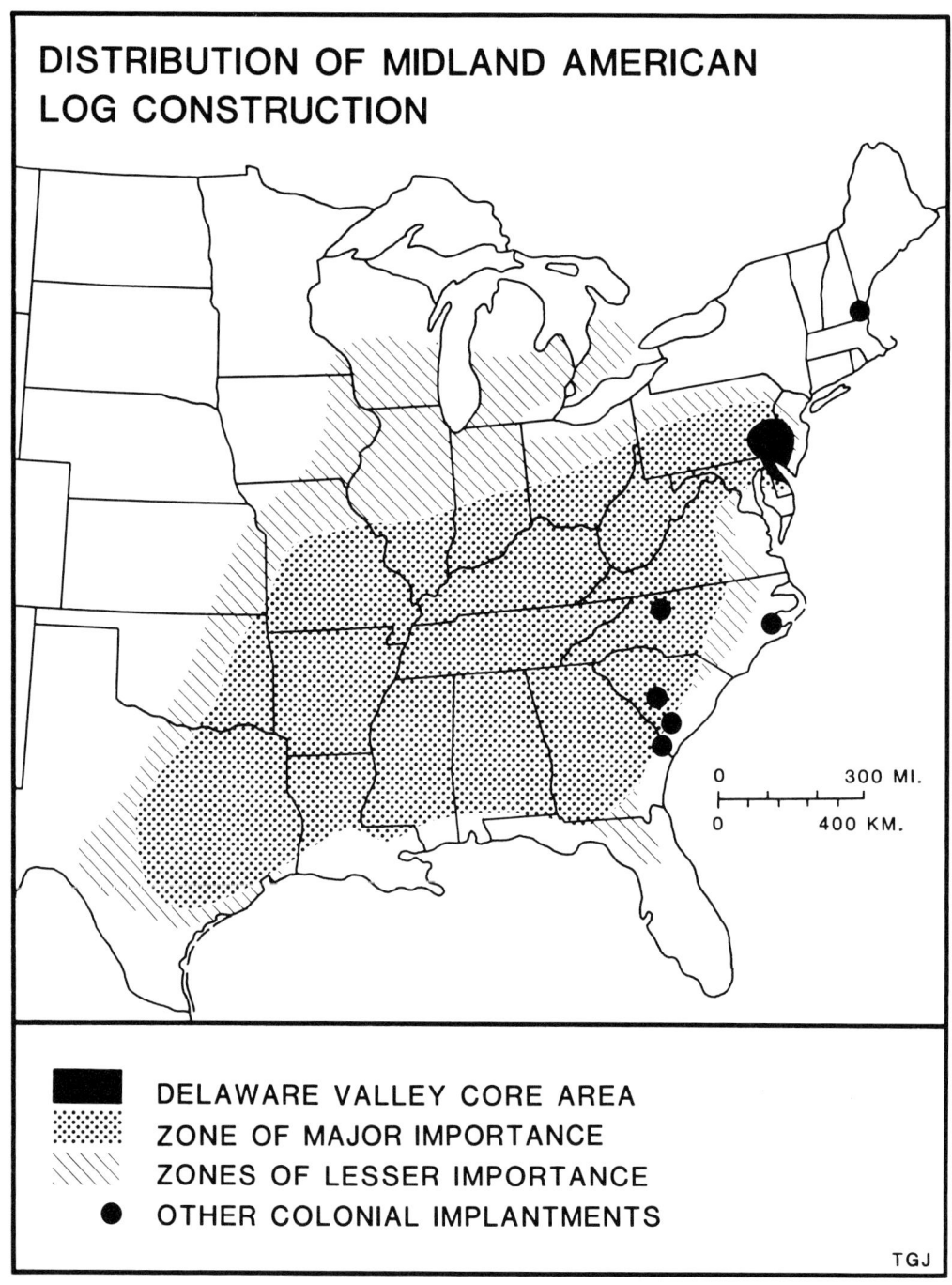

Figure 1.2. Midland log construction appears in most of the eastern half of the United States. It was also implanted in much of the Rocky Mountains, Pacific Northwest, and even northern Mexico.

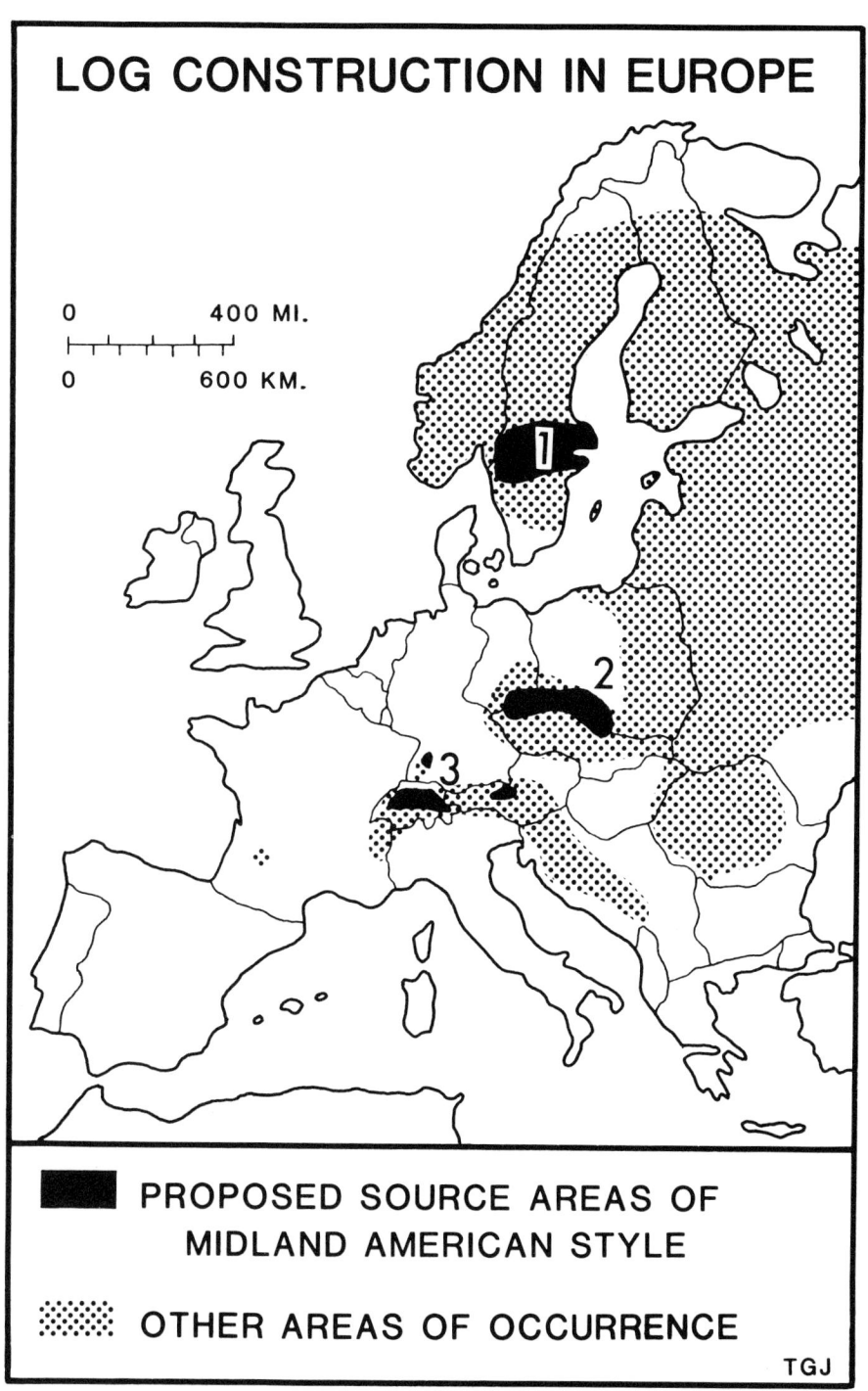

Figure 1.3. The three potential source areas of Midland American log construction are (1) central Sweden, (2) the Czech–Polish–East German borderland, and (3) portions of the Alpine-Alemannic region in southern central Europe.

Figure 1.4. Storage crib in central Sweden, now in Zorns Gammelgård, Mora, Dalarna province. (Photo by T.G.J., 1981.)

Scandinavian origin and those who favor German antecedence.[27]

Traditionally, the Scandinavians, who were the first carpenters skilled in log construction to arrive in colonial America, received credit for implanting the styles and techniques that subsequently spread through the Midland culture area (Figure 1.4).[28] Martin Wright, expressing this view, wrote that "it was the Swedes who accomplished the introduction of horizontal log construction into America."[29] Numerous form elements of Midland architecture and carpentry were attributed to the Delaware Valley Swedes and Finns, including house plans, notching techniques, wooden fence types, and log barns.[30]

This thesis of Fenno-Scandian origin came under devastating attack from certain folklorists, historians, and cultural geographers, most of whom argued for German antecedence of Midland log construction.[31] Lamenting that the idea of northern European origin was "difficult to kill," Henry Glassie declared that the Swedish and Finnish architectural influence on the Delaware was "apparently never of much importance" and by the middle eighteenth century "had been completely overwhelmed by the totally different kind of log construction ... introduced from central Europe."[32]

Among those who support the thesis of German origin no general agreement exists concerning the relative importance of the Alpine-Alemannic region and the Czech–Polish–East Ger-

Figure 1.5. Log barns in Saas in Prätigau, Canton Graubünden, Swiss Alps. (Photo by T.G.J., 1978.)

man borderland. Yet the log building traditions of these two groups of Germans were rather different, and it is necessary to avoid "the common practice of treating all the manifestations of German influence as a single, coherent tendency."[33] The use of such a term as "German" double-crib barn is both incorrect and misleading.[34]

Most writers championing Teutonic influence in Midland American log construction pointed to Switzerland and Alemannic southwestern Germany as the most important source region, both because settlers began coming to colonial America from these districts fairly early in the German immigration and because they constituted the largest group with experience in log construction to enter the colonies (Figure 1.5). Alpine-Alemannic influence has been suggested for such diverse elements of Midland American folk architecture as barn types, house forms, and bridge construction.[35]

Eastern German influence in the Midland tradition was first proposed by historian Thomas J. Wertenbaker. "From Saxony," he suggested, came an "attractive" and "peculiar method of log construction," imported to colonial America primarily by the Moravian Brethren, or Herrnhuters, religious descendants of Jan Hus.[36] Later, geographer Kniffen and folklorist Glassie proposed that the *primary* source area of Midland log construction lay in "Moravia, Bohemia, and Silesia" rather than in Sweden, Switzerland, or southwestern Germany.[37] Glassie then presented an even stronger statement of the thesis, declaring that only "in Bohemia, western Moravia, and Silesia" could "log construction of exactly the American type" be found.[38] To the Moravian Brethren he and Kniffen added the Schwenkfelders, Silesian pietists, as agents of diffusion.[39] From Pennsylvania, Glassie proposed, eastern German construction techniques began diffusing into the southern Appalachians in the 1730s, spreading ultimately to the Midland culture area at large.[40]

At the time of the migrations to America in the eighteenth century, the proposed eastern German source region constituted one of the most Slavicized parts of German-speaking Europe.[41] Even German ethnographers of the Nazi era acknowledged that the log construction of Silesia and the Sudetenland had Slavic roots.[42] In fact, the advent of Prussian rule had marked the decline of log building in areas such as Silesia, where Frederick the Great sought to lessen fire danger by restricting wooden construction.[43] Moreover, substantial numbers of the

Figure 1.6. Dovetailed corner of a log inn at Lanškroun (Landskron) in northeastern Bohemia, Czechoslovakia. (Photo by T.G.J., 1982.)

Moravian Brethren who came to colonial America were ethnic Czechs rather than Germans.[44] The eastern German methods of log carpentry, then, are partially or even largely Slavic, and the Kniffen-Glassie thesis needs to be restated in slightly different terms. Midland American log construction, in this view, is derived largely from a western Slavic type, implying that the Moravian Brethren, in retreating from religious persecution, brought with them not only the Czech Hussite faith but also a Slavic carpentry tradition.

Whatever the origins of American log carpentry, there is little doubt that these woodworking techniques were applied in the colonial setting to certain floor plans derived from other source areas, particularly the British Isles. Carpentry and plan can be independent variables. Even the most strident advocates of Scandinavian or German origin of log construction acknowledge the English and Scotch-Irish contribution to American folk architecture. While the focus of this volume is on the Fenno-Scandian, Alpine-Alemannic, and eastern German–western Slavic source areas of log architecture, the British connection will at all times be borne in mind.

Unlikely as it may seem, the academic debate concerning Old World origins proceeded over a period of four decades largely unsupported by in-depth, purposeful field research in the three proposed European source regions.[45] Proponents of one or another of the supposed hearth areas normally relied for evidence upon various illustrated publications by European scholars. Generally, these Old World researchers were unconcerned with the question of American diffusion and failed to ask the kinds of questions or to record the specific field data essential to solving the problem of transatlantic spread. As a result, the debate concerning origins remained unresolved.

The present volume is the result of an attempt to address the various theses of origin and evolutionary concepts through intensive field research, including four field seasons in northern and central European log construction areas, one season in the British Isles, and thirteen field excursions, over a full decade, through the eastern half of the United States.

This reliance upon European field

research depends upon two assumptions: that the American folk forms are introduced rather than indigenous and that the cultural landscape of Europe retains wooden buildings relevant to the seventeenth and eighteenth centuries. The diffusionist emphasis seems appropriate, given the conservative nature of folk culture and the uninventiveness of the American frontiersman. Probability and logic would seem to dictate that the appearance of elements of architectural form both in early Midland America and, contemporaneously, in European source regions of the colonial settlers is best explained by relocation diffusion rather than independent invention.

The assumption that log buildings of the proper eras survive in Europe is easily justified. The Alps and southwestern Germany display numerous eighteenth-century log buildings. Indeed, relict log dwellings dating even to the thirteenth century survive there.[46] Similarly, an abundant and venerable log construction tradition containing numerous eighteenth-century specimens can yet be seen in the German-Slavic borderland, in spite of the ravages of warfare and fire.

Scandinavia and Finland yielded material evidence more reluctantly, in part because the pertinent emigration period is more remote, in the seventeenth rather than the eighteenth century. Too, in collecting log structures for preservation in outdoor folk museums northern European ethnographers have been biased in favor of the more refined carpentry of the eighteenth and nineteenth centuries. As a consequence, the great majority of Nordic folk museums present a misleading and temporally biased image of northern European log construction. In Sweden and Finland, better specimens of earlier log buildings are to be found in the districts of recent pioneering, as in central Finland, and among groups, in particular the Lapps, who have only recently adapted to the modern world. Numerous examples of crude, hastily constructed log buildings representative of the pioneer period can be seen in these peripheral areas, but not in Stockholm's Skansen or even local folk museums.

The American landscape also yields a rich harvest for those interested in log buildings, though here, too, attrition introduces a temporal bias. The landscape evidence is abundant, though care must be taken not to read it too literally. One must not, for example, assume that the present relict distribution of a particular floor-plan type is representative of past times.

The data gathered in the field research, supplemented with an exploration of the pertinent primary and secondary sources, are presented here in an effort to resolve the question of European origins. That resolution in turn permits an evaluation of the four basic concepts of first effective settlement, overseas simplification, syncretism, and cultural preadaptation. In the process, we will see that the humble log cabin can teach us much about the evolution of traditional American culture.

Two
Midland American
Log Construction

The log carpentry and architecture of Midland America consist of a relatively small number of basic techniques and floor plans, most of which are rather simple or even crude by European standards.[1] Though regional and temporal variation is evident within the Midland culture area, the log construction retained a basic unity that renders it immediately recognizable wherever it occurs.[2]

Two Generations of Carpentry

The Midland log carpentry tradition encompassed two stages or generations. The first is identified with the initial, difficult years of pioneering and represents the Midland style at its most primitive. Often contemporary observers associated the word *cabin* with the dwellings of this generation. "With the early settler a cabin comes first," wrote an observer in 1837, describing a small, windowless house, built of round logs, crudely notched.[3] The cabin floor was earthen, and the chimney was made of log or mud and poles. Weighted boards formed the roof. A visitor to the newly established town of Dallas, Texas, in 1844 described this early stage of Midland construction, observing "two log cabins, the logs just as nature formed them, the walls just high enough for door heads." The roof "covering was clapboard held in place by weight poles, chimneys made of sticks and mud, and old mother earth served as floors."[4]

The second generation of log structures succeeded and largely displaced the first within a decade or so after initial settlement. Earlier pioneer structures were relegated to the status of outbuildings or removed. The word *house* was linked to the second stage, implying a much more refined structure. Logs carefully flattened before placement in the walls, notching done with care and precision, plank floors, and chimneys of mortared stone or brick characterized the second generation of dwellings. The walls were made tight, and the roof shingled. In contrast to the structures of the cabin stage, most of which were hastily erected by amateur communal labor, second-generation log buildings were normally the work of semiprofessional, often itinerant carpenters.

It is possible to overstate the contrasts between the two stages, however, implying a dichotomy instead of a continuum. Many structures display traits of both generations, and the influence of the cabin stage never entirely disappeared. By European standards, even the structures of the Midland house generation were crude and rather primitive.

Shaping and Placement of Timbers

The first step in erecting a log building, following the cutting and gathering of tree trunks, involves the shaping of timbers.[5] In Midland American construction, three major methods of preparing the log are common (Figure 4.2). The most primitive technique, linked to the cabin stage, employs logs left in their natural round shape, often with the bark intact, particularly if hardwood is used (Figure 2.1).

More commonly, especially in dwellings, the logs are hewn on two sides, producing a flat surface on the front and back of the timber. Normally the hewing is sufficiently severe to be described as "planking," with the thickness of the log reduced to half or less of the top-to-bottom dimension. The hewn timber is usually three to eight

Figure 2.1. Round log construction with undersided single saddle notching, Denton County, Texas. Pioneers used this crude technique extensively, and it survives today mainly on farm outbuildings. (Photo by T.G.J., 1969.)

inches thick, and the top and bottom retain their natural round shape (Figure 2.2). Representative of such planking is a house in Cades Cove, Great Smoky Mountain National Park, Tennessee, built of fifteen-inch logs planked to a thickness of six inches. Some large logs after hewing are only one-fifth to one-fourth as thick as tall (Figure 4.6). Certain other specimens of two-sided hewing, a minority, retain more nearly equal dimensions. Another house in Cades Cove, for example, employs 8½-inch logs only slightly hewn on two sides to a width of 7½ inches (Figure 2.3).

Figure 2.2. Square-notched logs that have been hewn to plank thickness on two sides, near Durant in Oklahoma's "Little Dixie" region. Note also the chink construction. (Photo by T.G.J., 1981.)

Figure 2.3. These V-notched logs in Cades Cove, Tennessee, have been hewn on two sides, but retain relatively great thickness. (Photo by T.G.J., 1980.)

The third major Midland shaping technique is half-log construction, achieved by splitting round timbers lengthwise and inserting them in the wall with the curved side facing outward (Figure 3.4). Half-log buildings are most common in the pine forests of the inner Gulf Coastal Plain of the South. More widespread is planked half-log construction, in which the curved outer face is hewn flat (Figure 4.2, sketch #3).

Traditionally, the shaping of logs was accomplished by scoring the curved surfaces with an ax, marking the desired hewing depth with a chalked string, and employing a foot adze, a hoelike cutting tool, to "hew to the line." An even cruder hewing could be achieved using an ax alone. In either case, the resulting faces displayed unsightly score marks and other surface irregularities (Figure 2.4). The folk term "rough hewn" accurately describes the Midland method. Only after about 1850 were milled timbers, easily detected by their smooth faces, regularly employed in American log con-

Midland American Log Construction

Figure 2.4. Ax score marks and the irregularities resulting from hewing with a foot adze are visible on this log dwelling in Sequoyah County, eastern Oklahoma. Two-sided planking is evident, and the notching is half-dovetailing. (Photo by T.G.J., 1981.)

struction, and even then the older, cruder methods remained dominant.

Barns and other outbuildings are more often built of unshaped logs than are dwellings, and the greatest survival of round-log structures occurs in mountain areas and among certain Indian groups. For example, an analysis of nearly five hundred Cherokee buildings in Georgia revealed that 56 percent consisted of round logs, 36 percent of hewn timbers, and the remainder of half-logs.[6] The revival of log construction in the decade of the Great Depression was also dominated by the use of round logs and may be interpreted as a regression to pioneer techniques.

Regardless of the shaping technique, two different methods of placing logs in a wall are possible. The carpenter can either fit the timbers tightly together by carefully shaping the top and bottom of the adjacent beams, forming a solid wall, or he can leave cracks, called chinks, between the logs, allowing the timbers to touch only at the corners. Chink construction requires less skill and work, permits slightly crooked logs to be used, and accommodates the natural taper of the timbers. In Midland American construction, chinks are almost invariably present, in both stages and on dwellings as well as outbuildings (Figure 2.5). A few chinkless houses and barns survive in the Delaware Valley hearth region and elsewhere in the Midland culture area, but they are exceptional (Figure 3.12).

On some structures, such as hay barns, open chinks are a desirable feature. Generally, though, the carpenter had to produce a tight wall, necessitating the use of some sort of filler, or chinking. Most commonly, slats, shingles, or small rocks were wedged into the chinks and then sealed, both inside and out, with a daubing of lime mortar or clay (Figure 2.2). If the local climate was mild, as in the Gulf Coastal Plain, the carpenter might instead simply cover the chinks with rived boards, using no filler at all. Chink construction—open, filled, or covered—is one of the hallmarks of Midland American log carpentry.

The completed log wall, particularly in the house stage of Midland construction, was normally covered with

Figure 2.5. Most of the chinking has fallen away in this house in northern Texas, revealing the chink construction typical of Midland American log carpentry. The chinks accommodate the irregularities and taper of the logs, simplifying the building process. Remnants of the chinking—board slats and lime cement—can be seen at the lower left. The logs are half-dovetailed. (Photo by T.G.J., 1975.)

board siding, either immediately or in later years. The lower socioeconomic groups usually employed vertical board-and-batten siding, while the middle class expressed its prosperity with milled horizontal siding. In either case, the log wall was hidden, to the extent that later generations of dwellers often did not know that the walls of their homes contained log cores. The siding also promoted survival of the structures, particularly in the humid subtropical climate of the southern coastal plain.

Corner Timbering

The key feature of Midland log craftsmanship is the joining of timbers at the corners of the structures.[7] In chink construction, the corner timbering not only prevents lateral slippage of the logs but also bears almost the entire weight of the building. If the corner is faulty, the structure cannot endure.

In Midland America, the typical means of corner joining is the notch, whereby timbers from adjacent walls are affixed directly to one another by a locking or pinned joint. While literally hundreds of notch styles are possible, only eight types occur in the Midland carpentry tradition, and only five of these are common (see Figure 4.7). If the logs are left round, "saddle" notching is normally used. Characterized by a saddle-shaped depression cut near the end of the log, on the top, bottom, or both sides, this notch is designed to accommodate the round shape of the adjacent log (Figure 2.6). Most common in the Midland tradition is under-sided saddle notching, which is superior because the inverted cut catches no rainwater. Saddle-notched logs project beyond the corners, giving the

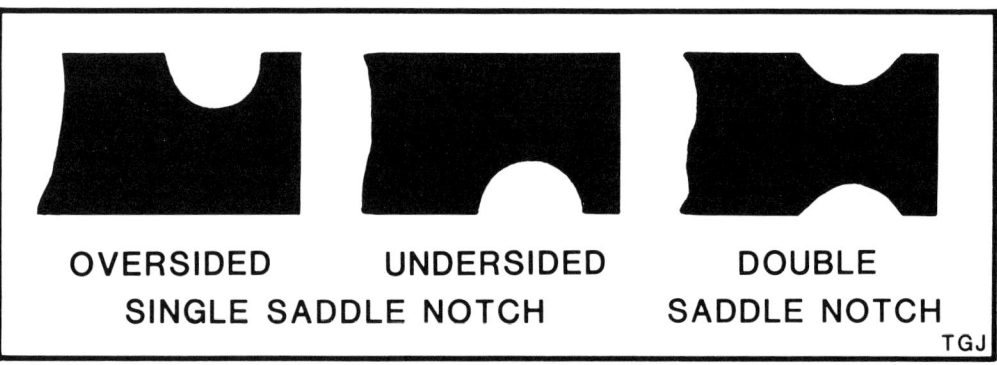

Figure 2.6. The most common Midland American type is undersided single saddle notching.

structure a rustic, crude appearance (Figure 3.4).

Very similar to the undersided saddle joint is a second common type, the "V" notch. The cut resembles, instead of a rounded depression, a steeple or inverted letter V, and the top side of the log below must be shaped to fit the notch. The V joint is often employed on round logs, in which case, as with saddle-notched timbers, the butt ends project beyond the corners (Figures 3.16, 3.17). V notching is also used on logs that have been hewn on two sides; in this more refined subtype the ends are usually sawn off flush at the corners (Figure 2.7). If hewn logs are to be V notched, carpenters often leave the timbers relatively thick, rather than plank them (Figure 2.3). V notching, on both round and hewn logs, is most common in a belt stretching from eastern Pennsylvania westward across the Ohio Valley, including the lower Midwest, Shenandoah Valley, and Kentucky. It also occurs frequently in Missouri and the interior part of Texas. This distribution clearly marks the directional flow of one major migrational thrust from the Delaware Valley hearth of the Midland culture. Generally, the further south one goes in the Midland region, the less often one encounters V notching.

The most sophisticated Midland notches are the "dovetail" joints, including two distinct types. "Full-dovetailing" resembles a cabinetmaker's joint and is distinguished by the splayed cuts on both the top and bottom of the log tongue (Figures 2.8, 5.20). Difficult to fashion, full-dovetailing is not common in most of the Midland culture area, being confined mainly to eastern seaboard states, particularly Pennsylvania, western Virginia, and a small section of the North Carolina Piedmont (Figure 2.9). Much more common is the half-dovetail notch, in which only the top side of the log tongue is splayed (Figures 2.4, 2.5). Overall, half-dovetailing may be the most common Midland notch, particularly on dwellings, and it is the dominant type in states as far-flung as Texas, North Carolina, and Indiana. It is, however, very rare in the eastern Pennsylvania cradle of Midland log

Figure 2.7. V notching applied to two-sided plank hewing, with chinked construction, Cooke County, Texas. (Photo by T.G.J., 1981.)

Figure 2.9. Full-dovetail notching on the Lick-Boner House, built in the eighteenth century by Moravian Brethren at Old Salem, in Winston-Salem, North Carolina. (Photo by T.G.J., 1980.)

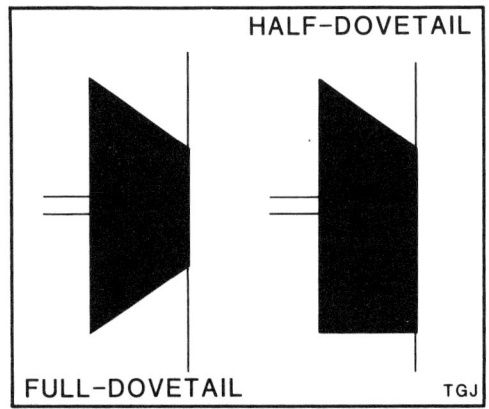

Figure 2.8. Midland dovetail notching.

construction. Both types of dovetailing are used almost exclusively on logs that have been hewn on two sides, and usually planked.

The "square" notch is a crude type occurring mainly in the inner Gulf Coastal Plain, though some examples can be seen in the Delaware Valley (Figure 3.12). Square notching does not form a locking joint, since it consists of right-angle cuts and flat surfaces (Figure 2.10). Small rectangles are cut from the top and bottom of the log butt, and the resulting joint is normally pinned to prevent lateral slippage (Figure 2.2).

Midland American Log Construction

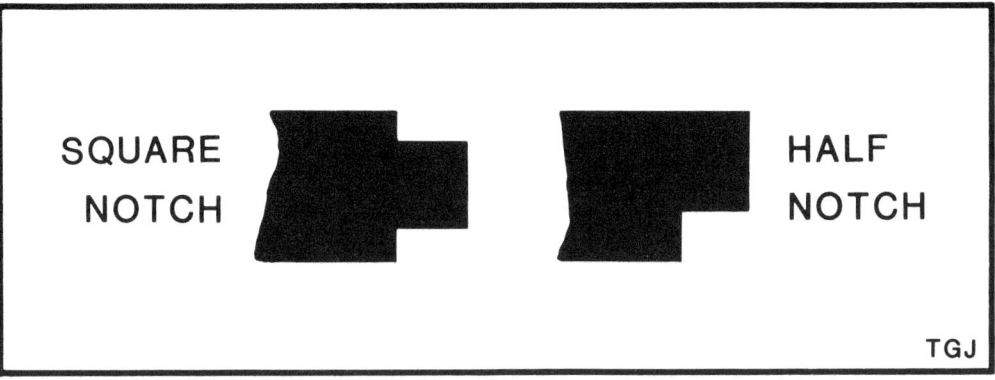

Figure 2.10. Midland square and half notches.

Even cruder and easier to fashion is the "half" notch, differing from the square type in that a cut is made only on the underside of the log end (Figure 2.10). Half notching is relatively rare in Midland America; when it occurs, it is often interspersed with the square notch as a technique for accommodating irregularities in log thickness.

"Semilunate," or "half-moon," notching is the type most commonly employed in unplanked half-log construction and is confined largely to the southern Piney Woods. The natural curvature of the outer wall faces is carried into the notch. While it superficially resembles full-dovetailing, the semilunate joint might better be regarded as half of the double saddle notch (Figures 3.6, 4.7).

The "diamond" notch, so named for the shape of the log tongue, is a rather rare form of Midland corner timbering (Figure 2.11). In the upper edge of the diamond-shaped tongue, a V cut is made to receive the lower edge of the log immediately above (Figure 3.14). Diamond notching, which is used on both round and hewn logs, occurs as a minority type, often on tobacco barns, mainly in southern Virginia and central North Carolina.

Figure 2.11. Diamond notching on hewn logs in a Franklin County, North Carolina, house dating from about 1800. Note also the chinking. (Photo by Catherine W. Bishir, 1974, used with the permission of the North Carolina Division of Archives and History.)

Figure 2.12. Rectangular single-pen dwelling representative of the cabin stage of construction, as evidenced by the round logs; wooden chimney; and ridgepole and purlin roof with board covering, weight poles, and cantilevered butting pole. The scene is in a Creek Indian village in the southeastern United States in the late eighteenth century. (Sketch by a Mr. Tidball, 1791, from Swanton, *Indians of the Southeastern United States*, plate 58.)

In a small minority of Midland American dwellings, the logs are secured by vertical corner posts instead of notching. Slots, or mortices, are cut into the posts, and the horizontal logs are tenoned at each end and inserted into the uprights (Figure 4.13). Such corner-posting is confined almost exclusively to southeastern Pennsylvania. Schaefferstown in Lebanon County offers some nice examples.

Gable and Roof

Midland log buildings are normally covered by gabled roofs, of which two major structural types occur.[8] The older and less common of the two is the "ridgepole and purlin" roof. Characteristically, the gable consists of logs that are notched into a ridgepole (Figure 3.24). Parallel purlins, or "rib poles" run the length of the structure and bear the weight of the roofing material. The pitch of such roofs is usually gentle, ranging from as little as 5 to 10 degrees in the "Anglo western roof" up to, at most, 30 degrees.[9] Originally, the covering of most ridgepole and purlin roofs consisted of rived boards, usually held in place by weight poles and a cantilevered "butting pole" at the eave (Figure 2.12). Short slats of wood called "knees" covered the cracks between the boards and acted as spacers for the weight poles. Ridge-

Midland American Log Construction

Figure 2.13. Log house with exterior rock chimney, rear shed room, front porch, board-enclosed gable, and roof pitch of about 35 degrees, in Sequoyah County, Oklahoma. (Photo by T.G.J., 1981.)

pole and purlin roofs covered with boards were most common on pioneer cabins, and few survive today.

The second Midland roof type lacks a ridgepole and has no log walls in the gables. Instead, the roofing rests on rafters seated on the "plates," or top logs, in the two eave walls. The rafters are either round poles or hewn beams, pinned together at the ridge, and lathing is affixed to them at right angles, running from gable to gable. Broad wooden shingles, the most common Midland roofing, are then laid down over the lathing, a practice still employed in suburban tract housing. Raftered roofs are steeper than the ridgepole and purlin type, ranging between 30 and 40 degrees in pitch. In the gables vertical studs reach from the top log to the outer rafter, and boards are affixed to close in the attic (Figure 2.13).

Floor Plans in Midland Dwellings

Builders working in the Midland tradition of log construction held to a relatively small number of house types, all of which can be understood as retention, subdivision, or multiplication of the basic four-walled log unit, or "pen" (Figure 2.14).[10] Simplest are the "single-pen" dwellings, represented by five basic types.[11]

The "English" single-pen is square

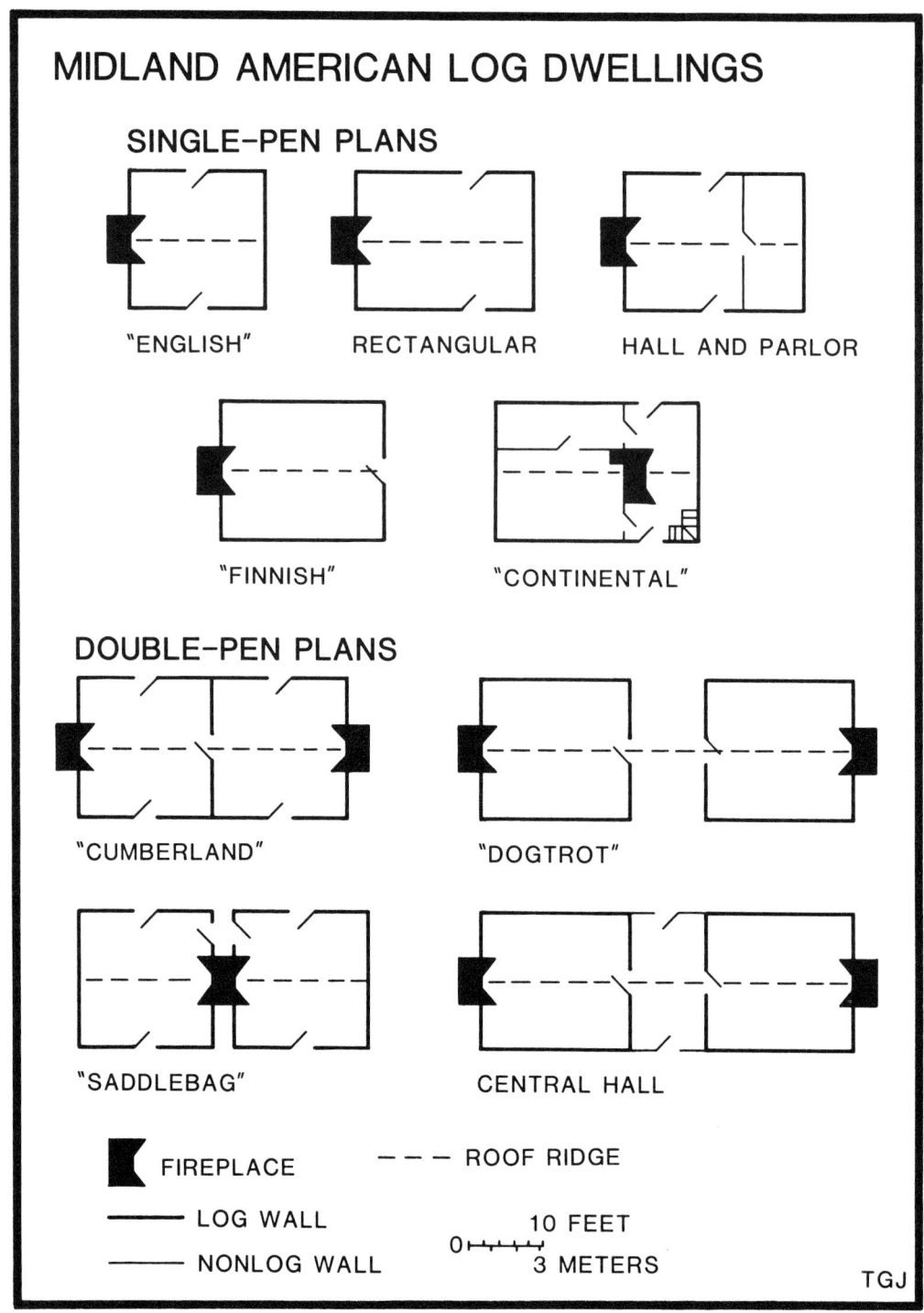

Figure 2.14. The term "Cumberland house" is derived from Riedl, Ball, and Cavender, *Survey of Traditional Architecture*. Dimensions shown represent a norm; departures of up to five or six feet occur.

Midland American Log Construction

Figure 2.15. Single-pen "English" log house, Mecklenburg County, North Carolina. The English type is distinguished by square plan, centered door, and exterior gable-end chimney. (Photo by T.G.J., 1983.)

in plan, about sixteen to eighteen feet on each side, with side-facing gables, aligned front and rear doors on the eave walls, and a fireplace with exterior chimney centrally positioned in one gable end (Figure 2.15). A second type, oblong or rectangular in plan, is very similar to the English single-pen, differing mainly in the elongation of the eave walls so that they exceed the dimension of the gable ends by six feet or more. The aligned doors are usually off center in the oblong plan (Figure 2.12). Many attribute this second basic type to the Scotch-Irish, who formed a fifth or more of the total Midland immigrant population by the time of the American Revolution. The "hall-and-parlor" plan is, in effect, an oblong single-pen with a log or board partition dividing the pen into two rooms of unequal size (Figure 2.16).

If the sole entrance to a square or slightly rectangular single-pen is placed in one gable end, so that the eave walls form the sides rather than the front and rear of the dwelling, the result is the "Finnish" plan (Figure 2.17).[12] In Midland America, however, the Finnish type has typically British chimney and fireplace positioning, central in the gable end opposite the door. The greatest present survival of the gable-entrance single-pen house

occurs in the Great Plains and Rocky Mountains, identifying it as a frontier type that did not persist in earlier-settled areas.

Largest and most complex of the single-pen plans is the "continental," or "German," house, distinguished by dimensions of roughly eighteen by twenty-five or thirty feet; internal division into three or, less commonly, four rooms; an interior, central oven and hearth; an off-center entrance; and side gables (Figures 2.18, 5.9).[13] Grouped around the massive central fireplace are an elongated kitchen, entered through the front door and running the entire depth of the house; a parlor, or *Stube*, usually occupying over half of the remainder of the dwelling and positioned on the front side; and the *Kammer*, or bedroom, behind the parlor. In spite of the fact that Ger-

Figure 2.16. Hall-and-parlor log house, near Charlotte, North Carolina. In this house, the parlor also has a front door, making it, in effect, two-thirds of a "central-hall" house. (Photo by T.G.J., 1983.)

(Opposite, top)
Figure 2.17. Gable entrance, single-pen log semidugout, West Texas, dating from 1891. Such structures likely represent survivals of the "Finnish"-plan dwellings of the cabin stage. This building is now at the Ranch Headquarters Museum, Texas Tech University, Lubbock. (Photo by T.G.J., 1972.)

(Opposite, bottom)
Figure 2.18. A German "continental" single-pen house with central chimney and internal division into three rooms, story-and-a-half height, and cellar. The house stands in the Oley Valley of Berks County, Pennsylvania, and dates from about 1740. It measures 19¼ by 29¾ feet, with the shorter walls on the gables. (Photo by T.G.J., 1980.)

Figure 2.19. Cumberland house near Nashville, Tennessee, with two exterior chimneys. (Photo by T.G.J., 1978.)

mans formed as much as 30 percent of the population of the colonial Midland core area, the continental house remained confined largely to southeastern Pennsylvania, with outliers down the corridor of the Great Valley in Maryland and western Virginia and in the North Carolina Piedmont around Winston-Salem.

Of these single-pen plans, the English and Finnish types lent themselves well to enlargement as "double-pen" dwellings, consisting of two full-sized square or slightly rectangular log units under a single roof. If a mirror-image second pen is placed adjacent to the first on the gable wall opposite from the chimney of an English single-pen, the result is a "Cumberland" house, so named because it is so common in the southern Appalachian Plateau (Figure 2.19). The Cumberland plan has two front and two rear doors and, normally, a chimney at each gable. If both pens are constructed at the same time, rather than the house evolving from a single-pen, the two rooms are separated by only one log dividing wall and the timbers forming the front and rear of the structure run the entire length (Figure 2.19).

Attachment of the second room to

Figure 2.20. A massive chimney and double fireplace stand between the two pens of a saddlebag house at Fort Washita in southern Oklahoma. (Photo by T.G.J., 1981.)

Figure 2.21. Open dogtrot of a central Texas log house. In the subtropical climate of the Gulf Coastal Plain, the dogtrot served as a breezeway, making it a place of both work and rest during the long summer. (Photo by T.G.J., 1970.)

the chimney gable of the original pen, so that the fireplace becomes central in the enlarged dwelling, produces the "saddlebag" house, a type common in areas with cold winters, such as the Ohio Valley and mountain South (Figure 2.20).[14] The gaps between the pens to the front and rear of the chimney are usually devoted to a closet, stairs, or a passageway between the pens.

If the second pen is placed on the gable end opposite from the chimney, separated from the first room by an unwalled passageway seven to twelve feet wide, the result is the well-known "dogtrot" or "dogrun" house, a type particularly common in the subtropical inner coastal plain from Georgia to central Texas (Figure 2.21).[15] Though the dogtrot seems best suited to a warm climate, specimens have been observed as far north as Pennsylvania, Ohio, Illinois, and Missouri. Enclosure of the open passageway, either at the time of construction or later, to form a parlor or hall, produces the "central-hall" house, a type common through most of the Midland culture area. Many dogtrots disappeared from the landscape in this manner, particularly in the present century.

Enlargement of these single- and

double-pen log houses could also be accomplished by the addition of rear shed rooms, usually half the width of the adjoining pen and not built of logs (Figure 2.13). Full-sized gabled rooms added to the rear produce L- and T-shaped houses perhaps best classified as triple-pens. Rarely, third pens are added on a gable end, producing greatly elongated dwellings. Counterbalancing a rear shed addition in many Midland houses is a front porch, often running the length of the house and helping shelter the log walls (Figure 2.13).

Also common are vertical enlargements, in the form of lofts, half-stories, and full second stories.[16] The continental single-pen plan, for example, implies at least a second half-story, and full two-story examples are not uncommon in America (Figure 5.26). If one of the four double-pen house types is enlarged by the addition of a full second story, an "I" house results. So named because it is common in Midwestern states beginning with the letter *I* and because its tall narrow gable-end profile resembles a block I, this Midland house type is characterized by single-room depth, double-pen width, and two-story height. The most common subtype, found widely in the Midland culture area, from the Delaware Valley to the Texas blacklands, is the central-hall I house. The Cumberland I and dogtrot I are less common, but still numerous (Figure 2.22).

Midland Log Barn Types

Midland American log construction was, in the main, a rural phenomenon, and the typical folk farmstead consisted of many log structures in addition to the dwelling. The most important among these was the barn, the key agricultural building which usually served as granary, stable, hay storage, and tool shed.[17] As with house types, a relatively small number of barn plans and form elements account for the great majority of such structures in the Midland culture area.

In the folk vernacular of Midland America, a four-walled log unit in an outbuilding is referred to as a "crib," distinct from the term "pen" used in describing houses. The smallest Midland barn consists of one unit and is thus called a "single-crib" (Figure 2.23). In its simplest form, the single-crib barn has only one level, usually devoted to grain storage, particularly corn (Figures 2.24, 3.45). Others are a bit taller, containing an attic hayloft, and most have a shed attachment on one or more sides for stabling and storage (Figure 2.25). Regardless of size, the barn is equipped with small hatch doors in a gable end, a pattern paralleling the Finnish single-pen house plan.

The next largest Midland type is the "double-crib" barn, centered upon a wagon runway and closely resembling the dogtrot and central-hall houses.[18] A variety of subtypes can be found, some linked closely to certain districts and regions. In some, the runway between the cribs is left open, in the manner of a dogtrot house (Figure 4.28), while certain others have doors front and rear. Cribs can be square or elongated, varying in size and shape even within individual barns (Figure 2.23). In all but one subtype, the "drive-in corncrib," gables face the sides of the barn. If the cribs are elongated along the axis of the wagon runway, the builders often subdivide them with board or pole partitions, forming

Midland American Log Construction

Figure 2.22. A Cumberland I house with single chimney, in the Shenandoah Valley of Rockingham County, Virginia. I houses result when double-pen houses acquire full second stories. Note the log splicing where the pens join. (Photo by T.G.J., 1980.)

four internal units instead of two. Shed additions are as common for double-crib barns as for the single-crib, to the extent that it is often impossible to see the log walls from the exterior.

Double-crib barns can also be elevated to multistory height, forming the equivalent of an I house (Figure 2.26). In this case, an earthen bank or ramp is often constructed to provide wagon access to the upper level, where hay and grain are stored (Figure 2.27). Below, on ground level, are found the stalls, poultry coops, and milking bays. To enlarge the upper level, allowing additional storage space, a cantilevered "forebay" is sometimes placed on the eave side opposite from the bank (Figure 2.28). This combination of double-crib plan, multilevel height, bank, and forebay produces the famous "Dutch" or Pennsylvania barn, a type closely linked to the German population of that state.[19] Copied in masonry and frame after the log construction era had passed, the Pennsylvania barn spread westward through much of the Midwest, south into the Shenandoah Valley, and north into Ontario (Figures 2.29, 2.30).[20] Farther

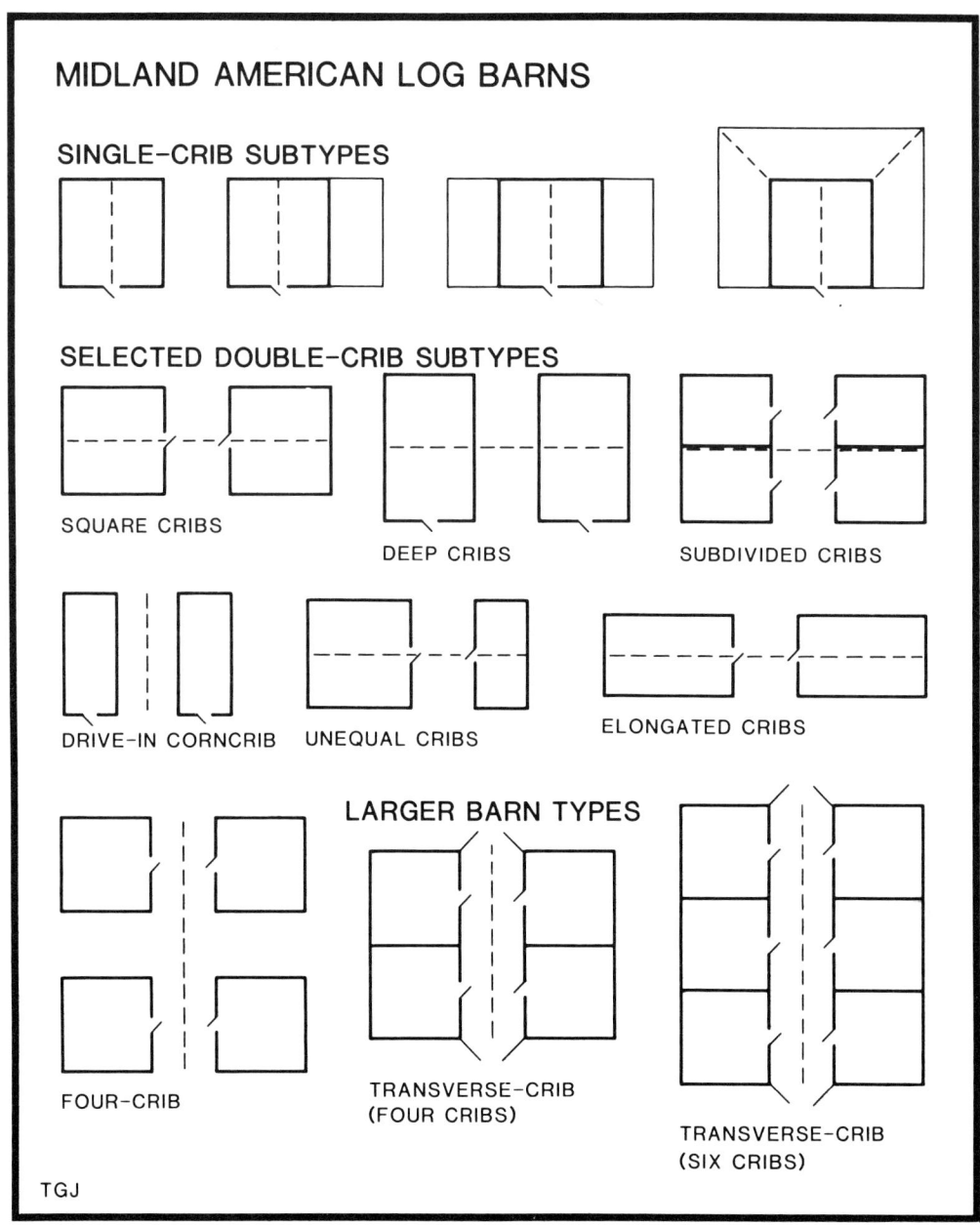

Figure 2.23. Crib hatch door placement varies, and the wagon runways of double-, four-, and transverse-crib barns may or may not be closed off with exterior doors. (Sources: Price, "Double-Crib Log Barns"; Glassie, "Old Barns of Appalachia"; Kniffen, "Folk Housing"; Riedl, Ball, and Cavender, *Survey of Traditional Architecture*.)

Midland American Log Construction

Figure 2.24. Small single-crib barn built in half-log construction, in the Big Thicket region of southeastern Texas. The small hatch door leads to a corn crib; a feed trough made of a hollow log stands under the near shed roof; and a chicken coop occupies the other shed. (Photo by T.G.J., 1972.)

Figure 2.25. A tall, two-level single-crib barn with shed rooms, central Texas. The lower level was once a corncrib and the upper level a hayloft, but the entire structure is now used for hay storage. (Photo by T.G.J., 1980.)

Midland American Log Construction

(Opposite, top)
Figure 2.26. A tall double-crib barn, with spacious haylofts, in northern Texas, near Gainesville. The change from V to saddle notching about halfway up the wall suggests that the barn was not built in one stage. (Photo by T.G.J., 1976.)

(Opposite, bottom)
Figure 2.27. A bank and covered "bridge" provide access to the upper level of this double-crib barn in Chester County, southeastern Pennsylvania. The lower level is of stone rather than wooden construction. (Photo by T.G.J., 1980.)

(Above)
Figure 2.28. Log barn with forebay, built about 1747 in Berks County, Pennsylvania. Compare it to Figure 4.17. (Photo date unknown, but at least as early as 1915; provided by Robert F. Ensminger and used with his permission.)

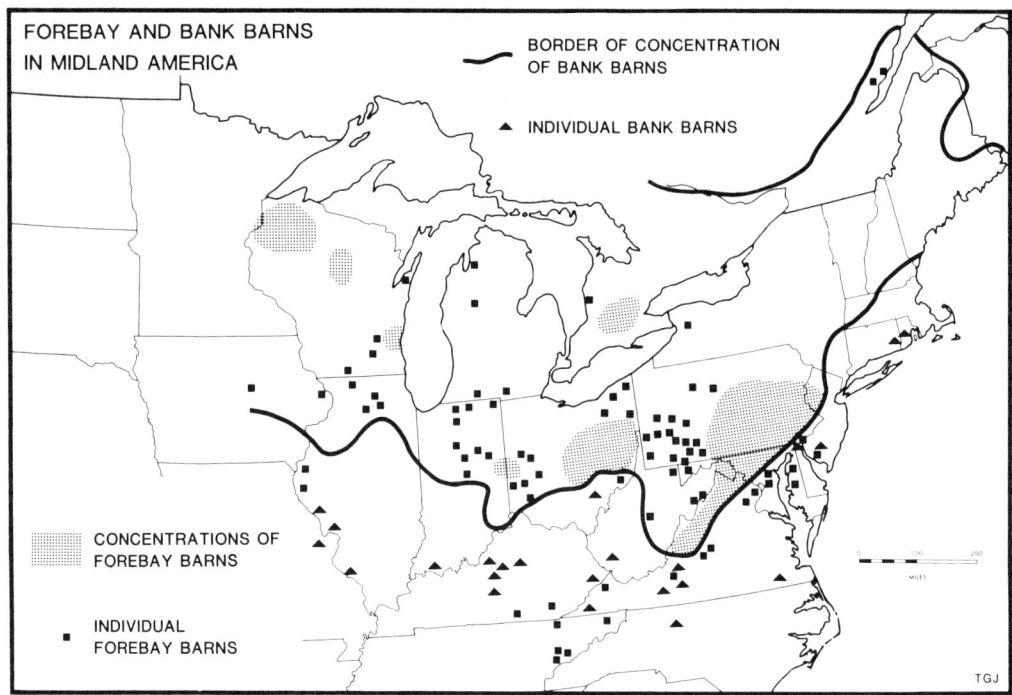

Figure 2.29. Note that bank barns occur more commonly than forebays. (Sources: field research and Ensminger, "Comparative Study"; Noble, "Barns as Elements"; Noble and Seymour, "Distribution of Barn Types"; Glassie, "Pennsylvania Barn in South"; Ennals, "Nineteenth-Century Barns"; Arthur and Witney, *The Barn*; Bastian, "Southeastern Pennsylvania and Central Wisconsin Barns"; Wilhelm, "Pennsylvania-Dutch Barn in Southeastern Ohio"; Wacker, "Traditional House and Barn Types"; Glass, "Pennsylvania Culture Region"; Ridlen, "Bank Barns in Cass County"; Kiefer, "Agricultural Settlement Complex"; Hutslar, *Log Architecture of Ohio*; and Montell and Morse, *Kentucky Folk Architecture*.)

afield, in some parts of the southern Appalachians, a multilevel double-crib log barn with massive forebays on all sides, but lacking a bank, developed from the Pennsylvania prototype, producing one of the visually most spectacular Midland structures (Figure 2.31).

While elevation of the double-crib type provided one logical method of enlargement, Midland barns could also be expanded by adding cribs as lateral additions. The "four-crib" barn is square in plan, with log cribs at each corner and two intersecting runways between (Figure 2.32). Like the single-crib barn and the drive-in corncrib, the four-crib has a front-facing gable, and the massive roof permits abundant attic loft space. Closely akin is the "transverse-crib" barn, differing from the four-crib type in that it has only one wagon runway, entered through the gable walls (Figure 2.33). Also, the transverse-crib barn can be more easily enlarged, and two, three, or even more cribs line each side of the runway.

Midland American Log Construction

Figure 2.30. Masonry and frame Pennsylvania barn, with projecting forebay, near Schaefferstown, Pennsylvania. Note the stair beneath the forebay and compare it to Figure 4.17. (Photo by T.G.J., 1980.)

Figure 2.31. Double-crib log barn with massive, four-sided forebay, Cades Cove, Tennessee. Such barns likely developed from the Pennsylvania type. (Photo by T.G.J., 1980.)

Figure 2.32. Four-crib log barn in the Ozark Mountains of Arkansas. The front-to-rear runway is enclosed only with slat gates. (Photo by T.G.J., 1979.)

Other Midland Log Structures

Log structures other than dwellings and barns in the Midland America tradition are too numerous to treat in detail in a survey of this scope. Included are such farm buildings as log smokehouses, cotton sheds, pigsties, tobacco barns, and springhouses. Some of these have highly distinctive forms which likely offer clues to Old World origins. One common type of Midland smokehouse, for example, is distinguished by a projecting, cantilevered gable on one end, providing a convenient sheltered place to butcher the slaughtered animals.[21]

The Midland culture area also once had large numbers of log gristmills, jails, taverns, schools, chapels, courthouses, stores, offices, free-standing kitchens, and similar structures. Most of these resembled one or another of the typical dwelling plans. Inns and taverns, for example, typically utilized the dogtrot plan, while free-standing kitchens were often very similar to the front-gable Finnish single-pen, as were most churches and schools.

One of the most distinctive special-purpose log structures in Midland America was the military blockhouse, now almost completely vanished from the landscape. Usually square in plan, the blockhouse was distinguished by a projecting upper story, jutting beyond the ground floor on two or, more commonly, all four sides and resting upon

Midland American Log Construction

Figure 2.33. Transverse-crib log barn with two cribs on either side of the runway, Middle Tennessee. This is the smallest transverse-crib subtype, and enlargement can be accomplished by adding cribs at the rear. (Photo by T.G.J., 1978.)

cantilevered logs. The roof was usually hipped rather than gabled. Some blockhouses stood alone, in the manner of fortified dwellings, often surrounded by palisade walls, while others were placed at the corners of forts.

The use of logs extended to other types of structures as well. Covered bridges, common in the northern half of the Midland culture area, often rested on notched log piers.[22] Fencing, too, derived from the log carpentry tradition. The "Virginia worm," or "snake," fence, built of split rails stacked in a zig-zag pattern without posts (Figure 2.34), enclosed most fields in the eastern half of the United States, while livestock pens usually consisted of the more durable "post-and-rail" fence, characterized by split rails or round poles stacked between posts set in pairs about six inches apart (Figure 3.48).[23]

In frontier times, then, entire Midland cultural landscapes consisted of horizontally laid logs, poles, and rails, producing a visual harmony and cohesiveness. So pervasive was the use of timbers that the term "log culture complex" can be used to describe the phenomenon. Such a landscape, even in remnant form, virtually demands genetic interpretation, while at the same time, in hundreds of form elements, it provides clues to its Old World roots.

Figure 2.34. Split-rail "Virginia worm" fence, Cades Cove, Tennessee. Such fences accompanied the log culture complex in Midland America and added visual reinforcement to the use of horizontal log construction. (Photo by T.G.J., 1980.)

Three
Northern Europe

Almost without question, the first log structures in the United States were erected by Scandinavian settlers. Through most of the colonial period, beginning in the 1630s, North America received immigrants from northern Europe, especially Sweden.[1] The principal focal point of settlement was the Delaware Valley, where the colony of New Sweden was established in 1638. Most parts of the extensive Baltic empire of the Swedes were represented in America, as were Norway, Denmark, and northern Germany, but the majority of the settlers came from the Swedish central lowland, particularly the old provinces of Värmland, Närke, Dalarna, Uppland, Södermanland, Dalsland, and Västergötland (Figure 3.1).

The ethnic composition of the seventeenth-century northern European immigration was complex. Swedes and Finns formed the largest groups, but Danes, Norwegians, and Germans from the Baltic coastal regions were also present. Finns who derived mainly from central Sweden, particularly Värmland and Dalsland, may even have formed a majority in the early Delaware Valley population.[2] They had been introduced as woodland pioneers in Sweden beginning about 1580 and soon became numerous.[3] Värmland place names such as Finnskogen (Finn's Woods) and Finntorp (Finn's Croft) are present-day reminders of these colonists from beyond the Gulf of Bothnia. All of these ethnic groups, with the exception of the Danes, could have influenced log construction in colonial New Sweden. Among the professional carpenters arriving in seventeenth-century America were Dirk Bensingh, a Swede, and Dirck Holgersen of Norway.[4] Few if any of the Finns were craftsmen, but it is probable that

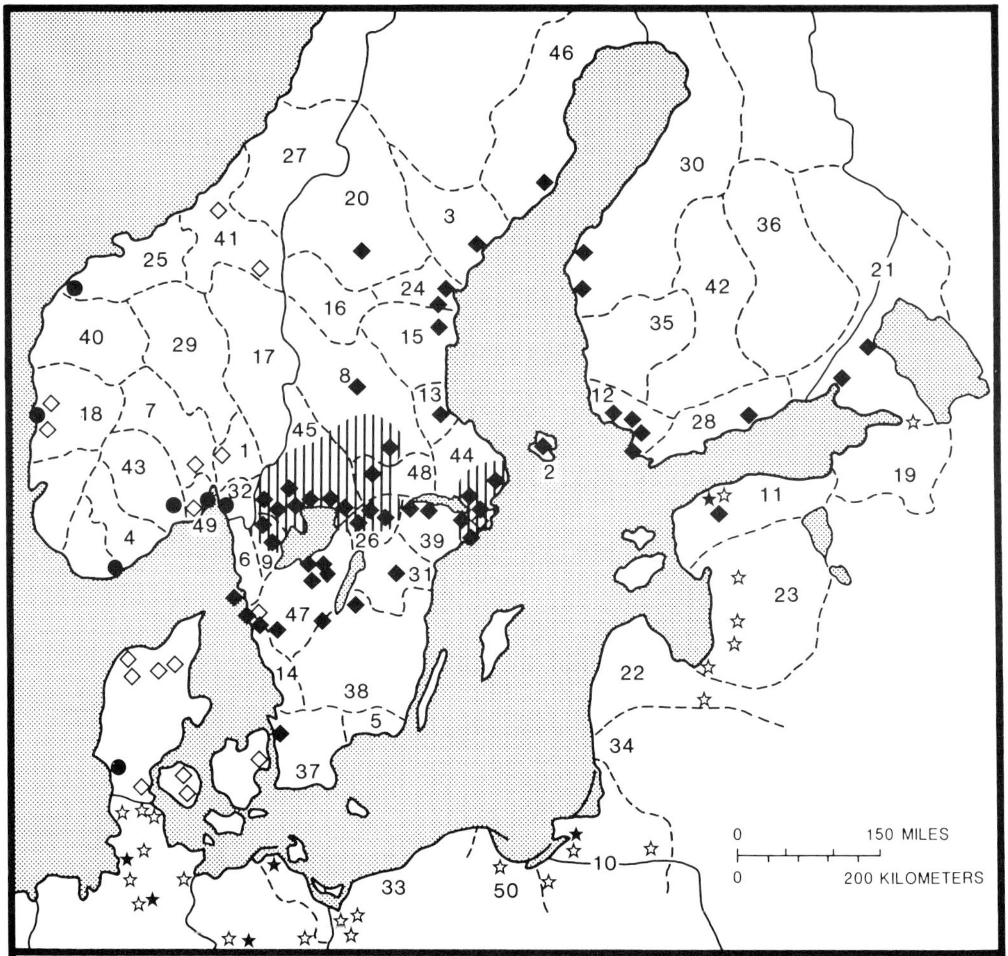

42 American Log Buildings

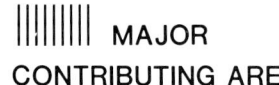

NORTHERN EUROPE : PLACES OF ORIGIN OF COLONIAL AMERICAN SETTLERS

- ◆ ETHNIC SWEDES AND FINNS, 1600s
- ● NORWEGIANS AND DANES, 1600s
- ◇ SCANDINAVIANS, 1700s
- ★ ETHNIC GERMANS, 1600s
- ☆ ETHNIC GERMANS, 1700s

|||||||| MAJOR CONTRIBUTING AREAS

TGJ

Northern Europe

(Opposite)
Figure 3.1 The numbers refer to traditional provinces or districts. Key: 1 = Akershus, 2 = Åland Is. (Ahvenanmaa), 3 = Ångermanland, 4 = Aust Agder, 5 = Blekinge, 6 = Bohuslan, 7 = Buskerud, 8 = Dalarna, 9 = Dalsland, 10 = East Prussia, 11 = Estonia, 12 = Egentliga Finland (Varsinais Suomi), 13 = Gästrikland, 14 = Halland, 15 = Hälsingland, 16 = Härjedalen, 17 = Hedmark, 18 = Hordaland, 19 = Ingermanland, 20 = Jämtland, 21 = Karelia, 22 = Kurland, 23 = Livonia, 24 = Medelpad, 25 = Möre og Ramsdal, 26 = Närke, 27 = Nord-Tröndelag, 28 = Nyland (Uusimaa), 29 = Oppland, 30 = Österbotten (Pohjanmaa), 31 = Östergötland, 32 = Ostfold, 33 = Pomerania, 34 = Samogitia, 35 = Satakunta, 36 = Savolax (Savo), 37 = Skåne, 38 = Småland, 39 = Södermanland, 40 = Sogn og Fjordane, 41 = Sör-Tröndelag, 42 = Tavastland (Häme and Keski-Suomi), 43 = Telemark, 44 = Uppland, 45 = Värmland, 46 = Västerbotten, 47 = Västergötland, 48 = Västmanland, 49 = Vestfold, and 50 = West Prussia. (Sources of origins data: Johnson, *Swedish Settlements on the Delaware*; Wuorinen, *Finns on the Delaware*; Evjen, *Scandinavian Immigrants in New York*; Nelson, *Swedes and Swedish Settlements*; J. Jordan, "Moravian Immigration to Pennsylvania, 1734–1765"; Fries, *Records of the Moravians*, vol. 1; Schultze, "Old Moravian Cemetery of Bethlehem"; Kluge, "Moravian Graveyards at Nazareth"; Beck, "Moravian Graveyards of Lititz"; Kalm, *Pehr Kalms Resa*; Louhi, *Delaware Finns*; Arfwedson, *Brief History of the Colony*.)

nearly all of them could erect the folk structures typical of pioneer settlements in interior Sweden.

In the eighteenth century a second immigration from Scandinavia and the Baltic lands reached the Midland American colonies (Figure 3.1). These later settlers were part of the influx of Moravian Brethren and consisted mainly of ethnic Germans from the Baltic area, though some Swedes, Danes, and Norwegians were included.[5] Among them was Erich Ingbretsen, a carpenter from the mining town of Röros in Sör-Tröndelag province, Norway, who settled at Bethabara, a Moravian colony in North Carolina. Another Norwegian Moravian, Evert Eversen, a joiner, was in Pennsylvania by 1748, as was a Swedish carpenter from Stockholm, Christian Tannewald. Johann Thomas, a German carpenter from Pyritz in Pomerania, settled at Bethlehem, Pennsylvania, in the eighteenth century.[6]

Because the origins of colonial northern European immigrants were so diverse, the field research for this study necessarily covered a wide area, although the focus was central Sweden. The only major gap in the regional coverage lay in the eastern Baltic provinces, from Estonia south to East Prussia, a source region of eighteenth-century Moravian immigrants.[7] In part, this gap was filled through the use of secondary sources, as well as displays at the Museum of Soviet Ethnography in Leningrad and the Nordiska Museet in Stockholm.[8]

The Shaping of Timbers

Of the three major Midland American timber shapes—round log, two-sided planking, and split log—only one oc-

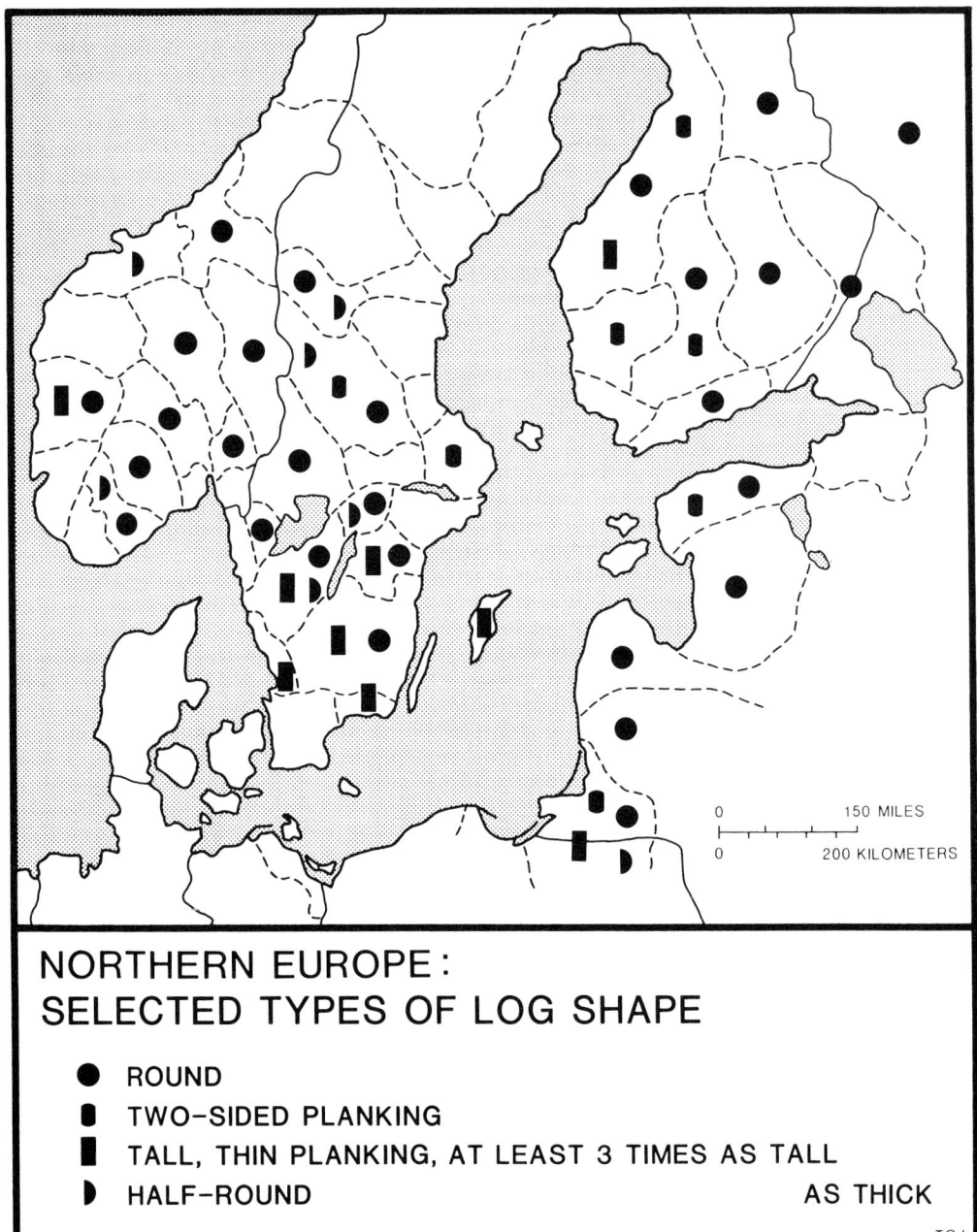

Figure 3.2.

Northern Europe

Figure 3.3. Round-log construction with saddle notching and chinks, from the province of Dalarna, Sweden, now at Skansen in Stockholm. Compare to Figure 3.4. (Photo by T.G.J., 1981.)

Figure 3.4. Round-log construction, saddle notched with chinks, in East Texas. It is almost identical to the Swedish structure shown in Figure 3.3. (Photo by T.G.J., 1973.)

curs with great frequency in northern Europe (Figure 3.2). Numerous houses and outbuildings constructed of peeled round logs are seen in Karelia, Savo, Värmland, and other peripheral, thinly settled provinces, as well as in Norway and along the eastern Baltic shore (Figure 3.3).[9] Round-log construction was, without question, also found in New Sweden and through most of Midland America (Figure 3.4).[10] Half-log construction appears only occasionally in northern Europe, most notably in Dalarna and Härjedalen, districts that do not appear to have been major sources of the Delaware Valley pioneers (Figure 3.5).[11] Even so, the similarity to Midland techniques is compelling (Figure 3.6).

Two-sided planking is a persistent minority type on outbuildings in parts of Fenno-Scandia and is sufficiently widespread that it could have been known to some of the settlers of New Sweden (Figures 3.7, 3.8).[12] By contrast, this shaping technique is unknown or very rare in the Alps and southwestern Germany, the primary source region of the Pennsylvania Germans. Most likely, Fenno-Scandian two-sided planking represents a crude medieval technique that later gave way

Figure 3.5. Half-log construction, from the province of Dalarna, now in Zorns Gammelgård, Mora, Sweden. Compare to Figure 3.6. (Photo by T.G.J., 1981.)

Figure 3.6. Half-log construction with semilunate notching in the Piney Woods of East Texas. Compare to the Swedish example shown in Figure 3.5. (Photo by T.G.J., 1973.)

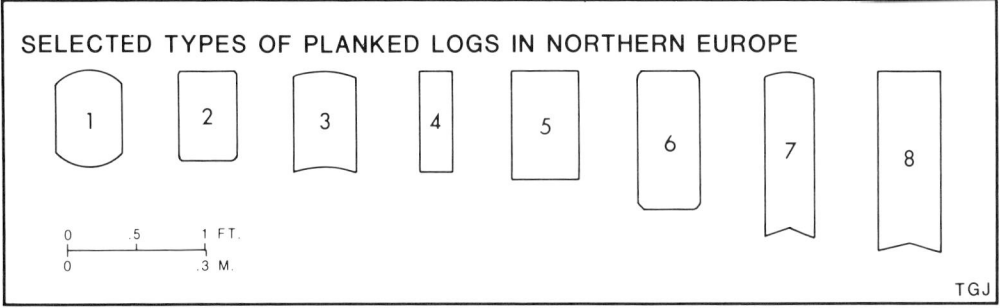

Figure 3.7. The locations are (1) Zorns Gammelgård, Mora, Dalarna; (2) Viby By, Uppland; (3) Ransäter, Värmland; (4) Blekinge (at Skansen in Stockholm); (5) Tavastland (Häme) (at Seurasaari in Helsinki); (6) Wadköping, Örebro, Närke; (7) Oktorp, Halland (at Skansen); (8) Södra Råda church, Värmland. Based on field observations. These samples, representing only a few types out of hundreds, suggest the highly varied character of shaped timbers in Fenno-Scandian log construction and reveal the danger inherent in using stereotyped views of northern European forms and methods.

Figure 3.8. Chink construction with two-sided planking, province of Dalarna, now in Zorns Gammelgård, Mora, Sweden. (Photo by T.G.J., 1981.)

Figure 3.9. January frost flecks this Finnish full-dovetail notching, with two-sided planking, Satakunta province, now in exhibit 25 at Seurasaari in Helsinki. (Photo by T.G.J., 1981.)

to more sophisticated methods. Too, the Fenno-Scandian hewing of this type produces not the thin, tall planking common in America but instead relatively thick timbers (Figures 3.8, 3.9). Thin planking does occur in Sweden, primarily on oaken buildings in southern provinces such as Halland and Blekinge, but it is more elaborate than the two-sided type and, in any case, these provinces sent few if any colonists to colonial America because they did not at the time belong to Sweden (Figure 3.7).[13]

In America, the planking of logs was generally achieved by means of ax and adze, a technique which left telltale score marks and other surface irregularities on the hewn faces of the timbers. Nowhere in Europe except in the Fenno-Scandian region did the field study encounter similar hewing, and it is rare even there (Figure 3.10). Most likely hewing with ax and adze represents a crude, archaic pioneering technique in Sweden and Finland, because later Nordic craftsmen removed the unsightly marks with a drawknife. It is noteworthy, though, that both the broadax and foot adze—the two primary Midland American hewing tools—are part of the traditional Fenno-Scandian tool ensemble.[14]

Midland American log shapes and

Figure 3.10. Ax and adze marks scar a hewn log wall near the Stora Gatan (main street) in Sigtuna, Uppland province, Sweden. Note also the two-sided planking and moss chinking. Compare to Figure 3.12. (Photo by T.G.J., 1981.)

shaping techniques, then, closely resemble certain primitive and relatively uncommon Fenno-Scandian types and methods. The more sophisticated and widespread northern European forms are unknown or rare in Midland America.

Chinks and Chinking

A similar pattern of possible kinship between the two carpentry traditions is revealed through an analysis of the manner in which logs are placed in the wall. In Midland America, as was described earlier, cracks called chinks are normally left between the timbers. The Fenno-Scandian region offers relatively few surviving examples of chink wall construction (Figure 3.11). Instead, adjacent logs are normally shaped so as to fit snugly together, with thin layers of moss or oakum placed between.[15] The Finns and Swedes along the Delaware built some chinkless log houses of this type (Figure 3.12).[16]

In northern Europe open chinks appear mainly on hay barns and certain other special-purpose structures, such

Northern Europe

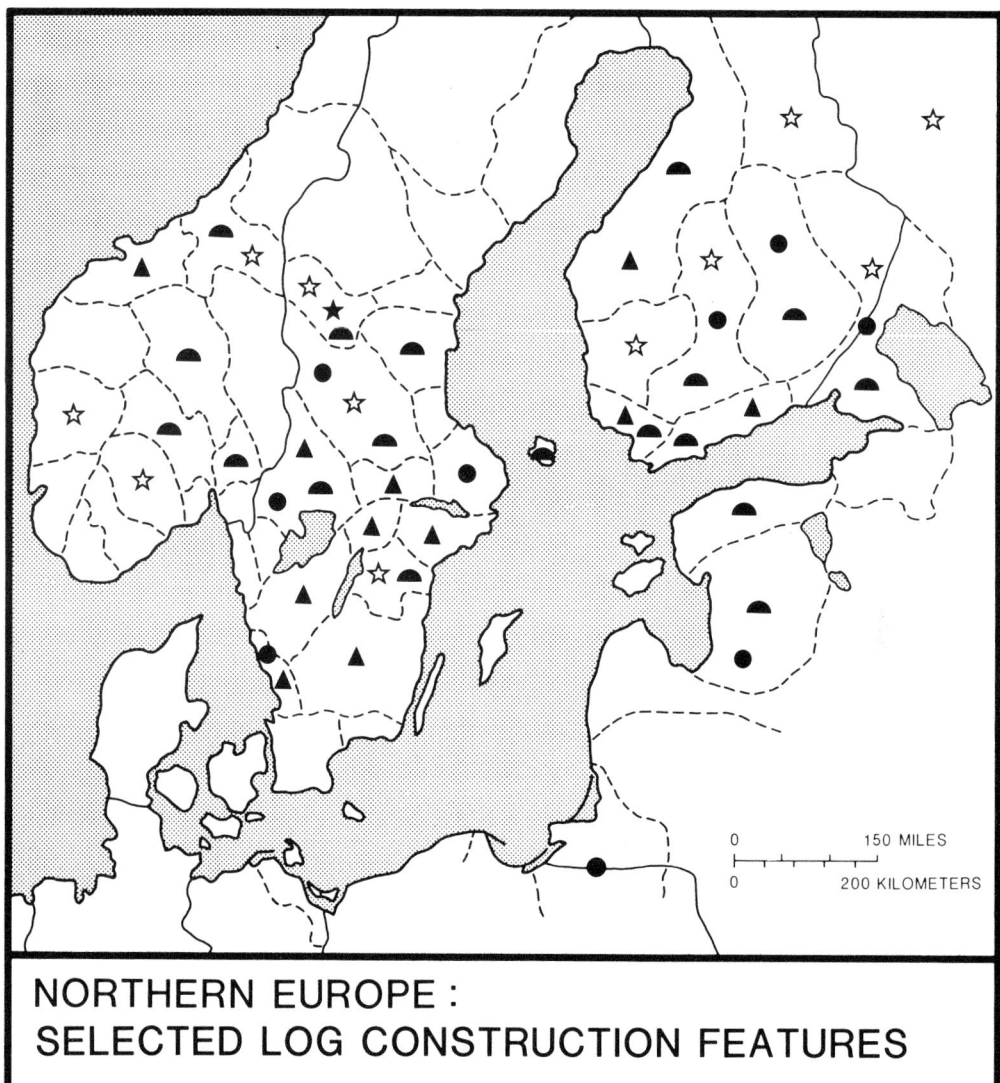

Figure 3.11.

Figure 3.12. Square notching, ax and adze hewing, and chinkless construction occur on the Morton House, a seventeenth-century Fenno-Scandian structure in Prospect Park, Pennsylvania. (Photo by T.G.J., 1980.)

as boat houses, charcoal huts, and windmill towers (Figure 3.3). Scattered examples can be seen in most of the area, from northern Russia to Norway, particularly in districts still bearing the imprint of the woodland pioneering era, such as central Finland and Karelia.[17] In such chink wall structures, no attempt is made to fill the cracks and produce a tight wall, and the chinks allow a desired or harmless ventilation.

Filled chinks are extremely rare in present-day northern Europe. One highly atypical structure, a sawmill in Härjedalen province, displays chinks filled with stones and daubed with clay, in the Midland style. The practice was once more common, at least locally. In western and southwestern Finland, for example, clay chinking was employed in the first century A.D., and it is possible that this technique survived in northern European frontier districts as late as the seventeenth century, particularly among ethnic Finns, who introduced it into the Delaware Valley.[18] In the middle eighteenth century the Swedish traveler Peter Kalm observed that some of the log houses of his fellow countrymen near Philadelphia had "the crevices stopped up with clay, instead of moss, which we make use of for that purpose."[19] A Delaware Swedish cabin on display at the National Museum for Science and History at Washington, D.C., has clay chinking of the type Kalm described, and several scholars have documented the practice in the early Delaware Valley.[20] It is certainly possible that under the pressure produced by frontier life and faced with the necessity to use hardwoods instead of the customary, easier-to-work conifers, the early Finnish and Swedish colonists erected chinked walls for their crude dwellings and that the practice persisted in the fringe areas of the colony, where it was subsequently adopted by the Scotch-Irish, Rhenish Germans, and other immigrants who had no previous experience with log construction.[21] The Rhinelanders, drawing upon their experience with clay and straw daubing in half-timbered construction, could have refined the primitive Scandinavian art of chinking in Pennsylvania.

We should remember, too, that the large majority of log buildings surviving in the modern countryside of northern Europe, with the exception of interior Finland, are not pioneer structures. In that context, it is noteworthy that central Finland, together with Karelia, contains the largest observed concentrations of chink wall construction.[22]

Types of Corner Timbering

Possible prototypes for the major types of Midland American corner notching occur at least locally in northern Europe. The oldest and most primitive form, saddle notching, is found in a broad belt from Soviet Karelia to the fjord coast of Norway (Figure 3.13).[23] On both sides of the Atlantic, saddle notching is almost invariably linked to the use of round logs and more crudely constructed buildings (Figures 3.3, 3.4). Värmland offers numerous examples, many of which are of Finnish origin. In the most common Fenno-Scandian subtype, a saddle-shaped depression is cut only into the top side of the log, the opposite of the preferred American practice, but inverted saddle notching like that common in the Midland tradition does occur, primarily in Värmland, Västergötland, Östergötland, Småland, Karelia, Österbotten, and parts of Norway.[24] The occurrence of saddle notching on log structures in the lower Delaware Valley leaves little doubt that this style, too, was introduced by the Swedes and Finns.[25] By contrast, semilunate notching, which would appear to be derived from the saddle notch, appears very infrequently in Sweden (Figure 3.5).

V notching, the most common type in eastern Pennsylvania and widespread in the Midland culture region, has been interpreted as a German type.[26] The field research revealed, however, that it is of northern European origin, reinforcing a venerable but discredited thesis first proposed by Henry Mercer.[27] V notching occurs in a major source region of the American Finns and Swedes as well as in the lower Delaware Valley.[28] More exactly, I propose that Midland V notching is derived from Dalsland and western Värmland and that ethnic Finns were the most likely agents of diffusion.

Two American subtypes of V notching are common: a primitive, round-log form with projecting crown and a refined, hewn type sawn off flush at the corners (Figure 3.14).[29] The round-log form is older and of Scandinavian origin.

Swedish ethnographers long ago documented the presence of V notching in their country, classifying it as one kind of inverted or reversed notch, an *underhaksknut*, or "undersided" joint. They interpret it as a Norwegian type that spread very early into Swedish border districts west of Lake Vänern, in Dalsland and western Värmland (Figure 3.13).[30] There, Finnish pioneers likely adopted it in the period between 1580 and 1640. Indeed, the Finnskogen district extends over into Norwegian Hedmark, permitting Finnish-Norwegian contacts over a wide area. V notching seemingly represents the "strong Norwegian influence" visible in the folk culture of upper western Sweden.[31]

The Norwegian heartland of V notching appears to lie in Buskerud province, where field research found the best examples. A photographic comparison of Norwegian and American round-log V notching reveals a striking similarity (Figures 3.15, 3.16). If the comparison is extended to include V notching on surviving Swedish-Finnish houses in the Delaware

52   American Log Buildings

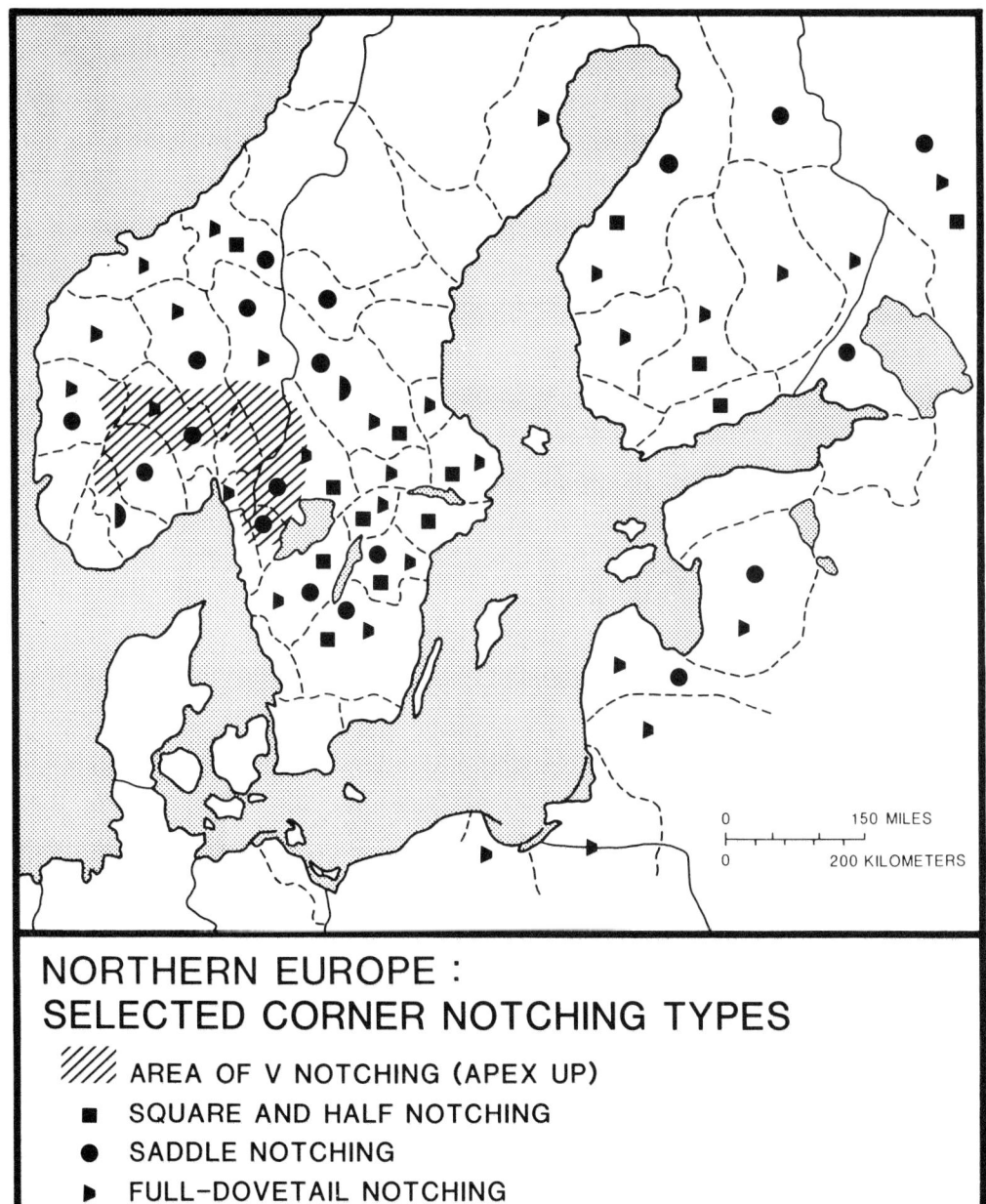

Figure 3.13.

Northern Europe

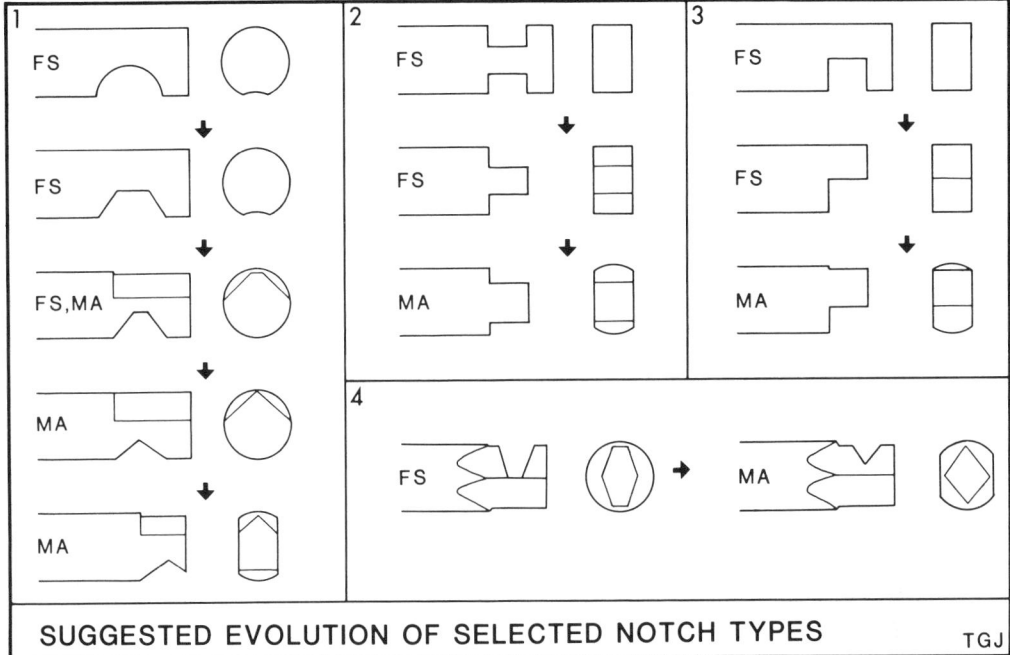

Figure 3.14. Key: 1 = V notch; 2 = square notch; 3 = half notch; 4 = diamond notch; FS = Fenno-Scandian; MA = Midland American. The distributions of the proposed Fenno-Scandian prototypes for types 1, 2, and 3 are shown in Figure 3.11. Type 4 is known in Sweden as a "Gothic groove notch" and is common in Dalarna. See Arnstberg, *Datering av knuttimrade Hus*, p. 99.

Valley, the argument for Scandinavian origin becomes compelling (Figures 3.15, 3.17). Interestingly, V notching also occurs among Finnish immigrants in the upper Midwest in structures dating from the 1880–1920 period. In addition, an inverted form of round-log V notching, in which the blunted apex of the V points downward, is very old and rather common in the Fenno-Scandian tradition. Major survival districts for this "groove notch" include central Sweden, especially eastern Värmland and Dalarna.[32]

The field research discovered no examples of the hewn, sharp-pointed, flush-cornered V notch in northern Europe. Pennsylvania Germans probably developed this American variant from the older, more primitive Dalsland-Värmland type, a modification that probably occurred between 1710 and 1730. Geographer Robert F. Ensminger has noted a venerable German log barn, undated, in Berks County, Pennsylvania, displaying both subtypes of V notching (Figure 3.18).[33] In America, round-log V notching traveled in company with saddle notching, not with hewn V notching, suggesting a common Finnish origin for the round-log types but not for the hewn form.

Diamond notching, a relatively rare Midland American type confined largely to the Piedmont and inner coastal plain of Virginia and North

Figure 3.15. Round-log V notching in Hallingdal, Buskerud province, now in the Hallingdal Folkemuseum in Nesbyen, Norway. Compare to Figures 3.16 and 3.17. Also compare to illustration in Wright, "Log Culture in Hill Louisiana," p. 74. (Photo by T.G.J., 1981.)

Figure 3.16. Round-log V notching in Cooke County, Texas, very similar to the Norwegian type shown in Figure 3.15. The structure was built by Anglo-Americans of Arkansas origin. (Photo by T.G.J., 1981.)

Carolina, is almost certainly derived from the *gotisk rännknut* ("Gothic groove joint") of central Sweden.[34] The similarity between these two forms of corner timbering is striking, and the Swedish form is common in Dalarna, a source of Delaware Valley Finns (Figure 3.14).[35] Families such as the Thomasons and Justices, who moved along the Piedmont in their migration southward from New Sweden, were perhaps responsible for the diffusion of diamond notching.

A more common Midland American corner-timbering method is square notching (Figure 3.14, sketch no. 2). Previously described as an Americanism, square notching, together with the closely related but less common half notching, could well be of Fenno-Scandian origin (Figure 3.19). In Sweden these two types are collectively referred to as the *slätknut* ("flat corner") or *bladknut* ("leaf notch").[36] Though widespread in northern Europe, from the Soviet Union to Norway, square notching seems to be most common in Västergötland, northern Småland,

Northern Europe

Figure 3.17. Round-log V notching on the seventeenth-century "Lower Swedish Cabin," Creek Road, Clifton Heights, Pennsylvania. The notching is almost identical to the blunt-apex Norwegian–western Swedish type shown in Figure 3.15. (Photo by T.G.J., 1980.)

Figure 3.18. Two types of V notching on a German barn near Fleetwood in Berks County, Pennsylvania. The Germans probably developed hewn-log V notching from the cruder round-log variety introduced by the settlers of New Sweden. (Photo by Robert F. Ensminger, 1981, used with permission.)

Närke, and eastern Värmland, including the heart of the major Delaware Valley source region (Figure 3.13).[37]

The oldest known surviving specimen of Swedish square notching, the Södra Råda church, built in 1323 of pine, stands in southeastern Värmland.[38] Construction details visible on this remarkable structure indicate not only that square notching was of Fenno-Scandian origin but also that the notch was first produced by sawing the projecting crowns from the much more common double notching, or *vertikal dubbelhaksknut* (Figure 3.14). Such sawing yielded a flush corner that could more easily be covered with board siding or, as at Södra Råda, with shingles. The log walls of the church, like those of numerous other structures in west-central Sweden, display a mixture of double and square notching (Figure 3.20). In northern Europe, square notching is generally concealed beneath vertical boards, even if the remainder of the structure is not covered by siding.[39] For this reason, a casual observer would likely fail to record square notching as a common northern European type.

The suggestion that Midland American square notching is of Swedish origin gains powerful additional support from the presence of this type of corner timbering in the portions of New Jersey and Pennsylvania once ruled by Sweden, as well as in the Finnish settlements founded in the upper Midwest in the late nineteenth and early twentieth centuries.[40] The earliest surviving American specimen is found on the late-seventeenth-century addition to the Morton (Mårtinsson) House at Prospect Park, Pennsylvania (Figure 3.12). American square notching should properly be regarded as the American survivor of European double notching. The extreme rarity of the double notch in Midland carpentry long puzzled students of diffusion, particularly in view of its widespread occurrence in several source regions of colonial immigrants, including northern Europe. A desire to conceal log walls beneath siding so they would not appear alien in the British host culture of the American colonies perhaps encouraged descendants of the Finnish and Swedish settlers along the Delaware to saw off the remaining log crowns. At least one log structure, in West Virginia, retained a mixture of double and square notching into the twentieth century, providing tangible evidence of the evolutionary sequence suggested above.[41]

Half notching appears less frequently than square notching in northern Europe, but in the same general areas. The medieval log church at Pelarne in northeastern Småland is half notched, as are individual joints in many square-notched buildings.[42] Both half and square notching in Scandinavia and Finland gain structural

Figure 3.19. Square notching on a Småland market booth. This notch occurs consistently through the lowlands of central Sweden. The structure is now at Skansen in Stockholm. (Photo by T.G.J., 1981.)

strength from wooden pins set vertically in each joint, a technique also common in Midland American construction.[43]

The dovetailed joint, with boxed corner, so common in the Midland American log construction style, is supposedly alien to the Fenno-Scandian tradition, a point made repeatedly by debunkers of the thesis of northern European origin. The field research for this study, however, revealed abundant examples of full-dovetail notching in both Sweden and Finland (Figure 3.13). Swedish ethnographers refer to it as the *sletknut* or *slätlaxknut* ("plane dovetail joint"); together with other

Northern Europe

Figure 3.20. A forebay juts from the upper level of an outbuilding in the Wadköping Museum, Örebro, Närke province. Note the gatehouse in the background, which provides access to the courtyard of the farmstead. The outbuilding shows square notching on the forebay, while the bearing wall is double notched. (Photo by T.G.J., 1981.)

northern European scholars, they regard dovetailing as a relatively recent introduction from Germanic central Europe (Figure 3.9). While they admit that the northward diffusion of dovetailing occurred, on a limited basis, in medieval times, long before the American migration, they feel that its adoption by farm folk occurred later, in the 1700s and 1800s.[44] The Angherdshestra church in Småland provides an excellent early example of dovetailing, and in some rural parts of Närke, in central Sweden, full-dovetailing is as common as double notching.[45] It is not impossible that the spread of dovetailing from church-building craftsmen to peasant carpenters occurred in certain districts as early as the 1600s, especially in Närke, a pivotal area for the American migration.

Curiously, the northern Europeans who migrated to the Delaware Valley apparently built more full-dovetailed structures than any other type, to judge from their surviving log buildings.[46] The 1654 original room of the Morton House is a good example. Perhaps the explanation lies in the polyglot nature of New Sweden, which in turn reflected the multiethnic character of the Swedish Baltic empire. The few blatantly Teutonic features of New Sweden's log architecture, particularly

Figure 3.21. Gently splayed half-dovetailing, mixed with a few full-dovetail joints, on a storage shed alongside highway 62 near Munkfors in Värmland province, Sweden. Note also the two-sided hewing. (Photo by T.G.J., 1981.)

Figure 3.22. The hooked half-dovetail notch, a relatively rare Scandinavian type possibly antecedent to Midland American half-dovetailing. This structure is in Gamla Uppsala, Uppland province, Sweden. (Photo by T.G.J., 1981.)

dovetailing, may be the work of such seventeenth-century immigrants as Konstantin Grünenberg from Mark Brandenburg, Hans Janeke from East Prussia, Hans Lüneburger from Pomerania, or Johan Schalbrick from Estonia.[47] In other words, a northern German influence in log carpentry could have been present in the Delaware Valley as early as the middle 1600s.

Half-dovetailing, long regarded as an Americanism, also occurs in northern Europe, though extremely rarely (Figure 3.21). The field study discovered examples only in Värmland, mixed with full-dovetailing on a few newer structures. This would seem an inadequate prototype for Midland American carpentry. A related and much more common Scandinavian type, the hooked half-dovetail, also likely bears no kinship to the American method (Figure 3.22).

To conclude, four of the five major Midland American types of corner timbering, as well as diamond and half notching, also occur frequently in northern Europe. No Midland notch,

Northern Europe

major or minor, lacks a potential prototype in the Fenno-Scandian realm, but the strongest cases for northern European origin can be made for V, square, and diamond notching. To be sure, many widespread Fenno-Scandian notches do not occur in Midland America, a fact that led many experts to dismiss the possibility of Swedish and Finnish influence, but certain primitive, even archaic, regional varieties of northern European corner timbering offer links to a variety of Midland types.

Gable and Roof

In northern Europe the log walls normally extend up into the gables, providing support for purlins and a ridgepole, upon which the roofing material rests. The great majority of Midland American structures, particularly those of the second, or "house," stage have logless gables and no ridgepole (Figure 3.23). Fenno-Scandian roofs display a gentle pitch, ranging from as little as 13 degrees up to about 27 degrees in slope, sufficient to permit, in Norway, a living grass and turf covering. These basic contrasts to the prevalent Midland style have been cited as additional proof that Fenno-Scandian influence is absent in American log architecture.[48]

Overlooked by the debunkers of the thesis of northern European origin are the gently pitched, ridgepole-and-purlin roofs of the crude Midland "cabin" stage. Upon close inspection, this Midland minority type proves to be virtually identical in construction and pitch to the Fenno-Scandian roof (Figure 3.24).[49] In the western half of the United States, where larger numbers of structures representing the early pioneer stage survive, a crude form of the northern European gable and roof are so common as to be labeled the "Anglo-Western roof."[50] The Swedes and Finns on the Delaware almost certainly introduced a style of gable and roof that characterized crude, early log construction on the Midland frontier. Logless gables and rafter roofs prevailed in the postpioneer house period, representing later, more refined German or British techniques. The survival of more houses than cabins in the Midland landscape presents a misleading picture of traditional roof construction.

This thesis receives additional support from an analysis of roofing material. Shingle roofs are relatively rare in northern Europe, and wide, large shingles and shakes like those of Midland America do not appear on traditional structures. Split logs or boards cover most older Swedish and Finnish structures (Figures 3.11, 3.25).[51] Loose board roofs very similar, if not identical, to those of northern Europe typified the cabin stage in Midland America.[52] Related features such as cantilevered butting poles to prevent the boards from slipping and weight poles for additional stability occur in both Fenno-Scandian and early Midland roof construction.[53]

In addition, not all northern European gables are made of logs. Particularly in Finland, logless gables occur on some outbuildings, and the ridgepole is supported by an upright post resting on the top log in the wall.[54] Vertical boards occasionally cover gables in both Finland and Sweden, including some dating from the sixteenth century, though in many such cases logs may be concealed beneath the boards (Figures 3.11, 3.26).[55] In East Prussia

Northern Europe 61

(Opposite, top)
Figure 3.23. Typical low-pitched ridgepole and purlin roof and log gable, Säkylä parish, Satakunta province, Finland, now in exhibit 25 at Seurasaari in Helsinki. Compare to Figure 3.24. (Photo by T.G.J., 1981.)

(Opposite, bottom)
Figure 3.24. Low-pitched ridgepole and purlin roof, with log gable, on a restored house in Cades Cove, Great Smoky Mountains National Park, Tennessee. The roof and gable represent a survival of Fenno-Scandian influence in Midland America. Compare to Figure 3.23. (Photo by T.G.J., 1980.)

(Above)
Figure 3.25. Double-crib forebay bank barn at Torpo in the Hallingdal, Buskerud province, Norway. Note also the board roof. While very similar to the Pennsylvania barn, these Buskerud structures are apparently not the prototypes of the American forebay bank barns. (Photo by T.G.J., 1981.)

Figure 3.26. Swedish gable covered with vertical boards, in a manner common in Midland America. The structure is in the Äskhults By outdoor museum, Halland province. Corner-posting replaces the more common notching. (Photo by T.G.J., 1981.)

board gables are the prevalent form.[56] Again, the diversity of construction techniques in northern Europe renders stereotypes useless and potentially misleading.

Vertical boards are used widely in northern Europe to cover entire log structures, not just the gables (Figure 3.11). Perhaps it is noteworthy that a similar use of vertical board siding is common on Midland houses belonging to persons of the lower socioeconomic class. This could represent yet another link between the Fenno-Scandian style and the pioneer phase of Midland log construction.

Shed-roof front porches similar to those of the Midland American style also occur in Sweden and Finland (Figure 3.27). A broad, post-supported porch, referred to by the Finns as a *katos* or *keula*, appears on some outbuildings in Tavastland, Karelia, and other parts of interior Finland. Similar appendages, often cantilevered as in the American South, can be seen in Dalarna. Entrance porches on northern European dwellings are most often gabled, but houses occasionally have small shed porches (Figure 3.28).[57] To be sure, other possible prototypes for the Midland shed porch exist, particu-

Northern Europe

Figure 3.27. In northern Europe, a shed porch is often attached to an eave side of storage buildings. Together with the foundation piers, these porches produce a visual effect that reminds an American of the architecture of the inner coastal plain South. (Photo © 1947 Nordiska Museet, Stockholm, used with permission.)

larly in the West Indies, but it would be foolish to ignore the northern European examples. Perhaps the Finnish *katos* represents a trait preadapted to success on the southern, subtropical frontier of the United States.

Dwelling Floorplans: The I House

A leading student of American colonial vernacular architecture, Richard Pillsbury, recently suggested that the area encompassing southeastern Pennsylvania, southern New Jersey, and northern Delaware constitutes one of three early Midland house-form regions.

The area's major defining trait, according to Pillsbury, is the local dominance of one-room-deep dwellings, both single story and multistory. The so-called I house, a dwelling two full stories in height, one room deep, and at least two rooms wide, with side-facing gables, shares dominion with a variety of single-story types. Particularly common is the central-hall I house. Pillsbury, following Kniffen, argued that one-room-deep housing was "basically a British building tradition" and concluded that the lower Delaware Valley was shaped architecturally by English Quakers and the other British settlers.[58] Most of the

Figure 3.28. A Swedish "cell-type cottage" from Västmanland province, Sweden, in the open-air museum at Västerås. Consisting of two full-sized rooms with a fireplace in the middle, two front doors, and a shed porch, these dwellings resemble the Midland American "saddlebag" house. (Photo © 1947 Nordiska Museet, Stockholm, used with permission.)

remainder of the huge Midland American culture area, excluding only the districts most directly influenced by colonial German immigrants, is also characterized by one-room-deep housing, suggesting that the lower Delaware Valley is typical of and presumably antecedent to the Midland at large.

Pillsbury's lower Delaware house-form region coincides almost exactly with colonial New Sweden. Most types of one-room-deep housing occurring along the lower Delaware, and later on the Midland frontier, are also found, abundantly, in northern Europe (Figure 3.29).[59] The log I house, in a form very similar to the Pennsylvania central-hall type, is particularly common in Scandinavia, including the central Swedish source area (Figure 3.30).[60] I houses are more common in Sweden and Norway than in England or the Celtic highlands.

I houses are the largest form in the category referred to by Swedish ethnographers as the *parstuga*, or "pair cottage." One I house in Uppland province measures about forty-seven feet across the front, almost identical to the forty-six-foot Delaware Valley standard described by Pillsbury.[61] Unlike most Pennsylvania I houses, however, those in northern Europe have a wide hall that is sometimes subdivided along the axis of the roof ridge, and the chim-

Northern Europe

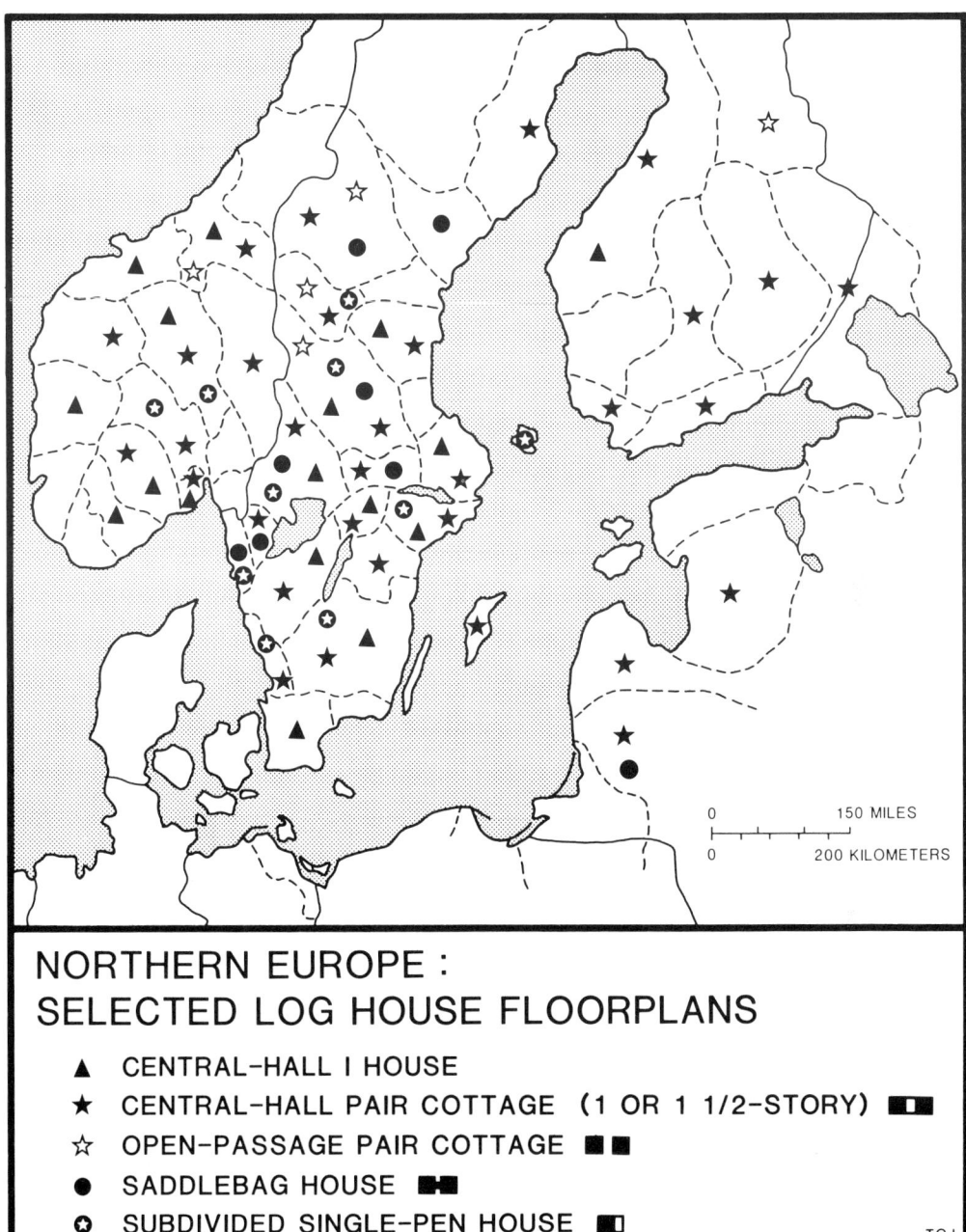

Figure 3.29.

Figure 3.30. Swedish central-hall log I house at the Disagården outdoor museum, Gamla Uppsala, in Uppland province. While slightly asymmetrical, Swedish I houses closely resemble those of Midland America, both in layout and dimension. Note also the post-and-rail fence. (Photo by T.G.J., 1981.)

neys are placed flanking the hall instead of on exterior gable walls. Still, the similarities are striking. I houses with chimney placement similar to that common in Sweden can still be seen today in the Great Valley of the Appalachians, and Kniffen lists such a plan among his variants of the typical American I house.[62] It is known that "houses of two stories" were built in New Sweden, and it is not unreasonable to conclude that some were probably I houses.[63] A central-hall I house of stone construction, built by Måns Jonasson (Mouns Jones) in 1716, still stands at Douglassville, Pennsylvania.

Of course the central-hall log I house of Midland America is not purely a Swedish introduction. It is more likely that the American type, and particularly the interior chimney variety, resulted from a blending of Fenno-Scandian and British traditions. At the very least, the Delaware Valley Swedes and Finns, whose descendants scattered widely through the Midland culture area, were culturally preadapted to accept the British I house by virtue of having known a similar northern European type.

Dogtrot and Central-Hall Houses

Essentially the same argument, suggesting Fenno-Scandian influence, can

Northern Europe

Figure 3.31. Open-passage pair cottage, Sunnfjord Folkemuseum, near Förde, Sogne og Fjordane province, Norway. A common woodland pioneer form, the open-passage cottage, like its American "dogtrot" counterpart, is now rare. (Photo by T.G.J., 1981.)

be made for certain one-story and story-and-a-half varieties of Midland folk houses. Martin Wright and Richard Hulan previously proposed the Swedish *parstuga* as the origin of the American "double house" or "dogtrot," a traditional dwelling readily identified by an open central breezeway. As Wright stated, an open-air hall running at right angles to the roof ridge in a two-room house is widely known in northern Europe (Figure 3.31).[64] Closely related is the Fenno-Scandian gatehouse, known in Sweden as a *portlider*, containing a driveway, or *gångsport*, to permit vehicular access through living quarters or outbuildings into the courtyard of a farmstead.

Sometimes the driveway occupies the first-story hall in an I house (Figures 3.20, 3.32).[65]

A story-and-a-half Fenno-Scandian pair cottage, its dogtrot now enclosed, still stands near the banks of the Delaware in Prospect Park, Pennsylvania (Figure 3.33). Completed in the 1690s, this house offers persuasive evidence that the New Sweden settlers and their descendants built open-passage double-pen dwellings (Figure 3.34).[66] The only question would seem to be whether the Delaware Valley pair cottages served as a prototype for the Midland dogtrot. New Sweden is far removed from the stronghold of the dogtrot in the inner Gulf coastal plain of

Figure 3.32. Gatehouse leading to the courtyard of a farmstead in Dalarna province, Sweden. Structurally, such gatehouses resemble the American "dogtrot." Note also the log roof, complete with butting pole. The structure is now at Zorns Gammelgård in Mora. (Photo by T.G.J., 1981.)

the South, a gap offering relatively few documented examples of the open-passage dwelling. Those who regard the dogtrot as an Americanism have placed its hearth area in the backcountry of North Carolina, the southern Appalachians, or the interior of Virginia, but the occurrence of open-passage log houses in Ohio, West Virginia, and the valley of Virginia suggests an origin in or near Pennsylvania.[67] It seems quite likely that the American dogtrot is another Fenno-Scandian frontier form element, one which persisted into postpioneer times only in the South. Most specimens along the diffusionary path from the Delaware Valley were likely demoted to double-crib barns or converted to the central-hall plan by the addition of walls in the passageway. In northern Europe, as in America, few open-passage houses remain, and in both areas they are regarded as an archaic frontier type. Even the Swedish vernacular term for such dwellings, *dubbelhus*, may have survived in America, rendered as its cognate, "double house."[68]

A remarkable dispersal of Swedish and Finnish families from the Delaware Valley brought them into every area where the dogtrot house has been reported, and their early intermarriage with Scotch-Irish, Germans, and English could have facilitated the spread of the double house to the Midland population at large. Perhaps it is noteworthy that the clusters of Thomasons,

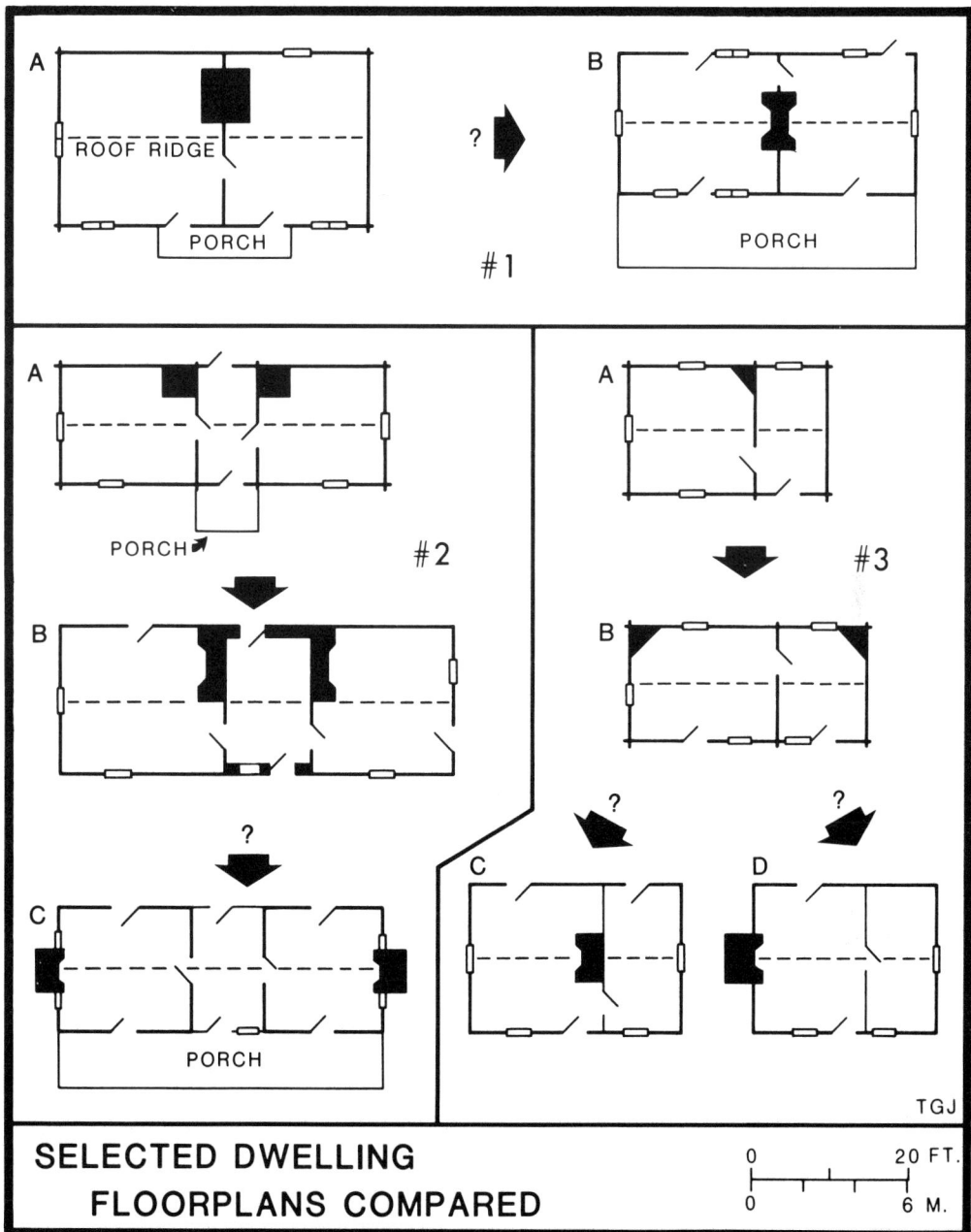

Figure 3.33. Key: 1A = "cell-type" cottage, Mora, Dalarna; 1B = "saddlebag" house, Howard Co., Missouri (after Marshall, *Little Dixie*, p. 52); 2A = pair cottage, Uusimaa province, Finland; 2B = Morton House, Prospect Park, Pennsylvania; 2C = central-hall house, Cooke Co., Texas; 3A = partitioned single-pen cottage, Småland (in the Jönköpings Läns Museum, Jönköping, Sweden); 3B = "Lower Swedish Cabin," Clifton Heights, Pennsylvania; 3C = "hall-and-parlor" house, Monroe, Co., Missouri (after Marshall, *Little Dixie*, p. 51); 3D = subdivided rectangular single-pen house, Buncombe Co., North Carolina. Both 2B and 2C were once "dogtrot" houses.

Figure 3.34. A pair cottage on the Delaware. The Morton House, a seventeenth-century structure, once had an open breezeway. The two pens were reputedly built in 1654 and 1698. (Photo by T.G.J., 1980.)

Freelands, Stalcups, Justices, and several other Delaware Valley families had appeared by 1790 in the North Carolina Piedmont, a proposed hearth area of the dogtrot house.[69] In this context, one can only wonder whether the regional pronunciation of the word *house* in the Carolina-Virginia Piedmont—rendered as *hoose*—might be derived from Swedish *hus* instead of representing Scottish influence as some linguists believe. In any case, the accumulated evidence—material, verbal, and circumstantial—that the dogtrot house of Midland America is derived from the Scandinavian *dubbelhus* is abundant. The British familiarity with enclosed central-hall houses could have encouraged the Scotch-Irish, Welsh, and English settlers to adopt the dogtrot plan, but the inspiration for an open passage was very likely Scandinavian.

Similarly, we should not shut our eyes to the possibility that the enclosed-hallway pair cottage of northern Europe, widespread both in one-story and story-and-a-half forms, might be related to the ubiquitous Midland American central-hall house (Figure 3.35). Like those of its Midland counterpart, specimens of this type of

Northern Europe

Figure 3.35. An enclosed-hall pair cottage, Savolax (Savo) province, Finland, now in exhibit 29 at Seurasaari, Helsinki. Note the stone skirting around the foundation, similar to practice in the upper South. (Photo by T.G.J., 1981.)

parstuga often began as open-passage houses and only later were converted to the enclosed central-hall plan.[70] Too, some American houses have the fireplaces flanking the central hall rather than at the gables, closely resembling the northern European placement.

Other Double-Pen House Types

Another common Midland American log dwelling, the "saddlebag" house, consists of two full-sized pens flanking a massive central chimney, with fireplaces opening into both rooms. The origin of the saddlebag house is undetermined, but some scholars have depicted it as an Americanism or suggested a link to British types or to the asymmetrical, central-chimney log house of the Pennsylvania Germans.[71] Instead, the American saddlebag house could be derived from a Swedish type (Figure 3.29). A particularly fine example stands in the Vallby open-air museum in Västerås, Västmanland, and the Swedish saddlebag, known as the *stuga av celltyp*, or "cell-type cottage," is found mainly in western and northern provinces (Figure 3.28). Dalsland and Värmland, important source re-

Figure 3.36. This double-pen cabin, or *fä-bod*, in Ångermanland province, Sweden, bears a striking resemblance to crude, early forms of the Midland American "Cumberland" house. Similarities include the two equal pens, each with a front door, and the placement of the chimney and fireplace in one gable end. (Photo 1917, © 1947 Nordiska Museet, Stockholm, used with permission.)

gions of the Delaware Valley colony, offer numerous examples, and some occur as far afield as Lithuania. The Swedish ethnographer Sigurd Erixon documented a seventeenth-century, story-and-a-half Västmanland saddlebag with a corner stairway, and Matti Kaups found an almost identical house among the Finns of the upper Middle West, in Michigan.[72] Both Swedish and American saddlebags have two front doors, a shed porch, and two rooms of roughly equal size (Figure 3.33). The placement of the chimney and fireplace is slightly different, and no rear doors occur in the Swedish type, but the Scandinavian and Midland examples closely resemble each other.

Similarly, the Midland American double-pen plan labeled in chapter 2 as the "Cumberland" type has a potential Scandinavian prototype. In certain fringe areas of settlement, such as Ångermanland, where vestiges of pioneer folk architecture remain more vivid, primitive double-pen huts with a low chimney and fireplace in one gable corner survived into the twentieth century. Sigurd Erixon published a photograph of one taken in 1917 and called it a *fäbod*, or summer pasture hut (Figure 3.36).[73] This building is amazingly similar to a "Cumberland" cedar chopper's cabin still standing in the early 1970s in Jack County, Texas (Figure 3.37).[74] Both the Swedish and

Northern Europe

Figure 3.37. Cumberland cabin built by cedar choppers in Jack County, Texas. Compare it to Figure 3.36. (Photo by T.G.J., 1972.)

Texan specimens had two tiny adjacent rooms occupied seasonally by seminomadic people and entered by separate front doors, employed saddle-notched round logs, were covered by low-pitched roofs, and stood less than six feet tall at the eaves. Here, then, is another primitive backcountry Scandinavian form element that spread to the colonial American frontier and survives today in its purest Old World form only in cedar brakes and other poverty pockets. The larger and more refined Cumberland house of the postpioneer period in America could have evolved from the Scandinavian cabin prototype, likely under Scotch-Irish influence.

Single-Pen Houses

The simplest Fenno-Scandian house, and the type likely prevalent among the Finns who came to the Delaware Valley, is the *pirtti*, consisting of a single, undivided, square room; a corner chimney; gable entrance; and sleeping loft.[75] A fine example of a Finnish *pirtti* from Värmland, source of many of the Delaware settlers, is preserved at Skansen in Stockholm. True, the typical single-pen cabin in America has the door on an eave side and the chimney at one gable, but a persistent minority type linked to the earliest pioneering phase did indeed have a gable door. Some of these were quickly en-

Figure 3.38. Rectangular single-pen cottage, Julita Gård museum, Södermanland province, Sweden. (Photo by T.G.J., 1981.)

larged to become dogtrots, and the door then opened onto the passage. Others retained their single-pen plan and were converted into barns. Here and there, in places as remote from the Delaware Valley as West Texas and British Columbia, gable-entrance single-pen cabins similar to the *pirtti* prototype still stand, possibly additional reminders of the Scandinavian influence in American pioneer architecture.[76]

Another simple northern European single-pen house, a type of Swedish *enkelstuga*, consists of one unpartitioned, rectangular pen with side-facing gables and an off-center door (Figure 3.38). It closely resembles one of the most common types of Midland single-pen house, differing mainly in the corner placement of the chimney and fireplace. In America, the rectangular-plan single-pen has usually, and probably correctly, been attributed to the Scotch-Irish.[77]

Also found in Sweden is a dwelling type closely resembling the Midland American "hall-and-parlor," or "Quaker," house (Figure 3.33).[78] Classified as a subdivided *enkelstuga*, this house consists of one full-sized room adjacent to an entrance hall.[79] It amounts to two-thirds of a central-hall pair cottage and was often enlarged to

Northern Europe

Figure 3.39. A Swedish *fatburen*, or fortified storehouse from Östergötland, now at Skansen in Stockholm. Such buildings may have served as prototypes for the American frontier blockhouse. (Photo © 1947 Nordiska Museet, Stockholm, used with permission.)

become such. As in the enclosed-passage *parstuga*, the hall was sometimes partitioned to provide a storage room.[80] Two surviving examples of this Swedish house type can be seen in the "Lower" and "Upper" cabins on Darby Creek in Clifton Heights, Pennsylvania.[81] While it is unlikely that this northern European hall-and-parlor served as a model for the Midland type, the similarity cannot be denied (Figure 3.33).

The various *enkelstuga* and *parstuga* dwelling plans of northern Europe are sometimes accompanied by another American feature, the free-standing kitchen, or, more exactly, summer kitchen.[82] In Sweden, for example, such cook houses are common in most southern and central provinces, including Värmland, Närke, Dalsland, and Västergötland.[83] The Swedes also occasionally place the kitchen in a rear shed room, a feature typical of some Midland American plans.[84]

Blockhouses

Sweden also offers a possible model for the Midland American frontier blockhouse, although the potential prototype served a somewhat different function in Scandinavia. The Swedish *fatburen*, or fortified storehouse, is virtually identical in form to the Midland blockhouse (Figure 3.39).[85] The storehouses were provided with loopholes, and the exterior was reminiscent of medieval Swedish knights' castles. Conceivably, the Delaware colonists might have retreated to the easily defended community storehouse during an Indian attack, found the structure admirably suited for such a purpose, and subsequently used it in that manner.

However, the origins of the American blockhouse may lie instead in the material military culture of the British army, as is suggested by the presence of chinkless log garrison houses on the New England frontier. That British tradition could, in turn, have a German origin, possibly conveyed by Teutonic military engineers in the employ of the English crown. The name "blockhouse" strongly suggests derivation from the German cognate *Blockhaus*, meaning simply "log house."

Barn Form Elements

Certain major form elements of Midland American barns also appear in

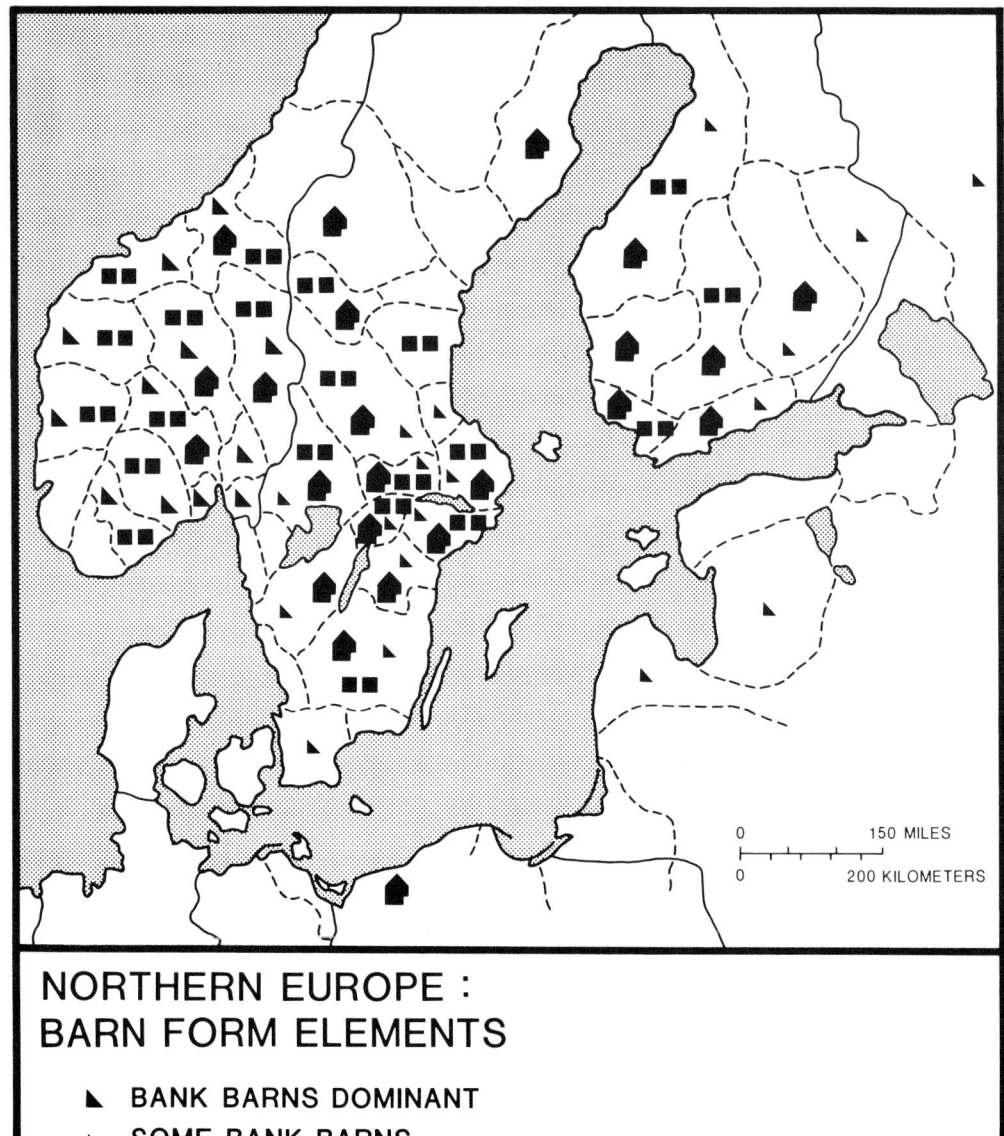

Figure 3.40.

Figure 3.41. Multilevel double-crib bank barn, at Vinstra in the Gudbrandsdal, Oppland province, Norway. (Photo by T.G.J., 1981.)

northern Europe. Most notable among these are the double-crib plan, characterized by two log cribs separated by a wagon runway or threshing floor and covered by a side-gable roof; the bank barn, a multilevel structure equipped with a bank and ramp for wagon access to the upper story; the forebay, a cantilevered projection on an eave side of the upper level; and the combination of double-crib, bank, and forebay on some individual structures to produce a close equivalent to the "Pennsylvania" barn.

Bank barns appear consistently across most of northern Europe, from Soviet Karelia to the Norwegian fjord country (Figure 3.40).[86] Only in the western Swedish coastal provinces of Halland and Bohuslän, both of which were under Danish rule during the colonization of New Sweden, are bank barns apparently lacking. Close field investigation reveals bank barns to be most common in Norway (Figure 3.41). Only a minority of Swedish and Finnish barns are equipped with banks and ramps, but in Norway these features are almost universal. Rarely does one encounter a national boundary so clearly reflected in the cultural landscape. To cross from Sweden to Norway is to enter the heartland of northern European bank barns.

A cantilevered forebay, or *överkragning*, jutting from one eave side on the upper level of outbuildings, is a common Swedish form element (Fig-

Figure 3.42. Single-level double-crib barn, near Nesbyen, Hallingdal, Buskerud province, Norway. (Photo by T.G.J., 1981.)

ure 3.20). Interior Norway and southern Finland also offer some forebays, but the spatial distribution and concentration strongly link this architectural feature to the Swedes.[87] An outlier in Pomerania, on the southern Baltic shore, may owe its origin to the former Swedish rule of that province.[88] Northern European eave forebays occur on barns, stables, sheds, and gatehouses, appearing in various sizes and serving a variety of functions. Often the forebay is merely a sheltered walkway, connected to the ground by stairs tucked beneath the overhang, but in some other structures the forebay provides additional storage space.

The double-crib plan occurs widely in Sweden, Norway, and parts of Finland (Figure 3.40). Without question, log double-cribs are much more common in northern Europe than in the German-populated regions of log construction in central Europe (Figures 3.42, 3.43). The typical Swedish-Finnish double-crib barn is single level, while in Norway two or even three stories are more common (Figure 3.41). In a minority of the single-level barns observed in the field study the central runway is left open, in the manner of small double-cribs in the Gulf Coastal Plain and Upper South. This similarity led Martin Wright to postulate a Swed-

Northern Europe

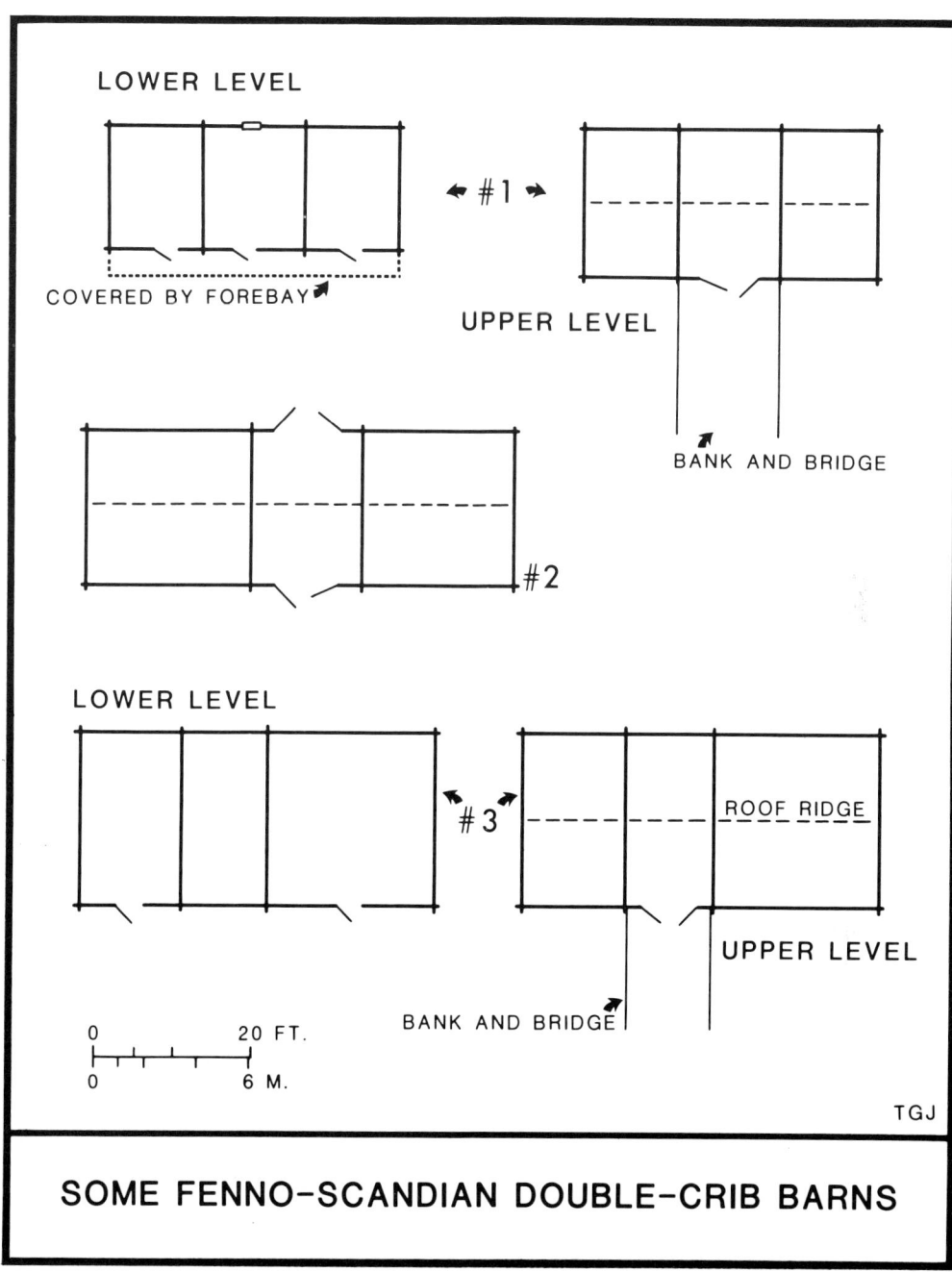

SOME FENNO-SCANDIAN DOUBLE-CRIB BARNS

Figure 3.43. Key: 1 = double-crib forebay bank barn, Numedal, Buskerud province, Norway, now in exhibit 17, Norsk Folkemuseum, Oslo; 2 = single-level double-crib barn, Viby By museum, Uppland province, Sweden; 3 = two-level double-crib bank barn, Gudbrandsdal, Oppland province, Norway, now in Sandvig Maihaugen collection, Lillehammer.

Figure 3.44. A Swedish *ängslada*, or meadow barn, near Leksand in Dalarna province. Such structures closely resemble Midland American single-crib barns, or corncribs, even to the details of hatch door construction. Compare to Figure 3.45. (Photo © 1947 Nordiska Museet, Stockholm, used with permission.)

ish origin for the double-crib barn of the American South, though a detailed analysis reveals certain Alpine forms to be more like the American type.[89] The Swedish term for open-runway double-cribs is *dubbellada med port*, or "double shed with portal."[90] Most northern European types, though, are equipped with doors, and some have no rear entrance to the threshing floor.[91]

The combination of double-crib plan, bank, and eave forebay in the same barn, producing a structure closely resembling the Pennsylvania type, is common in only two small districts in the Norwegian province of Buskerud. There, in the Hallingdal and, above all, in the Numedal, many splendid double-crib forebay bank barns line the valley floors and adjacent slopes (Figure 3.25).[92] In one major respect, however, these Buskerud barns differ from those of Pennsylvania and the Midwest. The banked entrance leads into the forebay on the front eave side rather than into the rear. This difference, coupled with the fact that the Numedal and Hallingdal provided no known emigrants to colonial America, argues convincingly against a Norwegian prototype for the Pennsylvania barn.

Singly and in combination, all of these barn form elements also appear in Alpine source regions of the colonial

Figure 3.45. Southern single-crib barn, or corncrib, in Denton County, Texas. Note the similarity to the Swedish barn in Figure 3.44. (Photo by T.G.J., 1973.)

Germans, and a more precise prototype of the Pennsylvania barn has been found in the Prätigau region of Canton Graubünden, Switzerland.[93] Still, the occurrence in northern Europe of bank, forebay, and double-crib plan leads one to wonder whether at least some of these basic Midland forms might not predate the German arrival in Pennsylvania, and particularly whether the Delaware Finns and Swedes did not erect double-crib outbuildings.

Much more likely to be of Fenno-Scandian origin is the Midland single-crib barn, the smaller forms of which are usually referred to as corncribs.[94] Consisting of one roughly square crib and a small hatch door on one gable end, the American single-crib barn has an almost exact prototype in the Swedish-Finnish meadow barn, or *ängslada*.[95] Like many Midland single-cribs, these Old World storage sheds are saddle notched and have a board floor wedged between the lower logs (Figures 3.44, 3.45). Many even have open chinks like those in rural America. Measuring six to twelve feet on a side and often not more than five or six feet tall to the eaves, the Scandinavian sheds instantly remind a native Southerner of a corncrib.

To test this possible linkage between Scandinavia and America, I showed the photograph in Figure 3.44 to an aged

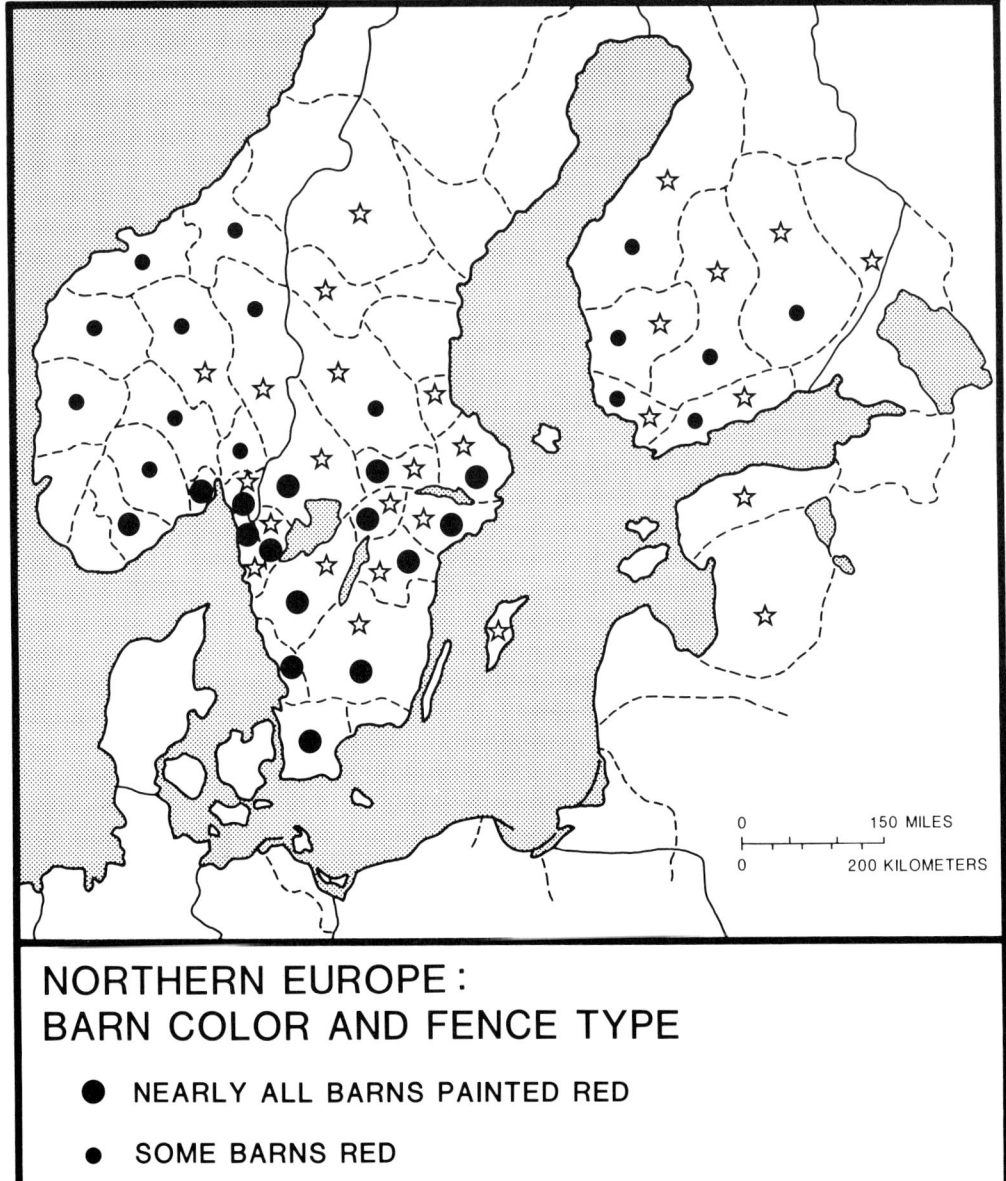

Figure 3.46.

farmer in northern Texas who still used log buildings on his place. Without identifying the Swedish meadow barn or disclosing its location, I asked the farmer what sort of structure it might be. Without hesitation, he replied that it was a "corncrib" and wondered whether it was the one on the "Cason place," some five miles distant. He felt that the hatch door was placed a bit too high, but regarded the structure as something entirely familiar.[96] Apparently, neither the Alps nor the eastern German lands offer so satisfactory a model for the smaller single-crib barns. Since no clear distinction exists between small corncribs and larger single-crib barns in the American vernacular, a common origin is likely.

Certain other log sheds in northern Europe, both in Sweden and Finland, have a cantilevered projection of the roof at the entrance gable end, creating a compelling similarity to the Midland American smokehouse.[97] In the Baltic lands such buildings are most often milk sheds, saunas, or storage cribs, but a modest change in function could have converted them into smokehouses on the American frontier.

Another intriguing characteristic of northern European barns is the red paint applied to the exterior (Figure 3.46). In Sweden this practice is almost universal, and in Finland it is said to reflect Swedish influence.[98] The preferred rust or dark red color, derived from the wastes of copper mines, is almost precisely the same seen on countless barns in the American Midwest and Pennsylvania. Swedish ethnographers believe that red paint became fashionable for outbuildings among the peasantry no earlier than about 1700, well after the Delaware colonization. The gentry, however, had adopted it in the early 1600s and the nobility even earlier.[99] Certainly, an opportunity for diffusion to the Delaware Valley existed, but such a spread does seem unlikely. The painting of log structures seems inconsistent with a frontier setting, and the Finns, who likely bore the brunt of the woodland pioneering in the New Sweden colony, apparently did not share the red paint tradition.

Fences

Part and parcel of the log culture complex in Midland America are a variety of traditional wooden fences. One of these, dubbed the "type I post-and-rail fence" by geographer H. F. Raup, consists of rails or poles stacked between pairs of closely-set posts spaced about six feet apart.[100] These primitive post-and-rail fences served to enclose stock pens, particularly in the American South.

A similar post-and-rail fence occurs widely in northern Europe, particularly in Sweden and Finland (Figure 3.46).[101] The basic support principle of this Fenno-Scandian fence is identical to the American type, in that pairs of posts are set in the ground (Figure 3.47).[102] Most often, though, the posts are small and round, made from young trees, while the American posts are more substantial. A further difference is seen in the northern European practice of setting the rails at a slant, supported by withes, while American post-and-rail fences have horizontal rails and no withes (Figure 3.48). Only a minority of Swedish fences have the rails lying horizontally, but some of these are Finnish and occur in the Värmland source region.[103]

Figure 3.47. A post-and-rail fence, highlighted by new snow, at the Seurasaari museum in Helsinki. In the background are several low-pitched ridgepole and purlin roofs. (Photo by T.G.J., 1981.)

According to Peter Kalm, who traveled among the Delaware Valley Swedes in the middle eighteenth century, the early settlers had erected "fences from posts and rails such as those in common use throughout Sweden," though problems with rotting had caused later generations to cease building northern European fences. Possibly, however, the type had simply migrated with the frontier, disappearing by 1750 from the older-settled districts, a sequence suggested by the fact that Kalm did observe post-and-rail fences on the settlement periphery of New York.[104] In the process the fence could have acquired massive posts, both to retard rotting and to add the strength necessary for its New World function of enclosing livestock pens.

It is also possible that the prototype of the ubiquitous American "worm," or "snake," fence, consisting of split rails laid in a zigzag manner, can be found in Sweden. Amandus Johnson made such a claim in an article published in 1955 and included a photograph of such a rail fence in northern Sweden.[105] I saw no fences of this type during the course of my field research, but it is possible that they represent a nearly vanished pioneer type in Scandinavia.

Northern Europe

Figure 3.48. Post-and-rail fence in northern Texas, possibly derived from the Swedish type. Compare to Figure 3.47. (Photo by T.G.J., 1977.)

To a far greater extent than previously recognized, then, the pioneer culture of Midland America and its architectural component seem to be of northern European origin. We should award the Delaware Swedes and, above all, the Finns who accompanied and perhaps outnumbered them, their due credit, too long denied by the Germanists. At the same time, as we shall see, Teutonic immigrants made major contributions to Midland American log architecture.

Four
The Alps and Southwestern Germany

The second, and largest, contingent of colonial American immigrants with knowledge of log construction came from the Alpine-Alemannic region of southern central Europe, including portions of the Swiss and Austrian Alps, the Swiss Plateau, and the Black Forest.[1] Forealpine portions of cantons Bern and Zürich in Switzerland, as well as the Austrian Alpine province of Salzburg, were major source areas of the German-speaking settlers coming to America between 1700 to 1760 (Figure 4.1).

An estimated twenty-five thousand ethnic Germans left Switzerland for America in the eighteenth century in a migration that peaked in the 1734–44 period. In addition to Zürich and Bern, cantons such as Graubünden, Aargau, Appenzell, St. Gallen, Solothurn, Basel, and Schaffhausen contributed significant numbers of colonists. Adjacent provinces and states to the north, in particular Alsace, the Rhenish Palatinate, and Württemberg, also served as major source regions.[2] The majority of these Alpine and Alemannic emigrants had no previous experience with log construction. Those settlers with knowledge of log carpentry came predominantly from the Bern, St. Gallen, Salzburg, and Graubünden regions, though a tiny minority was derived from the Hochschwarzwald, or Upper Black Forest. The destination of most of these German-speaking settlers was southeastern Pennsylvania, but the Salzburg Protestants chose Georgia as their principal goal, some of the Swiss went to the Carolinas, and a minority of Palatines occupied the Mohawk Valley of upstate New York.

In order to allow for the inspection of every possible source region of these Swiss, Austrian, and German

The Alps and Southwestern Germany

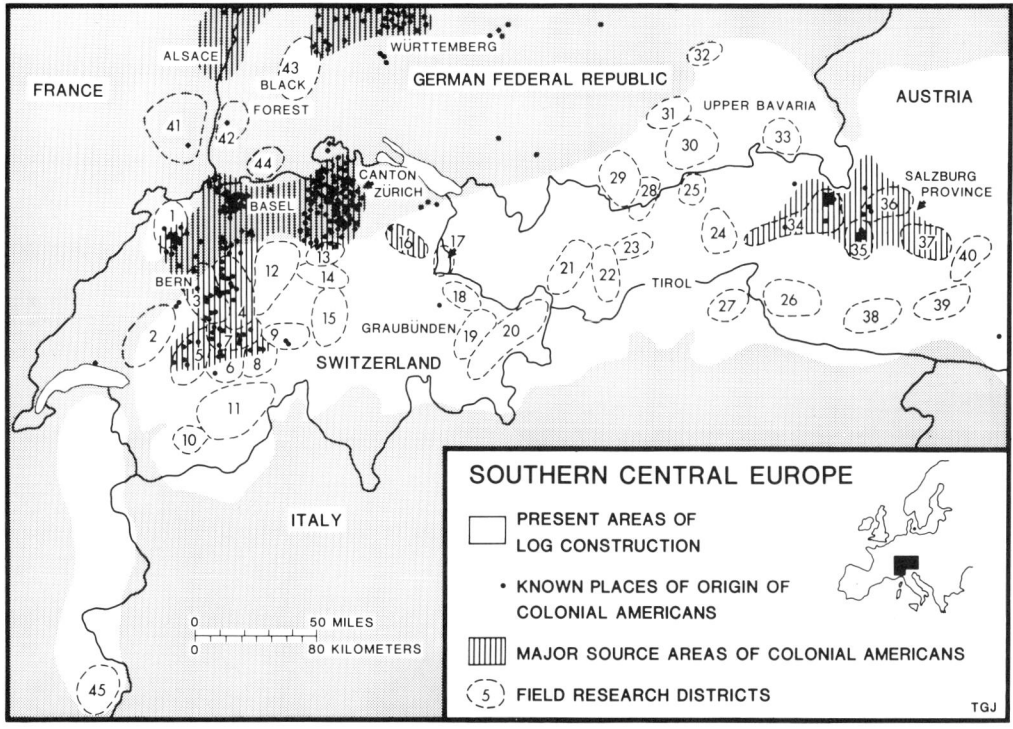

Figure 4.1. The forty-five field research districts are (1) Bernese Jura, (2) Canton Fribourg, (3) Aaretal, (4) Emmental, (5) Simmental, (6) Engstlingental, (7) Thunersee-Brienzersee, (8) Lauterbrunnental-Lütschental, (9) Gadmental-Haslital, (10) Val d'Hérens, (11) eastern Wallis (Valais), (12) Canton Luzern, (13) Canton Zug-southern Zürich, (14) northern shore of Lake Luzern (Vierwaldstättersee), (15) Canton Uri, (16) Toggenburg, (17) Liechtenstein, (18) Prätigau, (19) Landwasser and tributary valleys, (20) Engadin, (21) Oberinntal, (22) Ötztal, (23) Sellraintal, (24) Zillertal, (25) Achental, (26) East Tirol, (27) Antholzertal, (28) Oberisartal, (29) Oberloisach-Ammergau, (30) Tegernsee-Isartal, (31) Diesenhofener Forest, (32) In der Au, (33) Chiemgau, (34) Pinzgau, (35) Gasteinertal, (36) Pongau, (37) Lungau, (38) Oberdrautal, (39) Obergurktal-Millstättersee, (40) Obermurtal, (41) Sundgau, (42) western Breisgau, (43) Hochschwarzwald (upper Black Forest), (44) Hotzenwald, and (45) Queyras. Districts 1 and 3–9 lie in Canton Bern, 18–20 in Canton Graubünden, 21–27 in Tirol, 28–33 in Upper Bavaria, 34–37 in Salzburg Province, and 38–39 in Kärnten. Adequate records for village of origin were available only for Württemberg and cantons Basel, Bern, and Zürich. (Sources: Faust and Brumbaugh, *Lists of Swiss Emigrants*; Yoder, "Emigrants from Wuerttemberg"; Brantley, "Salzburgers in Georgia"; Schultze, "Old Moravian Cemetery of Bethlehem"; Fries, *Records of the Moravians in North Carolina*, vol. 1, pp. 68–69, 131; Beck, "Moravian Graveyards of Lititz"; Kluge, "Moravian Graveyards at Nazareth"; Jones, *Henry Newman's Salzburger Letterbooks*, pp. 319, 366–71, 412–13, 482–83, 592–93.)

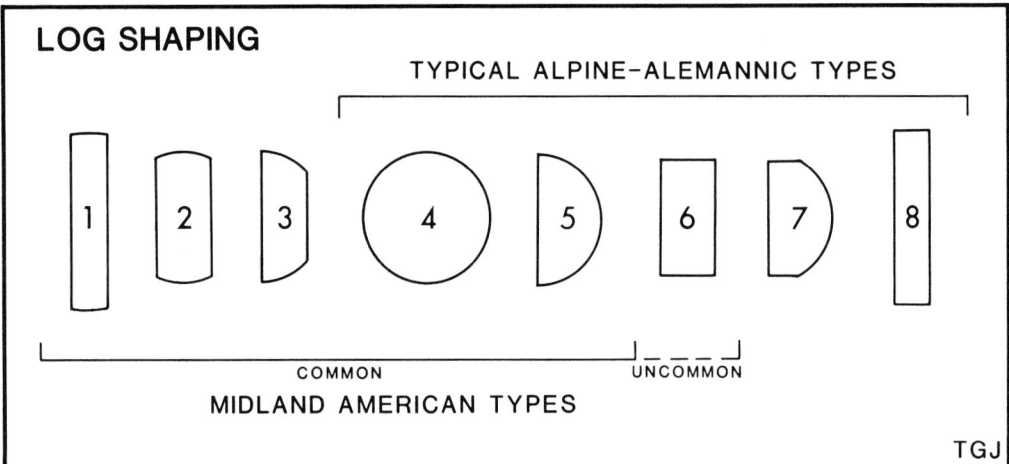

Figure 4.2. The types are (1) tall, thin, two-sided planking, (2) two-sided planking, (3) planked half-log, (4) round-log, (5) half-log, (6) four-sided planking, (7) half-log shaped for chinkless construction, and (8) tall, thin, four-sided planking. In addition to the kinship suggested by types 4 through 6, type 8 is probably antecedent to type 1.

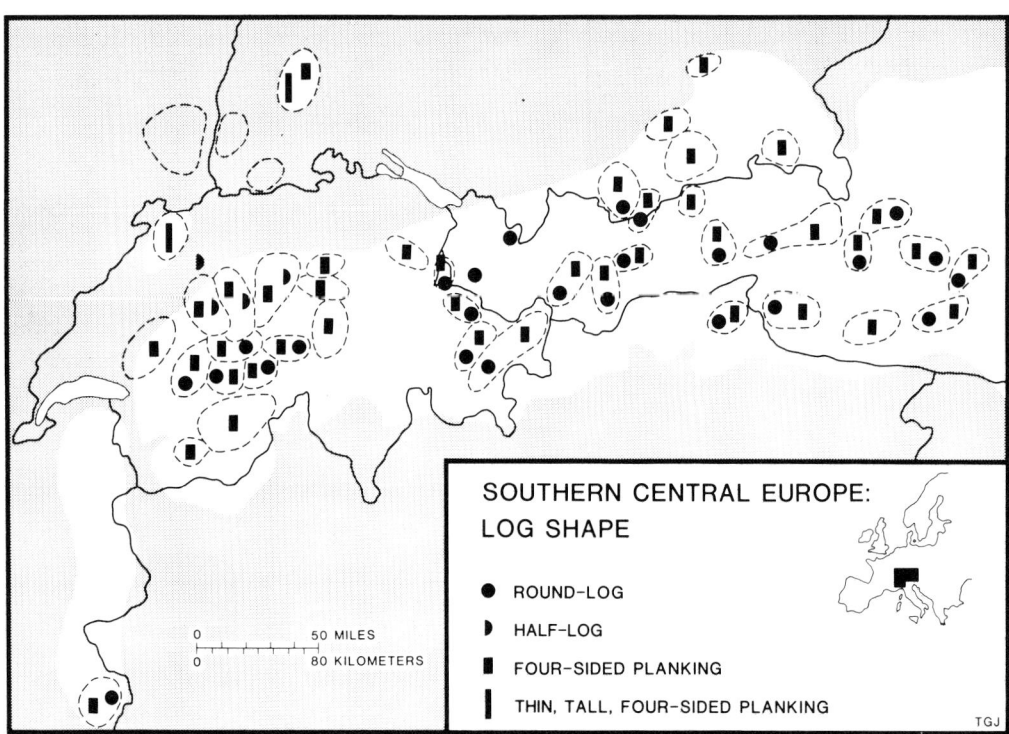

Figure 4.3. For sketches of the types, see Figure 4.2. "Half-log" on the map includes both types 5 and 7. Symbols placed outside field research districts represent data acquired from published secondary sources and not verified in the field.

The Alps and Southwestern Germany

emigrants, as well as adjacent regions where log folk architecture remains a viable part of the cultural landscape, the field research in the Alpine-Alemannic realm included visits to forty-five separate districts from Austrian Steiermark and Kärnten in the east to Alsace and the Bernese Jura in the west (Figure 4.1). These visits revealed a wealth of diversity in regional forms; each province, district, and valley offered a distinctive style. Some of these displayed close affinity with certain Midland American forms, while others were clearly unrelated to New World types.

The Shaping of Timbers

The Alpine-Alemannic techniques of shaping logs are both varied and regionalized.[3] As in the Midland United States, round logs are frequently used in outbuildings and, although rarely, even turn up in house construction. In southern central Europe, though, this crude method is confined to valleys within the Alps proper and is not seen in the Foreland, Jura, or Black Forest (Figures 4.2, 4.3).[4] In the large majority of cases, round-log construction is limited to barns and hay sheds. Half-logs, locally called *Hälblinge*, appear on storage sheds, or *Spycher*, in the forealpine sections of cantons Bern and Luzern, extending northward into Solothurn, where today log construction is very rare.[5] In particular, the Emmental, former Bernese home valley of the American Amish, contains many half-log *Spycher* (Figure 4.4). There is a splendid half-log storage shed from Kiesen in the Aare Valley of the Bernese foreland, possibly dating from the seventeenth century, at the Schweizerisches Freilichtmuseum at Ballenberg, near Brienz. Another half-

Figure 4.4. A farm storage building, or *Spycher*, constructed of half-logs with semilunate notching, in Langnau, Emmental, Canton Bern (field research district 4). Such construction is common on outbuildings in the Alpine foreland of cantons Bern, Solothurn, and Luzern, and closely resembles a type found in the American South. (Photo by T.G.J., 1978.)

log *Spycher*, in the foreland of Canton Luzern, dates from about 1600. In these districts, as in the southern United States, the rounded side of the half-log forms the outer side of the wall, providing a smooth surface on the interior.

By far the most common type, occurring on all kinds of structures, is a rectangular planked timber, carefully flattened on all four sides and measuring

Figure 4.5. Thin, tall planked timbers with full-dovetail notching on a farm storage shed near St. Blasien in the upper Black Forest, West Germany (field research district 43). Note also the chinkless construction. (Photo by T.G.J., 1978.)

Figure 4.6. Tall planking similar to Alemannic European construction, in Cherokee County, North Carolina. (Photo by T.G.J., 1980.)

about four to six inches in thickness by six inches to a foot in height. While similar in dimension to Midland two-sided planking, these differ in that the top and bottom sides are flattened. Occasionally, half-logs are also similarly flattened (Figure 4.2).

A highly distinctive Alemannic method of timber shaping is a tall, thin, board-style planking seen most frequently in the Black Forest and Jura (Figure 4.5). A typical thin-planked log storage shed, representative of the upper Black Forest, is on display at the Vogtsbauernhof open-air museum, near Hornberg in the Gutach district of Baden-Württemberg. The planks in such structures measure as little as about three inches in thickness, but can be as much as two feet in height, and the planks are also flattened on top and bottom to produce a tight wall. Alemannic planking was apparently implanted in Midland America, though derivation from a British sawn-plank tradition is possible. In contrast to either Alemannic or British prototypes, American tall, thin planking retains the natural curvature of the log on top and bottom.

The Alps and Southwestern Germany

One particularly noteworthy American concentration of tall, thin planking exists in the Great Smoky Mountains of North Carolina and Tennessee (Figure 4.6). At Oconoluftee in Swain County, North Carolina, stands a log house built of planks measuring four and one-half by twenty-one inches, and hewn logs with twenty-five-inch faces can be seen on Little Greenbrier School in the Great Smoky Mountains National Park. Diminished tree size west of the Mississippi River reduced the spectacular dimensions of Alemannic planking, but even in the westernmost belt of oak woods in Texas, in Parker County, one can see logs measuring five by thirteen inches.

Two-sided hewing, the most common Midland American shaping technique, is extremely rare in southern central Europe. The handful of examples observed during the field study were all in the Austrian Alps. The Ötztal in Tirol offers some specimens, as does Salzburg Province.[6]

Invariably, even on the oldest Alpine-Alemannic log walls, the ax score marks and slight surface irregularities produced by the adze, so typical of Midland hewn-log construction, are absent. Instead, the planked logs, regardless of width or height, display smooth surfaces apparently produced by ripsawing.

Some Alpine and Alemannic log buildings, then, consist of timbers shaped in a manner identical or similar to Midland American forms. The best cases for diffusion from southern central Europe to the United States can be made for Alemannic thin planking, for Swiss foreland *Hälblinge*, and for Alpine round-log construction. Since Finns and Swedes earlier introduced the use of round logs, the Alpine contribution should probably be interpreted as a reinforcement rather than an initial introduction.

Corner Timbering

In most of southern central Europe, as in Midland America, the dominant means of corner construction is the notch, with timbers from adjacent walls affixed directly to one another by a locking joint.[7] Close inspection, however, reveals relatively few similarities between the two regions in corner timbering (Figure 4.7). Two very common Midland types, the half-dovetail and V notches, are altogether absent in the Alpine-Alemannic tradition. Saddle notching, usually the topsided variety that is a minority type in America, appears on outbuildings and occasionally on houses within the Alps proper, but never in forealpine Switzerland or southwestern Germany, the major source regions of Pennsylvania Germans (Figure 4.8).

Instead, most southern central European houses are double notched, a type virtually unknown in the Midland American subculture.[8] Double notching has long been prevalent in Switzerland, where venerable examples include the Chüechlihus (1408) in the Emmental, the Haus zur Sonne (1409) in Küssnacht am Rigi on Lake Luzern, and a 1565 dwelling at Teufi near Davos, in Canton Graubünden (Figure 4.9).

Also common on houses in some Alpine-Alemannic districts is the full-dovetail notch, a relatively uncommon American type. While rare in Switzerland, full-dovetailing increases in frequency northward into Germany and eastward into Austria (Figure 4.8). Local ethnographers regard full-dovetailing as a newer, alien type in Switzerland and Austria, though it appears on

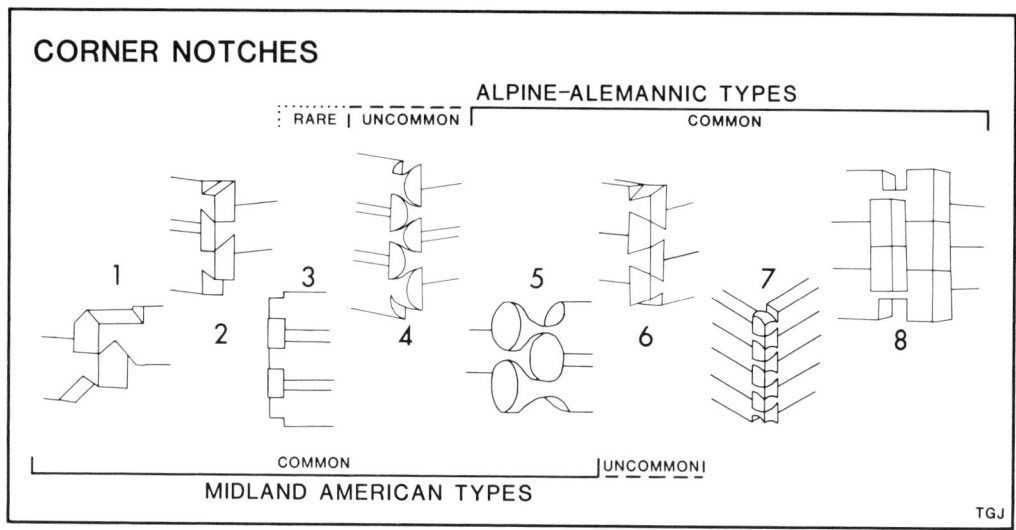

Figure 4.7. The types shown are (1) V notch, (2) half-dovetail, (3) square, (4) semilunate, (5) saddle, (6) full-dovetail, (7) flared full-dovetail, and (8) double.

the thirteenth-century Zwingli birth house in Canton St. Gallen (Figure 4.10).[9] It is most common in Upper Bavaria, a strongly Catholic region that sent few colonists to colonial America, and in the Black Forest. Many examples of Bavarian-Austrian dovetailing contain flared or rounded surfaces, a subtype unknown in America (Figure 4.7).[10]

The few scattered examples of square notching in southern central Europe normally occur only on individual logs within walls otherwise dovetailed or double notched (Figure 4.11). These few specimens were seemingly either double notches with the projecting end sawn off or incorrectly fashioned dovetail joints. A connection to New World square notching is highly unlikely. More impressive evidence of possible antecedence is seen in the semilunate notching on storage sheds in the Bernese foreland (Figure 4.4).[11] Most outbuildings, though, bear the same full-dovetail and double notches typical of dwellings in the area. Clearly, dissimilarities prevail in this common comparison of American and southern central European corner notching.

Another common Alemannic method of securing the joints, one not involving notching, is corner posting, in which the logs from adjacent walls are tenoned and fitted into slots fashioned in vertical corner beams (Figure 4.12).[12] In effect, corner posting, or *Blockständerbau*, is a transitional type between notched-log construction and half-timbering. In Midland America, corner posting is rare. One notable example is the 1741 lower story of the famous Golden Plough Tavern in York, Pennsylvania (Figure 4.13).[13] Perhaps the builders of the Golden Plough remembered the corner posting of the Black Forest or cantons Bern, Luzern,

The Alps and Southwestern Germany

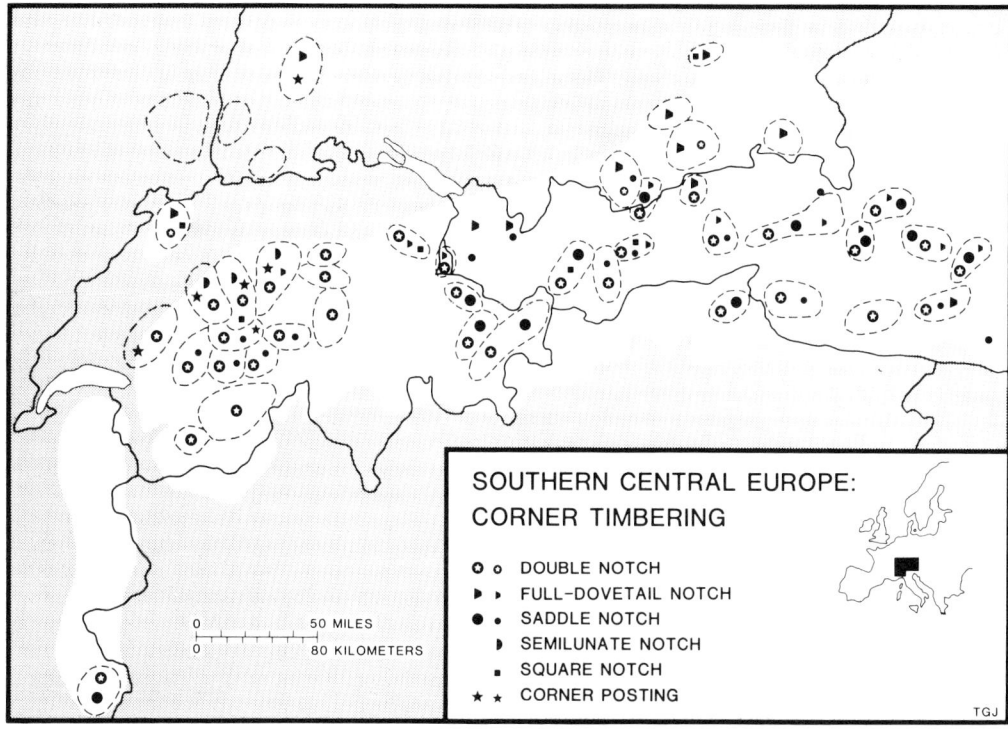

Figure 4.8. For sketches of the notch types see Figure 4.7. Large symbols indicate that the type occurs frequently in the district shown; small symbols indicate less frequent occurrence. Full-dovetailing includes both the regular and flared subtypes. Square notching is extremely rare, and each symbol designates only one occurrence. Symbols placed outside field research districts represent data acquired from published secondary sources and not verified in the field.

Figure 4.9. Double notching on a log granary in the village of Evolène in the Val d'Hérens, Canton Valais (field research district 10). This notch is the prevalent type on both dwellings and outbuildings in most of southern central Europe. (Photo by T.G.J., 1978.)

Figure 4.10. Full-dovetail notching, in places becoming square notching, on the seven-hundred-year-old Zwingli birth house, Wildhaus, Toggenburg district, Canton St. Gallen (field research district 16). The four-sided planking permitted chinkless construction. Double notching is found on the second story of the Zwingli house. (Photo by T.G.J., 1978.)

Figure 4.11. Square notching on a barn near Kuhtai in the Sellraintal, North Tirol (field research district 23). A very rare type in the Alps, this corner-timbering method probably resulted from the sawing off of double-notched logs. (Photo by T.G.J., 1978.)

Zürich, or Fribourg (Figure 4.8).[14] The field study recorded a corner-posted Black Forest house dating from 1502 and one in the Emmental built in 1408. In any case, the rarity of corner posting in America argues against significant Alemannic carpentry influence in the Midland tradition.

The Spacing of Logs in the Wall

Alpine-Alemannic carpenters usually build chinkless walls, so tight that a razor blade normally cannot be slipped between the logs of a Swiss chalet or Black Forest house (Figures 4.5, 4.9, 4.12). The American observer, accustomed to "prison-stripe" chinked log walls—thick gray lines of weathered wood alternating with thinner stripes of earthen chinking cement—finds the solid wooden walls of most Alpine-Alemannic houses visually alien.

In southern central Europe, chink walls do occur in some areas, but these are almost invariably on hay sheds,

The Alps and Southwestern Germany 95

Figure 4.12. Corner-posting on a Black Forest house in the Gutach (field research district 43). Common in southwestern Germany and the Alpine foreland of Switzerland, this method is a transitional type between log construction and half-timbering. (Photo by T.G.J., 1978.)

Figure 4.13. Corner-posting dating from 1741 on the Golden Plough Tavern, York, Pennsylvania. This is one of the few examples of corner-posting found in the Midland hearth area. While the corner post is typically Alemannic, the filled chinks are not. (Photo by T.G.J., 1976.)

where the unfilled chinks permit air to reach and dry the hay (Figure 4.14). The Swiss aptly describe such walls as *lockerer Blockbau*, or "loose log construction."[15] Not infrequently, Alpine log barns have tight walls in the lower level and chinks in the hayloft above (Figure 4.15).

Only in the Obergurktal of Kärnten province in Alpine Austria did the field research detect houses with American-style chinked walls (Figure 4.16). They are concentrated in the region between the Millstättersee and the mountain pass called the Turracher Höhe. While these chinked Carinthian houses serve as ample warning against sweeping generalizations about Alpine log construction techniques, they seem an unlikely prototype for the Midland style. Kärnten sent few settlers to colonial America, though some Carinthian Protestants, including the Nüssen family from near Klagenfurt, migrated to Pennsylvania in the 1740s.[16]

The Alpine experience with open-chink haybarn construction could certainly have been applied to Midland American house building as an expedient frontier technique. If, however, American chinking is derived from European haybarn construction, then the Swedes and Finns, who arrived much earlier bearing an identical practice, are the more likely agents of diffusion.

Roof Construction

The most common Alpine-Alemannic roof structure, particularly prevalent in Switzerland, is the ridgepole-and-purlin type.[17] In this case the introduction of a log carpentry tradition from southern central Europe reinforced a trait implanted earlier as a frontier form by Finnish and Swedish colonists. Some other roof structure types completely unknown in Midland America also appear in Alpine regions, in particular a variety in which a ridgepole rests upon vertical beams and a purlin roof lacking a ridgepole (Figure 4.17).[18]

Raftered roofs without ridgepole or logs in the gables occur in some Alpine districts, particularly Kärnten and Steiermark provinces in Austria.[19] The gable openings are sometimes enclosed by vertical boards in the Midland American manner.[20] In general, however, the Alpine districts displaying the greatest similarity to American roof structures possess no substantial migratory links to the colonial New World. For the same reason that Carinthian chinked walls are an unlikely prototype for Midland construction, eastern Alpine roof types should be rejected as a model.

On the other hand, the Alpine region boasts many splendid shingle roofs, particularly on outbuildings within the Alps proper.[21] In almost every respect,

Figure 4.14. Hay barn with chink walls, four-sided planking, and double notching, Lauterbrunnental, Berner Oberland (field research district 8). The chinks are left open to permit air to reach and dry the hay. (Photo by T.G.J., 1978.)

(Opposite, top)
Figure 4.15. The chinked houses of Kärnten are unique among dwellings in the forty-five field research districts. The principal concentration of covered bridges is in the Emmental in Canton Bern, source of America's Amish. Symbols placed outside field research districts were derived from published secondary sources.

(Opposite, bottom)
Figure 4.16. A Carinthian chinked log house, near Ebene Reichenau in the Obergurktal (field research district 39). Such construction, very similar to that of the Midland American region, occurs on dwellings in only one of the forty-five Alpine-Alemannic regions. Note also the front-facing gable. (Photo by T.G.J., 1978.)

The Alps and Southwestern Germany

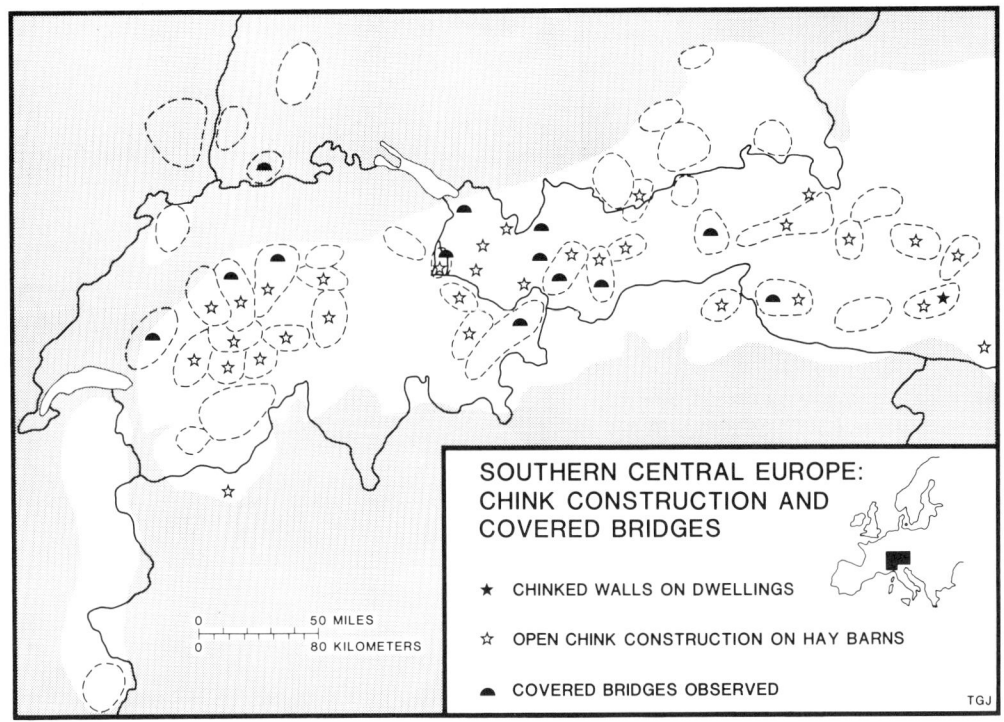

Figure 4.17. Gable view of the double-crib Alpine type 1 barn with large forebay, Saas im Prätigau, Canton Graubünden (field research district 18). The slope location is also typical of the Prätigau barns. Note the purlin roof without ridgepole and the stair beneath the forebay. Identical stairs are seen occasionally in Pennsylvania; see Dornbusch and Heyl, *Pennsylvania German Barns*, pp. 105–7. (Photo by T.G.J., 1978.)

these wooden roofs are similar to the traditional type of Midland America, even in details of construction such as the "capping" of roof ridges by allowing shingles on the windward side to project beyond the peak. Surely the American shingling tradition derives from the Alps, particularly since northern Europe, the eastern German lands, and the British Isles offer no equally acceptable prototypes.

Dwelling Floor Plans

Most Alpine and Alemannic house floor plans are fundamentally different from American types. The typical log dwelling of southern central Europe is massive and multistory, occasionally soaring to three or even four full stories. Lateral expansion is rare, even in areas of dispersed rural settlement. A front-facing gable, well exemplified by the Swiss chalet and Black Forest house, is most typical (Figure 4.16). Alpine-Alemannic houses generally contain more interior floorspace than their American counterparts and often include dwelling and barn under the same roof. Decoration is ornate and even spectacular. Clearly, such dwellings offer no prototypes for Midland American forms.[22]

The so-called German "continental"

log house of Pennsylvania, an asymmetrical dwelling with central chimney and side-facing gables, is rare in the Alpine-Alemannic realm.[23] In a raised form, referred to by some as the "Swiss bank house," it appears along the shady *ubac* slope of the northernmost of the two Alpine ridges, but is nowhere a dominant type. While the Swiss bank house was transferred to Pennsylvania, it never attained widespread acceptance in America.[24] Rather, it was one of those numerous form elements brought to the New World, only to vanish as the imported European cultures underwent a drastic simplification. To the north, well beyond the area of log construction, the "continental" floor plan, in both one-and-a-half and two-story height, is common in the Frankish-dominated Upper Rhine Plain. The diffusion to America was in all probability achieved from that area by Palatines, whose imprint on Pennsylvania Dutch culture is prevalent in dialect and many other aspects.[25]

Another log house type bearing some resemblance to American dwellings is the eastern Alpine *Rauchstubenhaus*. Consisting of two undivided log pens separated by an enclosed passageway and covered with a side-gable roof, the "smoking room house" bears a resemblance to the American central-hall house and to the Fenno-Scandian *parstuga*.[26] I observed no such houses west of Kärnten and Steiermark in the eastern Alps of Austria, and it seems highly unlikely that they could have reached America from those districts, so solidly Catholic and peripheral to the major source regions of colonial emigration.

The failure of the Alpine-Alemannic Germans to implant their traditional dwellings successfully in America is at first glance puzzling, given the large numbers of immigrants. Perhaps the answer lies in the ornateness, complexity, and huge size of their houses. Such forms were poorly suited to the frontier and, possibly more important, would have stressed the foreign character of their occupants at precisely the time when the colonial Germans were willingly adopting many features of the British-American host culture. The Frankish side-gable continental house was similar enough to the pre-existing British and Scandinavian types to blend into the Midland cultural landscape. A massive Black Forest or Bernese housebarn, on the other hand, would have drawn attention, and possibly derision, to its occupant. The most common Alpine-Alemannic dwellings were simply too spectacular for the American setting.

Barn Form Elements

Four major features of Midland construction occur in parts of the Alpine-Alemannic region. These include (1) two-level height, in which an upper level devoted to hay and feed storage rests atop a lower-level stable; (2) a banked ramp, or *Rampe*, providing wagon access to an entrance in the upper level of the barn; (3) the *Vorbau*, variously known in the United States as a "forebay," "forbau," or "overshot," a cantilevered projection jutting from one eave side of the upper level; and (4) the double-crib floor plan, consisting of two log cribs separated by a central runway or passage (Figure 4.18). The field study found numerous multi-level bank barns in Canton Bern and the Black Forest, but only to the east did they begin appearing in conjunction with forebays and double-crib plans.

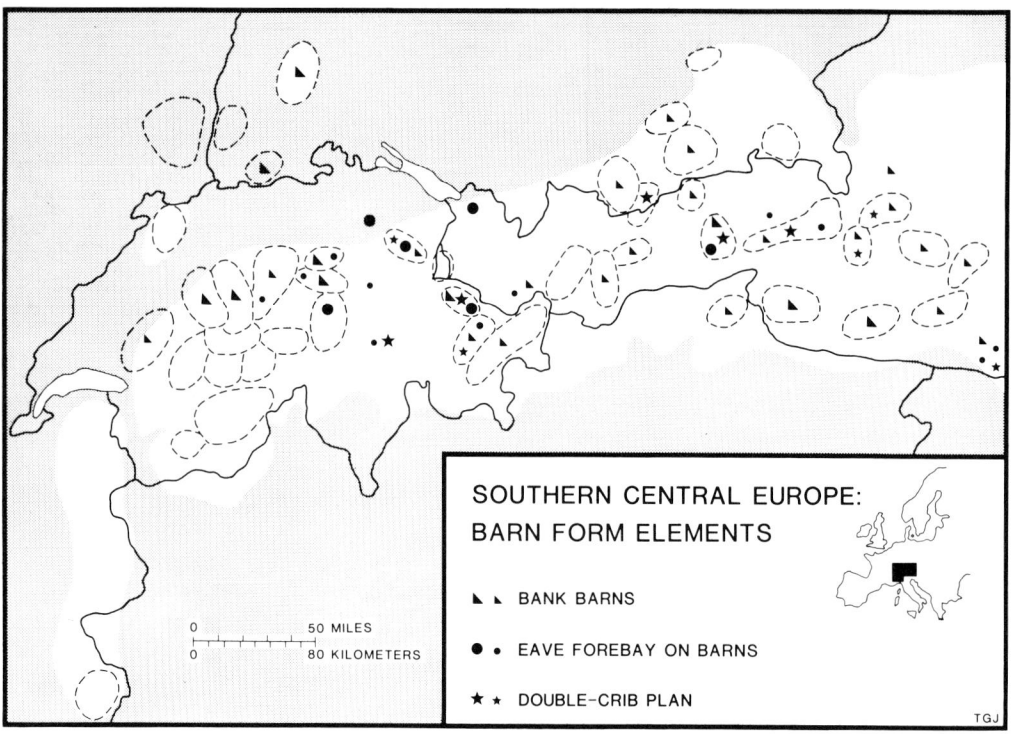

Figure 4.18. Large symbols indicate that the element occurs frequently in the district shown; small symbols indicate less frequent occurrence. Symbols placed outside field research districts were derived from published secondary sources, in particular Ensminger, "Search for the Origin," p. 67; Weiss, "Stallbauten und Heutraggeräte," map 1; and Gschwend, *Atlas der Schweiz*, sections 36 and 36a.

These four form elements—bank, forebay, two-level height, and double-crib plan—together constitute the major diagnostic traits of the famous "Pennsylvania barn."[27] The prevailing view has been that the Pennsylvania type evolved in Midland America through a combination of the log double-crib plan with bank and forebay.[28] Glassie proposed that this barn "was apparently developed in eastern Pennsylvania by building a log double-crib barn . . . on a hillside."[29] "Nowhere in the Old World," he declared, "can the precise prototype of the [Pennsylvania] bank barn be found."[30] John K. Heyl agreed, asserting that the Pennsylvania German barn had "no direct precedent in structures of similar use either in Britain or in western Europe."[31] The familiar stonemasonry and frame construction of the present-day Pennsylvania barns supposedly developed later, in post-frontier times, from the log prototype. The double-crib plan that contributed to the making of the Pennsylvania barn was, according to Glassie, an "ancient German" type, "brought by the Germans to Pennsylvania."[32] He implied that this ancestral log double-crib was a common central European type and suggested a possible Swiss prototype.[33]

Glassie and others believe, further,

that the imported German double-crib also gave rise in America to a variety of double-crib log subtypes and to "four-crib" and "transverse-crib" barns.[34] In other words, the diffusion of the Germanic double-crib barn was supposedly of crucial importance to the development of most major Midland types.

These traditional views must now be called into question. It seems likely that the Pennsylvania barn was fully evolved in log and possibly also masonry-frame forms before the migrations to America occurred; that the ancestral double-crib log barn is not a widespread type in central Europe or even the Alps, but instead occurs in relatively few districts; that various American subtypes of the double-crib log barn originated in Europe; and that the transverse-crib barn perhaps also has an Alpine prototype. Pennsylvania's role as a center of pioneer inventiveness has been exaggerated, and its importance as a cultural hearth area may have been overstated.

Forebays and Banks

Forebay, multilevel height, bank, and double-crib plan do not always or even normally appear in conjunction, either in southern central Europe or the United States. In America forebays are most common on bank barns in southeastern Pennsylvania, though "Dutch" migrants from the Delaware and Susquehanna valleys carried this form element southward into the Shenandoah Valley of Virginia, westward at least as far as Indiana, and across the Niagara frontier into southern Ontario.[35] The bank barn without forebay is much more widespread in North America, appearing throughout a broad belt from Québec to Iowa among people of Yankee, Midland, French-Canadian, and nineteenth-century European heritage.[36]

In southern central Europe, forebay barns are absent altogether in Alsace, southwestern Germany, and Canton Bern (Figure 4.18). The famous Emmental on the Bernese foreland, locally called the *Mittelland*, is devoid of forebays. Not surprisingly, the Amish, whose ancestors lived along the Emme, generally built barns lacking forebays in America.[37] Forebays begin appearing to the east, initially in non-log construction in cantons Luzern, Zug, and Zürich, become more common in Schwyz, St. Gallen, and the Vorderrheintal, and rise to prevalence in the Prätigau and Schanfigg, two adjacent valleys in Canton Graubünden (Figures 4.17, 4.19). Still farther east, forebay barns reappear at various places in Austria, especially the Zillertal, a lovely Tirolean valley, and a scattering can be seen even in Salzburg Province, Kärnten, and Steiermark.[38] A notable concentration of log forebay barns stands in the Toggenburg district of Canton St. Gallen, including the village of Wildhaus, birthplace of Reformation leader Huldrych Zwingli, many of whose religious descendants came to Pennsylvania (Figure 4.19). The Toggenburg was a source of emigrants to colonial America.[39] Almost certainly, the Midland American forebay is derived from central to eastern Switzerland. We should look among the immigrants from Luzern, St. Gallen, and, above all, Graubünden for the agents of diffusion.

Bank barns are much more widespread than forebays in the Alpine-Alemannic area (Figure 4.18). One encounters them from the Black Forest eastward at least as far as Steiermark and from the Alpine foreland of Bavaria southward to the Vorderrheintal

Figure 4.19. A log forebay barn in Huldrych Zwingli's birth village of Wildhaus, Toggenburg district, Canton St. Gallen (field research district 16). The forebay is very modest in size but still similar to those of Pennsylvania. (Photo by T.G.J., 1978.)

(Figure 4.20). Only in the southern and western perimeters of the study area, in districts bordering or within the Romance language regions, are bank barns rare or absent. So common are they in the major Swiss source regions of the Pennsylvania Germans that it is not difficult to accept Amos Long's suggestion that the Midland American type is derived from southern central Europe.[40] The bank barns of Scandinavia, as well as those found in northern England, are less satisfactory prototypes, since in both Britain and northern Europe the major concentrations of bank barns do not coincide with major source areas of American settlers.[41] Still, multiple diffusion quite possibly occurred.

Double-Crib Plans

Log double-crib barns, known to local ethnographers as *alpine Querscheunen*, or "Alpine lateral barns," are not nearly so widespread, either in the Alps or in central Europe at large, as Glassie and others would have us believe. They occurred in only eight of the forty-five districts inspected in this study, and

The Alps and Southwestern Germany

Figure 4.20. A gable-entrance bank barn in the hamlet of Fahrni, Canton Bern (field research district 3). Perched on heights above the Aaretal near Thun in the Bernese foreland, Fahrni was apparently the ancestral home of some colonial emigrants who went to America, since the family name Fahrni, often corrupted as Forney, appears among the Pennsylvania Germans. Bank barns are typical of most Alpine-Alemannic districts. (Photo by T.G.J., 1978.)

they can be termed common in but four (Figure 4.18). Such plans are numerous in the Prätigau, the Zillertal, the Pinzgau in Salzburg Province, and the Oberisartal in Upper Bavaria (Figure 4.21). From these we could select only two, the Prätigau and Pinzgau, where double-cribs are the prevalent type. To these we should perhaps add Graubünden's Schanfigg, where log double-crib barns are also dominant.[42] Some also occur in Kärnten in the eastern Alps.[43]

Further complicating the matter is the presence of at least five distinctive types of double-crib barn in these few Alpine areas (Figure 4.22). Of greatest interest to students of Pennsylvania Dutch traditional culture are multilevel double-cribs equipped with forebay and bank (Figures 4.17, 4.23). I will label this the type 1 Alpine double-crib. Robert Ensminger and I observed these barns independently and virtually simultaneously in 1978 in the Prätigau region of Graubünden, and we both concluded, without consultation, that they offered the most satisfactory prototype for the Pennsylvania barn.[44] Subsequently, an article pub-

Figure 4.21. A double-crib log barn with projecting forebay, Saas im Prätigau, Canton Graubünden (field research district 18). The upper level is for hay storage, as is revealed by the chink walls. Such structures are prototypes of the Pennsylvania barn. (Photo by T.G.J., 1978.)

(Opposite, top)
Figure 4.22. Five principal types can be distinguished among the double-crib log barns observed in the Alps. *Type 1* is two level, with bank and forebay (from Saas im Prätigau, Canton Graubünden, field research district 18); *type 2* is a raised two-bay with bank entrance (just south of Davos-Platz, valley of the Landwasser, Canton Graubünden, field research district 19); *type 3* has partitioned cribs and lacks a bank (near the Bad Hofgastein railroad depot, Gasteinertal, Salzburg Province, research district 35); *type 4* is an open-passage hay shed with square cribs (outskirts of Bad Hofgastein, field research district 35); and *type 5* is a front-gable bank barn with elongated cribs (on a mountainside above Zell am Ziller, Zillertal, Tirol, field research district 24).

(Opposite, bottom)
Figure 4.23. A view of the upslope side of a log double-crib forebay barn (type 1), Saas im Prätigau, Canton Graubünden (field research district 18). Note the chink walls, saddle notching, bank entrance, and doors closing off the central runway. (Photo by T.G.J., 1978.)

The Alps and Southwestern Germany

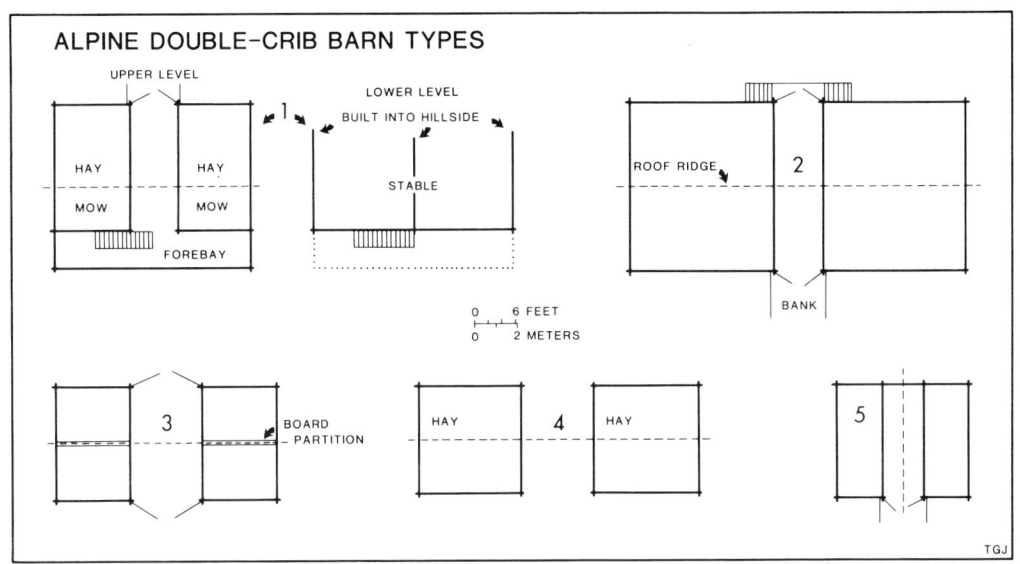

lished forty years ago by Swiss ethnographer Richard Weiss has come to my attention. In it, Weiss labeled the Graubünden forebay bank barn as his "type IIIb," noting that its concentration lay in the Prätigau and Schanfigg, with lesser clusters in the upper reaches of the Vorderrheintal, around Davos, and in the Montafon Valley of neighboring Vorarlberg Province, Austria. He judged the forebay bank barn to be a highly practical type, a virtue permitting its diffusion at the expense of other traditional forms. In his view, the Graubünden type IIIb gained its efficiency by minimizing the labor of hay delivery.[45]

This same efficiency would have given the Graubünden forebay bank barn an even greater advantage once implanted in Pennsylvania, a colonial setting where allegiance to ancestral regional European forms would have been weaker. Numerous eighteenth-century American settlers came from Graubünden, perhaps including some of the Prätigau *Walser*, descendants of medieval Alemannic immigrants from upper Wallis (Valais) among whom, as Weiss noted, the type IIIb barn is especially common.[46] It is known that natives of Chur, a town at the outlet of the Schanfigg Valley, came to colonial America.[47]

Conceivably, though, the Graubünden barn may not be Alemannic or even German-Swiss in origin. Romansh-speaking descendants of the soldiers of imperial Rome once dominated the Prätigau. The mountainside village of Saas, which contains an impressive cluster of log double-crib forebay bank barns, has a seventeenth-century public fountain bearing a Romansh inscription, though early nineteenth-century log houses there have German inscriptions. The word *Prätigau* itself is derived from the Romansh *protens*, meaning "meadows."

The Graubünden double-crib forebay bank type is a true barn, situated adjacent to farmhouses and combining the functions of stabling and feed storage. It contains an upper-level hayloft, normally distinguishable by its chink walls, a contrast to the chinkless construction of the stable level (Figure 4.22). Cribs, exclusive of the forebay, are elongated, averaging about ten to eleven feet in width by seventeen to eighteen feet in depth. The forebay projects two to six feet beyond the lower level. A stair is normally situated beneath the overhang of the forebay. Doors close off the sole entrance to the upper level, located on the up-slope side. Here, then, is precisely the log prototype of the Pennsylvania barn Glassie and Heyl claimed did not exist in Europe. We must discard the notion that the log forebay barn is a New World invention. The American barns of this type, still visible in the landscapes of Pennsylvania, Ohio, and other states, belong unmistakably to Alpine material culture.[48]

Nor are barns of the Pennsylvania type confined to Graubünden or limited to log construction. In the Zillertal, a staunchly Catholic valley in Austrian Tirol, stand barns similarly startling to the American eye. Particularly between Aschau and Zell, along the banks of the Ziller, one sees Pennsylvania-type forebay barns with the lower level built of masonry and the projecting loft above framed with vertical siding (Figure 4.24). In these and most other respects, the Aschau barns are identical to those of postfrontier Pennsylvania. Their presence in the Alps necessarily

The Alps and Southwestern Germany

Figure 4.24. This splendid barn would be at home in Pennsylvania, but its actual location is near Aschau in the Zillertal, North Tirol, Austria (field research district 24). Its similarity to the Pennsylvania barn includes forebay, masonry lower level, vertical boards on upper level, multiple doors and windows beneath forebay, and small windows on the forebay. In Pennsylvania, this barn would be called a "schottscheier" because of its narrow forebay. See Shoemaker, *Pennsylvania Barn*, p. 46. The small forebay windows are very common in Pennsylvania; see Dornbusch and Heyl, *Pennsylvania German Barns*, p. 133. (Photo by T.G.J., 1978.)

raises the question whether the classic Pennsylvania barn was not fully developed in Europe prior to the American migration.

Obviously, though, the Zillertal barns are in the "wrong" location if one accepts the notion that Tirolers did not emigrate to Pennsylvania. It is possible that we do not know enough about the origins of colonial Germans to validate this notion. To give an example of how diverse these origins may have been, one can document the migration of a German-speaking settler from the Siebenbürgen district of Romania to colonial York County, Pennsylvania.[49] Although the Zillertal today is Catholic, the valley once had an oppressed Protestant minority. Seeking religious freedom, many Zillertal Protestants emigrated. Some found their way to Silesia, where they implanted traditional Alpine architecture, complete with forebay barns, in and around the village of Zillertal, near Jelenia Góra (Hirschberg).[50]

Perhaps others found their way to America. It is possible, of course, that the Zillertal barns represent an independent invention, a parallel transition from log to masonry-frame. Too, the Pennsylvania forebay type is often called the "Sweitzer" barn, implying a Swiss rather than Tirolean origin.[51]

Ensminger suggests still another Swiss area, the Entlebuch in Canton Luzern, as a possible source of the Pennsylvania forebay barn. Containing the westernmost outlier of Swiss forebay barns, the Entlebuch has the advantage of being closer to the major Bernese foreland sources of Pennsylvania Germans.[52]

Other Alpine Double-Crib Types

Type 1 barns are by no means the only double-cribs found in both the Old and New Worlds. Alpine specimens similar or virtually identical to most other Midland American double-cribs can be found. Accordingly, a second objection to the traditionalist view centers upon the discovery of potential Alpine prototypes for various additional American forms of the double-crib barn.

Classification is an arbitrary and hazardous business at best, but perhaps four more Alpine double-crib subtypes, in addition to the Graubünden type already described, should be distinguished. The type 2 Alpine double-crib retains the multilevel character and bank entrance of type 1, but lacks a forebay and occurs exclusively along valley floors (Figures 4.22, 4.25).[53] The lower level is little more than a crawl space, possibly intended to accommodate springtime river flooding. Both ends of the narrow central passageway are closed with doors, and twin rear stairways provide access to the upper level on the side opposite the bank. The cribs are large and only slightly elongated, measuring about twenty by twenty-four feet. The field study located relatively few such barns, but some stand along the valley of the Landwasser near Davos in Graubünden. No doubt more once existed there, before the health resort and tourist boom overtook the Davos region earlier in this century. The Alpine type 2 is similar to the American "raised-three bay" barn of the northern United States, a type long assumed to be English in origin.

The type 3 Alpine double-crib is also a valley type, but smaller than type 2, single level, and lacking a bank. The elongated cribs, about ten by fifteen feet, are subdivided by log or board partitions along the axis of the roof ridge, and doors close off both ends of the runway (Figure 4.22). In America type 3 double-cribs, often without floors, are a very common southern Appalachian type and also occur west of the mountains. In the Alps type 3 barns seem confined mainly to the Gasteinertal, in the vicinity of the famous resort town of Hofgastein, Salzburg Province (Figure 4.26).

My type 4 double-crib is exclusively a hay shed, accordingly referred to as a *Heustadel* by Austrian Alpine farmers. This specialized function is revealed by its chink walls, top to bottom, and its location out in meadows away from farmsteads and villages. The single-level cribs are perfectly square and rather small, measuring about fifteen feet on each side (Figure 4.22). Normally, the runway, about eight to ten feet wide, is left open, but doors are sometimes present (Figure 4.27). Type 4 double-cribs are highly concentrated in the Pinzgau district of Salzburg

The Alps and Southwestern Germany

Figure 4.25. Double-crib bank barn without forebay (type 2), near Davos-Platz, valley of the Landwasser, Canton Graubünden (field research district 19). Note the multilevel plan, ramp, bank, and doors. For the exact dimensions of this barn, see Figure 4.22. (Photo by T.G.J., 1978.)

Province; the region near the Salzach in the vicinity of Mittersill revealed over fifty such barns along only one road. Lesser numbers exist in the adjacent Pongau and Gasteinertal, as well as around Mittenwald, in the Oberisartal, Upper Bavaria. Type 4, in its openrunway form, is a near duplicate of log barns seen widely throughout the southern United States (Figure 4.28).

Type 5 differs from all the others by virtue of its front-facing gable (Figure 4.22). Two highly elongated cribs flank the runway, causing the structure closely to resemble the "drive-in corncrib" of Appalachian America.[54] Unlike the corncrib, though, Alpine type 5 is most often a hay shed. Typically, it is built on a slope, becoming multilevel in the process, and a bank is usually present. Its most common location is in a hillside meadow far above the valley floor (Figure 4.29). This type occurs only infrequently, and mainly in two areas, the Zillertal and the Wagrain vicinity in the Pongau, Salzburg Province.

The Salzburg Protestants

Close American counterparts exist for all five of these Alpine double-cribs.

Figure 4.26. An Alpine type 3 double-crib barn, near Hofgastein, Gasteinertal, Salzburg Province (field research district 35). The small, elongated cribs are each subdivided by a log and board partition into two bins. Note also the "Dutch" doors, shingle roof, and roofing tiles awaiting installation. Very similar barns occur through much of the American upper South, and Hofgastein was a major source of Georgia Salzburgers (Jones, *Henry Newman's Salzburger Letterbooks*, p. 366). (Photo by T.G.J., 1978.)

(Opposite, top)
Figure 4.27. An Alpine type 4 double-crib hay shed, near Bramberg, on the Salzach River, Pinzgau district, Salzburg Province (field research district 34). In every respect—saddle notch, round logs, chink walls, open passage, square cribs, dimensions, and capped shingle roof—this barn is identical to hundreds in the American South (see Figure 4.28). Salzburg Protestants may have introduced this barn type into Georgia in the 1730s. The Pinzgau was the source region for some Georgia settlers (Jones, *Henry Newman's Salzburger Letterbooks*, pp. 366, 367, 412, 413). (Photo by T.G.J., 1978.)

(Opposite, bottom)
Figure 4.28. This double-crib barn in Tyler County, southeast Texas, is in almost every respect an Alpine type 4. Compare it with the barn in Figure 4.27. (Photo courtesy of Professor Francis E. Abernethy of Stephen F. Austin State University, Nacogdoches, Texas.)

The Alps and Southwestern Germany

Types 3, 4, and 5 all occur in Salzburg Province and could conceivably have reached the United States with the Salzburg Protestants, twenty thousand of whom were expelled from the mountain districts of Salzburg Province by the local archbishop in 1731–32. Most of these displaced Lutherans found new homes in Prussia and other religiously tolerant European lands, but some came to America, where they established a major, permanent foothold in Effingham County, Georgia. Moreover, even though there are few references to Salzburgers in colonial Pennsylvania, it is certain that some members of this oppressed minority did indeed find their way to Penn's religious haven.[55] Matthias Bacher, a native Salzburger carpenter, was in Pennsylvania by 1754, and certain other Protestants fleeing the archbishop's wrath came there as early as 1742.[56]

Conceivably, too, the Salzburger double-cribs could have been implanted by the Georgia settlers, particularly since that group is believed to have introduced other aspects of their Old World culture and settlement into the South.[57] The Alpine types 3, 4, and 5 double-cribs are most common in the southern states, but perhaps non-existent in Pennsylvania. In Texas, for example, type 4 open-runway double-cribs are prevalent, and type 3 barns abound in Appalachian northern Georgia, within 150 miles of Effingham County.[58] The Salzburgers had been a mountain people in Europe, and the lure of Georgia's green mountains eventually led some of them up the valley of the Savannah River to the Appalachians.[59]

The type 4 double-crib is very similar in floor plan to the open-passage "dogtrot" house type of the Gulf

Figure 4.29. An Alpine type 5 double-crib bank barn clings to a mountainside above the Gerlostal, a tributary valley of the Zillertal in North Tirol, Austria (field research district 24). Its front-facing gable and elongated cribs are similar to the Appalachian "drive-in" corn crib. (Photo by T.G.J., 1978.)

Coastal Plain, a type, as we have seen, likely of Scandinavian origin. Perhaps the Fenno-Scandian dogrun house was reinforced in Georgia by the presence of Salzburger type 4 open-runway double-crib barns. This might help explain why dogrun dwellings are so common on the Gulf Coastal Plain, but relatively rare in Atlantic coastal states north of Georgia.

Genealogists know that descendants of the Georgia Salzburgers live throughout much of the South.[60] That presence raises the question whether the role of colonial Pennsylvania in shaping the extended Midland subculture of the interior eastern United States has been overemphasized. Some form elements of Midland American log architecture could possibly have entered the upland South by way of German settlements in Effingham County, New Bern in North Carolina, and the Orangeburg area of South Carolina. Such heresy can be tempting when, rounding a turn in a Pinzgau highway, one sees a type 4 log barn identical in notching, log shape, chinks, dimensions, plan, height, and roof covering to the double-cribs prevalent in eastern Texas (Figures 4.27, 4.28). Another such barn, together with a type 3, stands on the outskirts of Bad Hofgastein. Significantly, a 1735 entry from the *Colonial Records of Georgia* mentions two hundred Protestants from Gastein in the Archbishopric of Salzburg who desired to come to Georgia.[61]

Salzburgers did build log structures in Georgia.[62] Their typical Old World house-wall construction, chinkless and double notched, survived in Effingham County at least as late as the 1880s.[63] It is likely that they also built the traditional Salzburg double-crib hay barns in Georgia, for we are told they made "rather much hay" there.[64] The long-vanished pioneer farmstead architecture of colonial Effingham County needs to be resurrected by archaeologists. Perhaps then we will learn that some of the regional diversity of Midland log architecture is the product of multiple colonial culture hearths rather than the work of inventive American pioneers tinkering with Pennsylvanian prototypes.

Nor should we overlook the fact that certain Midland American double-crib plans closely resemble the basic English "three-bay" barn, consisting of two square storage units separated by a central runway or threshing floor, the whole covered with a side-gable roof. In layout, this English barn is much like the Alpine type 4. Very likely, the presence of the three-bay barn, built in frame or stone construction, among the British settlers of the Middle Atlantic colonies facilitated and encouraged the implantation of structurally similar Alpine side-gable, log, double-crib types. Indeed, the highly successful diffusion of the double-crib Midland barn with square cribs (Figure 2.21) probably owes more to British than to Alpine influence, and the same may be true of other American side-gable types.

Other Barn Types

Another intriguing possibility is that the Midland transverse-crib barn, characterized by two or more cribs lined up along either side of a central runway parallel to the roof ridge, with entrances on each gable end, has eastern Alpine origins. Type 5 Alpine double-cribs are, in a few districts, sufficiently large to be close equivalents of the American transverse-crib barn. Local ethnographers call them *alpine Längscheunen*, or "Alpine long barns," and they occur from Swiss Graubünden eastward to Kärnten.[65] More likely, though, the Midland transverse-crib is an Americanism, developed simply by shifting the roof-ridge axis by 90 degrees on a "subdivided" double-crib barn (Figure 2.21), in order to facilitate adding more cribs.

Simpler forms, akin to the American gable-entrance, single-crib log barn, also occur in the Alps (Figure 4.30). These are the most elementary mountain meadow barns and are probably ancestral to the larger forms, particularly since they occur mainly in the same districts where double-crib forms abound. Kärnten and certain other eastern Alpine provinces seem to be the focal point of this simple type, known locally as a *Wiesenstadel* or *Heuschupfn*.[66] However, none of the Alpine specimens resembles the Midland corncrib as closely as does the Fenno-Scandian meadow barn, nor are they as abundant in the Alps as in northern Europe.

Related Features

Several other features of traditional material culture in the Alpine-Alemannic realm bear strong resemblances to elements in the Midland American landscape. Chief among these is the covered bridge, a particularly common type in a belt from forealpine Bern eastward to Tirol (Figure 4.15).[67] In America covered bridges extend from Pennsylvania into New England and westward across the lower Midwest, with outliers as far afield as Oregon.[68] G. M. Ludwig correctly attributed the midwestern and Pennsylvanian covered bridges to Switzerland, and one need look no further than the Bernese Emmental, the Amish homeland, for a prototype.[69] A bridge at Schaffhausen has also been cited as a possible model for the American structures.[70] Often the piers upon which the European covered bridges rest consist of notched-log pens filled with rock rubble, linking bridge building to the log construction culture.

Interestingly, the distribution of covered bridges is similar to that of bank barns, both in southern central Europe and in America, suggesting parallel diffusions (Figures 4.15 and 4.18). In all but two of the Alpine-Alemannic districts where one can observe covered bridges, bank barns are present also. Similarly, in the New World, covered bridges and bank barns both occur in the Midland, New England, and French Canadian subcultures.

The Alpine area of Austria also offers another possible prototype for the post-and-rail fence of Midland America. Kärnten, Tirol, and Salzburg Province contain fences similar to the American type, consisting of poles resting on withes between pairs of posts.[71] The greatest similarity to the Midland variety is exhibited by fences in the Tuxertal, Austrian north Tirol.[72]

The Alpine-Alemannic contribution to Midland American log architecture, the earlier introduction of selected Fenno-Scandian forms, and the many examples of British influence still do not provide satisfactory prototypes for every New World feature. The influence of southern central Europe seems to have been confined mainly to barn types. To complete the evaluation of possible continental European antecedents, we must turn to the east, to Saxony, Silesia, Moravia, and Bohemia, the source regions of the Moravian Brethren and Schwenkfelders, German religious minorities that emigrated to colonial America.

The Alps and Southwestern Germany 115

Figure 4.30. Single-crib log barn with board shed room addition, upper Emmental, Canton Bern (field research district 4). In many respects such Alpine single-crib structures have counterparts in Midland America. (Photo by T.G.J., 1978.)

Five
The German-Slavic Borderland

The third potential source region of Midland American log architecture lies in the borderland where Czechoslovakia, Poland, and the German Democratic Republic join, a zone of long-standing contact between Germans and northern Slavs.[1] Included are the provinces of Bohemia, Moravia, Silesia, and Saxony. The first two provinces lie in Czechoslovakia; Silesia is now largely Polish; and nearly all of the old Kingdom of Saxony is part of the German Democratic Republic.

An extensive secondary literature on the traditional architecture of this borderland contains many tantalizing suggestions of kinship with the American frontier (Figure 5.1). For example, in eighteenth-century Silesia "every farmer knew how to handle the ax and, with the help of a journeyman carpenter, to build his own house"—a description equally applicable to the Midland American pioneer.[2] Even after the Silesians began to build houses with other materials, they continued to construct log outbuildings, a sequence with precise parallels in Midland America.[3] In both areas, too, peasants regularly moved log buildings from one site to another.[4] Such similarities led Kniffen and Glassie, among others, to propose an eastern German origin of Midland log construction (discussed in chapter 1).

Field Research Areas

The proposed agents of diffusion from this region are the Moravian Brethren and Schwenkfelders, pietists who came originally from several small districts in Bohemia, Moravia, and Silesia, where log construction was common (Figure 5.2).[5] More specifically, the eastern German roots of the Moravian

Figure 5.1. A chinked "continental" log house with attached stall, at Horni Heřmanice (Ober-Hermanitz), a Brethren source village near Lanškroun in far northeastern Bohemia (field research district 3). Note the full-dovetailing, gable pent roof, and decoration. (Photo by T.G.J., 1982.)

Brethren lay in the Litice nad Orlicí–Litomyšl–Lanškroun (Lititz-Leitomischl-Landskron) area in far northeastern Bohemia and the Fulnek–Nový Jičín (Fulneck-Neutitschein) district in northeastern Moravia, near the border of Czech Silesia.[6] The latter district, straddling the strategic Moravian Gate near the headwaters of the Oder, was known to its German-speaking inhabitants as the Kuhländl (Czech Kravařsko), the "Kineland."[7]

In the 1600s, following a traditional path of Hussite refugees, many Brethren fled from these regions to Silesia and other lands to the north, seeking religious freedom. A century later another major migration brought Brethren to Herrnhut and nearby villages of Upper Lausitz, in the eastern part of the Kingdom of Saxony.[8] An informal census taken at Herrnhut in 1756 revealed that 62 percent of the Brethren claimed Moravian origin, while the remaining 38 percent declared Bohemia to be their ancestral home.[9] Also con-

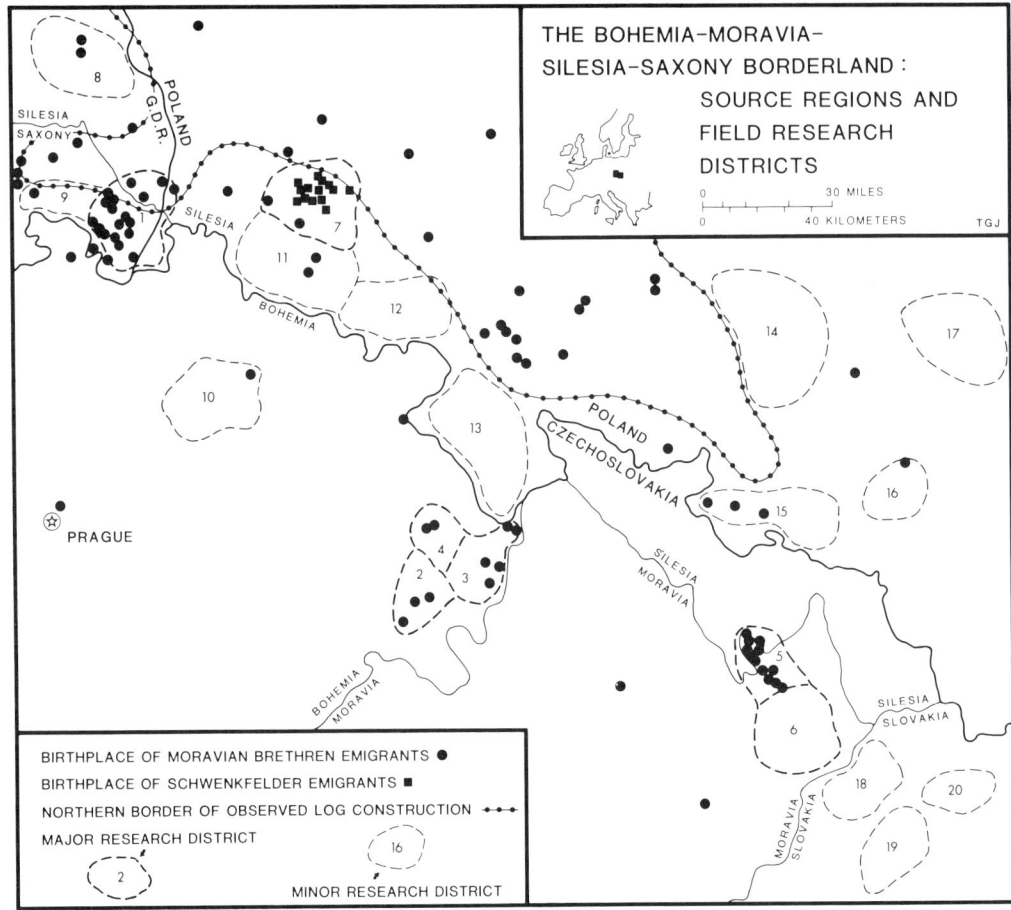

Figure 5.2. The field research districts are (1) Upper Lausitz, (2) Loučná headwaters, (3) Lanškroun (Landskron) area, (4) Litice nad Orlicí (Lititz) area, (5) Kineland-Moravian Gate, (6) Moravian Valachia, (7) Schwenkfelder source area, (8) Lower Lausitz-Spreewald, (9) Lausitzer Hills, (10) Český Ráj (Bohemian Paradise), (11) Karkonosze (Riesengebirge), (12) Wałbrzych (Waldenburg) area, (13) Kotlina Kłodzka (Glatz Hill Land), (14) Opole (Oppeln) area, (15) Racibórz-Glubczyce (Ratibor-Leobschütz) area, (16) Gliwice (Gleiwitz) area, (17) northern Katowice (Kattowitz) district, (18) Javorníky, (19) Rajčanka Valley, and (20) Varinka Valley. (Sources for birthplaces are Beck, "Moravian Graveyards of Lititz"; Kluge, "Moravian Graveyards at Nazareth"; Schultze, "Old Moravian Cemetery of Bethlehem"; Fries, *Records of the Moravians in North Carolina*, vol. 1, pp. 68–69, 130–31; Zeman, *Anabaptists and the Czech Brethren*, pp. 292–93; de Schweinitz, *History of the Church*, pp. 637–38; Brecht, *Genealogical Record of the Schwenkfelder*; Hopple, "Spatial History of the Schwenkfelders"; Eller, *Houses of Peace*, pp. 47, 52, 54; Hamilton, *History of the Church*, pp. 10–14; Reichel, *Moravians in North Carolina*; Kriebel, *Schwenkfelders in Pennsylvania*; and a field survey of epitaphs in the Hutberg cemetery at Herrnhut in the German Democratic Republic. Sources for the distribution of log construction, in addition to field research, are Richter, "Die Wand des Bauernhauses in Böhmen," p. 61, and Matuszczak, *Z Dziejów Architektury*, p. 160.)

Figure 5.3. Log wall with open chinks, thick two-sided hewing, and gently splayed full-dovetail notching, on a hay barn in Moravian Valachia (field research district 6), now in the Valašské Muzeum v Přírodě (Valachian Open-Air Museum) at Rožnov pod Radhoštěm (Roznau), Moravia. (Photo by T.G.J., 1982.)

tributing heavily to the Herrnhut colony were the Silesian settlements of the earlier Moravian diaspora. Church records and epitaphs in Brethren parishes at Herrnhut in East Germany; at Bethlehem, Nazareth, and Lititz in Pennsylvania; and at Winston-Salem in North Carolina provide abundant data on the specific origins.[10]

On the basis of these records, five Brethren source regions in the Czech– Polish–East German borderland were selected for intensive field research, including (1) the district of Litice nad Orlicí, (2) the Loučná headwaters area around Litomyšl, (3) the Lanškroun region, (4) the Kineland or Moravian Gate, and (5) Upper Lausitz (Figure 5.2). To these was added a sixth district, the northern part of Moravian Valachia, a hilly region bordering the Kineland on the south and a major survival area for log structures (Figure 5.3).[11] Fortunately, nearly all of the Brethren source areas proved to be rich in log architecture. Only the Kineland, where most of the surviving log structures are hidden beneath sheaths of masonry or plaster, was a disappointment (Figure 5.4). Near Litomyšl, even a source village unpromisingly named Kamenné Sedliště (Steinern Sedlitz), or "Sedliště built of stone," consists largely of log buildings (Figure 5.5). In Upper Lausitz, Herrnhut displays no visible log walls, but many nearby villages offer abundant examples (Figure 5.6).

The seventh district of intensive field research encompasses the source region of the Schwenkfelders, a Lower Silesian sect derived from the rolling plains between Lwówek Śląski (Löwenberg) and Złotoryja (Goldberg), in present-day southwestern Poland (Figure 5.2).[12] While not rich in log buildings, this Lower Silesian area has enough surviving specimens to permit analysis (Figure 5.7). Following the example of the Brethren, the Schwenkfelders sought religious haven in Upper Lausitz before coming to America. One of their principal refuge villages, Berthelsdorf, lies scarcely a kilometer from Herrnhut in Saxony.

In addition to the seven districts of intensive study, less rigorous field surveys were made in thirteen other areas

American Log Buildings

The German-Slavic Borderland

(Opposite, top)
Figure 5.4. Log house in Libhošt (Liebisch) in the Kineland (field research district 5). Note the chinkless construction, full-dovetailing, board gable, pent roof, and masonry covering a portion of the wall. Liebisch is a family name found among Pennsylvania Brethren derived from the Kineland, suggesting that this is an ancestral village of considerable antiquity. See Schultze, "Old Moravian Cemetery of Bethlehem," pp. 154, 164; Kluge, "Moravian Graveyards at Nazareth," p. 101. (Photo by T.G.J., 1982.)

(Opposite, lower left)
Figure 5.5. Chinked log house in the Brethren source village of Kamenné Sedliště (Steinern Sedlitz), near Litomšyl in the Loučná headwaters region of northeastern Bohemia (field research district 2). Note, in the place where the chinking has fallen out, that the logs are touching rather than being spaced apart. Note also the thickness of the logs, the two-sided hewing, the full-dovetailing, and the pegs to support the chinking. (Photo by T.G.J., 1982.)

(Opposite, lower right)
Figure 5.6. A log house in Saxony with hook and square notching, false chinking, and *Umgebinde* construction—typical features of wooden dwellings in Upper Lausitz—in Hirschfelde, near Zittau and Herrnhut, German Democratic Republic (field research district 1). (Photo by T.G.J., 1982.)

in Bohemia, Slovakia, Poland, and the German Democratic Republic (Figure 5.2). While none of these areas served as major source regions of colonial American immigrants, all are peripheral to the Brethren or Schwenkfelder homelands and contain abundant log buildings. They could not safely be ignored. Altogether, then, the field research encompassed twenty separate districts in and around the primary eastern German source regions of colonial American settlers.

Settlements in Colonial America

The eastern Germans arrived late in the Teutonic migration to colonial America. Lutherans, Calvinists, Dunkers, Mennonites, and Amish, mainly of Rhenish and Swiss origin, preceded the Moravians and Schwenkfelders, concentrating mainly in southeastern Pennsylvania. Individual eastern Germans, including Silesians, had arrived in the American colonies as early as the middle 1600s, but the Brethren and Schwenkfelders together constituted the first sizable group to immigrate from that region.[13]

Schwenkfelders led the way, abandoning their temporary refuge in Upper Lausitz in the mid-1730s to settle in Pennsylvania. Forty families strong, they occupied several contiguous townships northwest of Philadelphia, centered in Montgomery County (Figure 5.8). Their descendants, numbering about four thousand, remain concentrated there today.[14] The Schwenkfelders erected numerous log buildings in their new homeland, some of which survived into the modern era (Figure 5.9).

Following an abortive colonization attempt in Georgia, the Moravian Brethren, probably influenced by

Figure 5.7. Abandoned log and half-timbered *Umgebinde* house in the village of Raciborowice (Gross Hartmannsdorf) in the Schwenkfelder source region of Lower Silesia, Poland (field research district 7). The construction features hewn half-logs, double notching, and false chinking. (Photo by T.G.J., 1982.)

the Schwenkfelders, began migrating in strength to Pennsylvania in the 1740s.[15] Bethlehem and Nazareth, founded in 1741, were the mother colonies. Lititz, Emmaus, and Lebanon were soon added to the list of major Pennsylvania Moravian settlements, and the rapidity of Brethren diffusion is suggested by the fact that as early as 1752 they occupied at least thirty-five Pennsylvania sites with functioning schools (Figure 5.8).[16] A further scattering, including Indian missions, sent Brethren into eastern Ohio, New Jersey, and New York before 1790, and Moravian missionaries were active among other Germans as far south as the Shenandoah Valley and Piedmont of Virginia.[17] In the 1750s and 1760s, a second major implantation, Wachovia, was made in the North Carolina Piedmont, where Salem became the principal settlement.[18]

Like their Schwenkfelder counterparts, the colonial Brethren initially built log structures in America (Figure 5.10).[19] These buildings were the work of a relatively small number of professional and journeyman carpenters, including Anton Seiffert and Josef Bulitschek of Bohemia; Melchoir Schmidt, Georg Schindler, Michael Muenster,

The German-Slavic Borderland

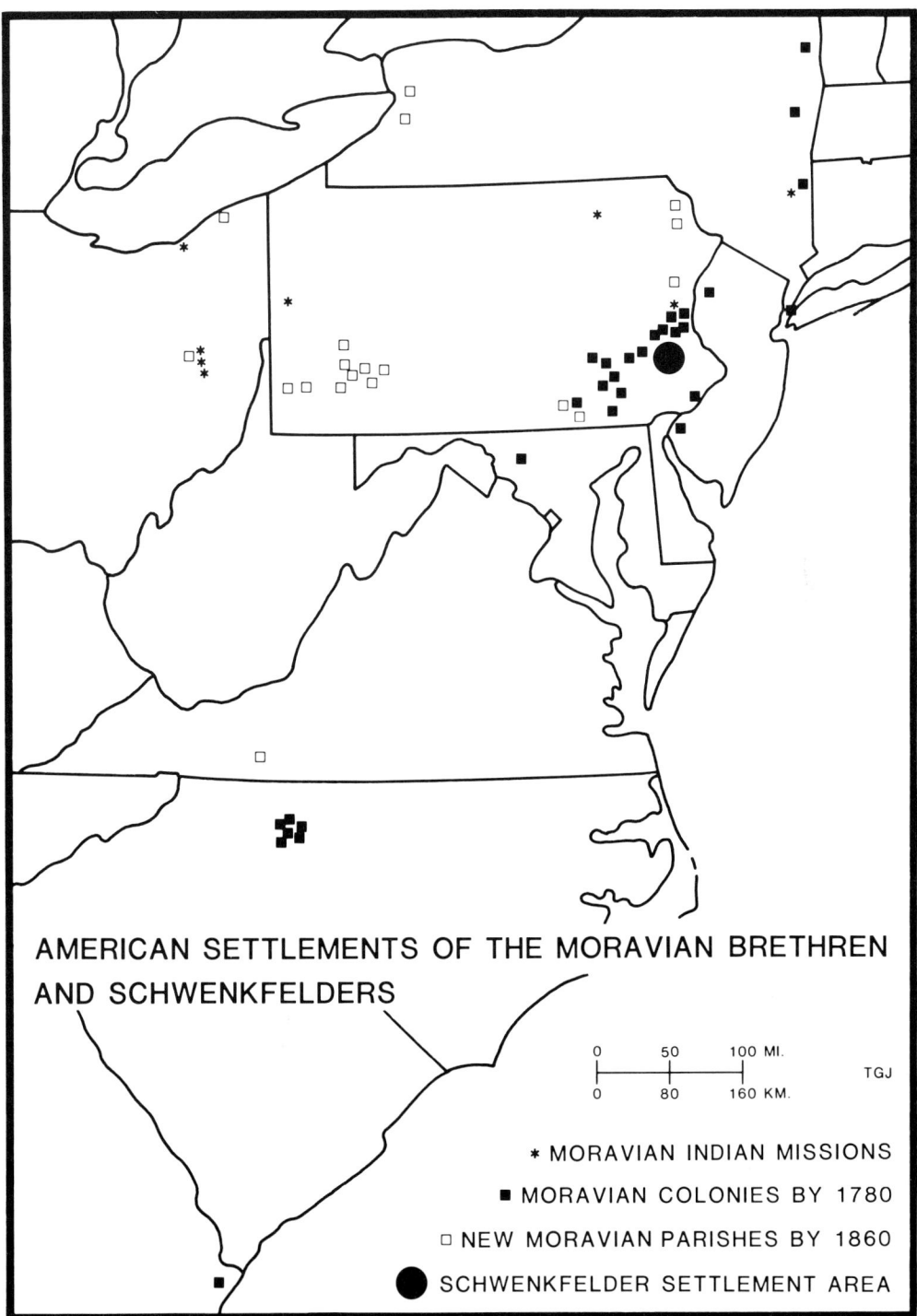

Figure 5.8.

Figure 5.9. Schwenkfelder two-story "continental" log house in Montgomery County, Pennsylvania. This dwelling, reputedly dating from 1737 and belonging to the Krauss family, no longer stands. The walls reveal a mixture of log shapes and notches, none of which are typical of the Lower Silesian source region of the Schwenkfelders. Were the house coupled with a stall, it would be similar to the basic Silesian Schwenkfelder house (see Figure 5.30). (Photo 1908, provided by the Schwenkfelder Library, Pennsburg, Pennsylvania, and used with permission.)

David Kunz, Paul Fritsche, and Melchoir Coumad of Moravia; Friedrich Beyer and David Tanneberger from Silesia; Tobias Hirte from Saxony; Christian Triebel; and Martin Lick. Schindler, Schmidt, Fritsche, Kunz, and Tanneberger were all natives of the town of Suchdol nad Odrou (Zauchtel, Zauchtenthal) in the Kineland; Hirte was an Upper Lausitzer from Eibau near Herrnhut; and Seiffert was born in Lipka north of Lanškroun.[20]

By and large, the Brethren constituted a higher socioeconomic group than the masses of colonial Germans, to the extent that "a majority of the group was of the craftsman class."[21] In North Carolina, Salem's master workmen instituted a system of apprenticeship beginning at age twelve.[22] These skills could have allowed the Moravians to exert a greater influence on colonial carpentry than their relatively small numbers and late arrival would suggest.

The German-Slavic Borderland 125

Figure 5.10. The first log house built by the Moravian Brethren in Bethlehem, Pennsylvania. Note the gable pent roof and "continental" plan, with a stall occupying the right-hand side of the structure. The drawing, by Rufus Grider, bears the date October 1850. It is owned by the Gemein Haus Museum of Bethlehem (index no. 257). (Photo courtesy Moravian Museum of Bethlehem, used with permission.)

Log-Shaping Techniques

The field study found six log shapes to be common on structures in the German-Slavic borderland, only one of which occurs frequently in Midland America (Figure 5.11). Two-sided hewing, the method dominant on dwellings in the United States, is far more common in the borderland, particularly Czechoslovakia, than in northern Europe or the Alpine-Alemannic region (Figures 5.3, 5.5). A Slavic origin for two-sided hewing is strongly suggested by its concentration in Slovakia and on the Czech side of the prewar linguistic boundary in Bohemia and Moravia. Two-sided hewing is among the least refined techniques observed in the area, suggesting a considerable antiquity.

Clearly, the occurrence of two-sided hewing in the eastern source regions supports the Kniffen-Glassie thesis. Closer inspection, however, reveals some basic differences between the

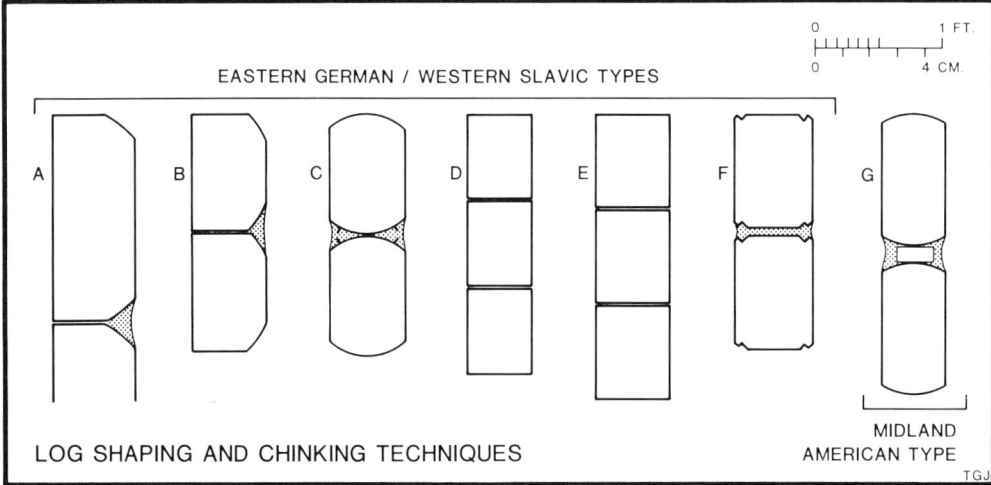

Figure 5.11. The examples are from A, Opole district, Upper Silesia; B, Upper Lausitz; C, Čičmany in western Slovakia; D, near Częstochowa in Upper Silesia; E, Saxon Upper Lausitz; F, Lower Silesian mountains; G, Midland American two-sided planking, North Carolina.

Midland and Slavic types. The Czech–Polish–East German technique produces a much thicker timber than is typical in America. Two-sided *planking*, the prevalent Midland hewn form, is absent altogether in the eastern source regions. In both Pennsylvania and North Carolina, most Moravian-built structures are clearly distinguishable from those of other groups by virtue of their thicker logs. The other five common Czech-Silesian-Saxon log shapes do not appear at all or are rare in the Midland tradition.

Another contrast is seen in the methods of hewing. The rather crude Midland technique, involving ax and adze, leaves irregular surfaces scarred by score marks. The log walls observed in the course of the field research bore no such marks. Sawn logs were known in the hill districts of east central Europe prior to 1800, and even the earlier shaping methods employed there, involving ax, hatchet, broadax, and cutting knife, produced a relatively smooth surface.[23]

Chinks and Chinking

The suggestion in chapter 3 that Midland chinked-wall construction is Fenno-Scandian in origin cannot be accepted unless a satisfactory prototype is not present in the German-Slavic borderland. Relying upon secondary literature, Glassie concluded that Midland-style chinking was indeed the rule among the eastern Germans and proposed, largely upon this basis, that the Moravians and Schwenkfelders had exerted a shaping influence in the carpentry tradition of the United States.[24] In fact, one might easily draw such a conclusion from a casual analysis of photographs of log buildings in Czechoslovakia, Silesia, and East Germany (Figure 5.1).[25] The same striped visual effect—dark logs alternating with white plaster—catches the eye both there and in America (Figure 5.7).

A close field inspection of log walls in the borderland, however, reveals that the techniques used there exhibit major contrasts to American methods. First, chinking is by no means universal in the Czech–Polish–East German region (Figure 5.12). Many log walls are chinkless, consisting of squared timbers tightly fitted together (Figures 5.4, 5.11D and E, 5.13). Even where chinking does occur, it is rather different from the Midland type. In lowland Silesia, including the Schwenkfelder source villages, as well as in Saxon Upper Lausitz and parts of northern Bohemia, a technique best labeled "false chinking" is employed (Figure 5.11A and B). It involves hewn split logs, placed in the wall with the curved sides facing outward. On top and bottom, the split logs are flattened to fit snugly together, so that the chinking fills only the indentation left by the natural curvature of the logs on the exterior side (Figures 5.11A and B, 5.14).[26] In many Saxon and Silesian houses, this indentation is left unchinked, clearly revealing the tight fit of the walls (Figure 5.15).

In Moravia and parts of eastern Bohemia, a second type of false chinking prevails, involving two-sided hewing (Figures 5.5, 5.11C). Here, too, most logs touch, and the chinking merely fills an elongated indentation. If individual logs are sufficiently irregular in shape that open chinks appear in places, then a small round pole is sometimes used to plug the gap (Figure 5.16). Slats and rocks, the typical Midland fillers, are absent. Instead a mud and straw daubing is held in place by small pegs inserted in the rounded surfaces of the logs (Figure 5.5). This type of false chinking is virtually impossible to distinguish visually from true chinking if the daub and plaster are intact, but when the filler is removed, the difference is at once evident (Figure 5.17).

True chinking, with cracks left between the logs, is most common in the hilly Silesian-Bohemian border district, but even there the technique differs from Midland American methods. The logs are hewn on four sides and grooved to anchor the daub and plaster. Timbers are placed in the wall in such a manner as to leave chinks of only .4 to .6 inch (Figure 5.11F). Wood plane shavings are driven into this narrow chink with a wedge at repeated intervals for several years, and only then is a plaster of oakum and lime mortar applied. In some Silesian districts, clay and moss provide the filler.[27]

American-style chinks can be observed only on hay barns among the eastern Germans and western Slavs, where their purpose is to provide ventilation for drying the hay. Chinking, or filling the cracks, is of course absent in such structures (Figure 5.3).

Still, the eastern German–western Slavic methods of chinking and false chinking resemble Midland techniques more than do other European types. Were no other evidence available, one would feel compelled to accept a Bohemian, Silesian, or Saxon prototype. As was mentioned earlier, however, some sort of chinking occurred on certain log houses erected by Swedes and

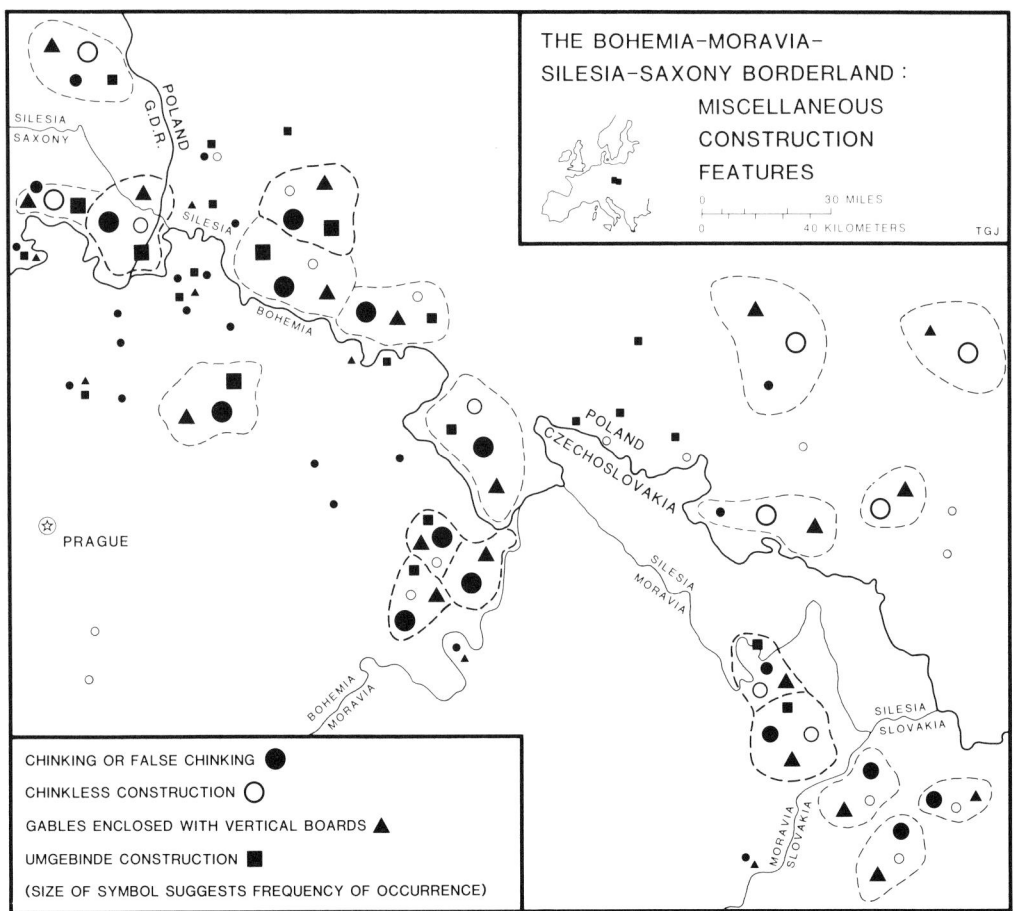

Figure 5.12. Locations shown outside research districts are based on individual field observations and on published secondary sources, in particular Schier, *Hauslandschaften und Kulturbewegungen*, and Richter, "Die Wand des Bauernhauses in Böhmen."

Finns along the Delaware River.[28] Since the Swedes settled in America almost a full century before the arrival of the eastern Germans, the case for Teutonic origin is weakened. The American-style wide chinking filled with solid material was perhaps a colonial Scandinavian adaptation to the use of hardwoods, particularly oak, an adaptation that may have occurred before the arrival of the Brethren and Schwenkfelders. In this case, the eastern German influence was apparently limited to reinforcement of an established trait.

The German-Slavic Borderland

Figure 5.13. Chinkless, hook-notched log house with *Umgebinde* construction, Hirschfelde, Upper Lausitz, German Democratic Republic (field research district 1). (Photo by T.G.J., 1982.)

Figure 5.14. False chinking on an *Umgebinde* log and half-timber house in Zbylutów (Deutmannsdorf), a village in the Schwenkfelder source region in Lower Silesia, Poland (field research district 7). The split logs touch, as can be observed at the corners where the logs project, and the chinking evident on the walls merely fills the indentation caused by the natural curvature of the logs. The joints are double notched. (Photo by T.G.J., 1982.)

Figure 5.15. The false chinking was left off this house in Neukirch, a Brethren source village in the Lausitzer Hills, Saxony, in the German Democratic Republic (field research district 9), revealing the chinkless nature of typical Saxon and Lower Silesian log construction. The timbers are hewn half-logs. Note the *Umgebinde* construction, also typical of the region. (Photo by T.G.J., 1982.)

Corner Timbering

Perhaps no other facet of log carpentry is potentially more revealing of antecedents than is the method of joining timbers at the corners of structures. Numerous cornering techniques occur in east-central Europe, some of which are closely identified with particular regions.[29]

Eastern Germans have been suggested as the agents of diffusion for several of the Midland notches.[30] Kniffen and Glassie proposed that American V notching was introduced from Lower Silesia by the Schwenkfelders.[31] That proposal must be discarded, for V notching occurs nowhere in Silesia or the remainder of the German-Slavic borderland, while it is found in Sweden, as was pointed out in chapter 3. All the log buildings inspected in the former Schwenkfelder villages display double notching, a type absent in Midland construction (Figure 5.18). Judging by the notching and other features of carpentry and design, it would seem that the Schwenkfelders

Figure 5.16. Log barn in Horni Sloupnice (Obersloupnitz), near Litomyšl in the Loučná headwaters region of northeastern Bohemia (field research district 2). Note the two-sided hewing, thick timbers, and open chinks, some of which are filled with poles and daubing. *Umgebinde* construction is rare this far east. (Photo by T.G.J., 1982.)

Figure 5.17. Chinkless wall of a log house in Životice (Seitendorf), just south of Nový Jičín in the Kineland, eastern Moravia (field research district 5). Note the gently splayed full-dovetailing, two-sided hewing, and thick logs. (Photo by T.G.J., 1982.)

made no contribution whatever to the Midland tradition.

A better case can be made for eastern German origin of the dovetailed notching forms. Full-dovetailing, in which both the top and bottom of the joint are splayed, is the prevalent type almost everywhere in Bohemia, Moravia, and Upper Silesia, where it is acknowledged to be a German rather than a Slavic type (Figures 5.1, 5.3, 5.19).[32] This type of dovetailing is also quite common in eastern Pennsylvania (Figure 5.20). By contrast, dovetailing is relatively rare in most of the Alpine-Alemannic and Fenno-Scandian source regions of American colonists.

Half-dovetailing, a simpler form involving a splaying of only the top side of the log tongue, is by far the most common Midland variety of the notch. Long assumed to be an Americanism and attributed by some to the Scotch-Irish, half-dovetailing appears consistently as a minority type among the western Slavs (Figure 5.19).[33] It occurs mainly on the Slavic side of the old linguistic border, in Bohemia, Slovakia,

Upper Silesia, and the southern perimeter of the Kineland. The hill town of Štramberk (Stramberg) overlooking the Moravian Gate offers some notable examples, but perhaps the best specimen is a venerable log church near Częstochowa (Tschenstochau) in Poland (Figure 5.21). In eastern Bohemia, half-dovetailing usually appears as individual joints in walls otherwise full-dovetailed, though some entire walls of inverted half-dovetailing can be seen there (Figure 5.22).

The spatial distribution of half-dovetailing in America—it is a rarity in the eastern Pennsylvania cultural hearth—suggests that this notch has correctly been interpreted as an Americanism. Too, no surviving Moravian structure in America displays half-dovetailing. Even so, the presence of this notch type in the German-Slavic source regions should caution against an unqualified acceptance of an American frontier origin for half-dovetailing.

Both types of dovetailing in the German-Slavic borderland are more gently splayed than their Midland American counterparts, a difference perhaps attributable to greater log thickness in the European regions. Moravian dovetailing in Pennsylvania normally reveals the same gentle splaying seen in the Old World (compare Figures 5.5 and 5.20).

Square notching, also presumed by many to be an Americanism, since it is one of the simplest forms to fashion, is a very common type in some parts of Slovakia, Saxony, and Moravia, rivaling dovetailing for dominance in Upper Lausitz and western Slovakia (Figures 5.19, 5.23).[34] An even simpler form, the half notch, also occurs as a minor type in both Midland America and the Czech–Polish–East German region (Figure 5.24).[35] These simplified types

Figure 5.18. Double-notched, chinkless log outbuilding in the Schwenkfelder source village of Nowa Wieś Grodziska (Neudorf), Lower Silesia, Poland (field research district 7). Note the vertical boards in the gable. (Photo by T.G.J., 1982.)

were probably known to Moravian Brethren carpenters, but it does not seem that they ever employed square or half notching on buildings erected in colonial America. As craftsmen, the Brethren perhaps regarded these inferior notching methods with contempt. In any case, the surviving Moravian log buildings in America, including the famous *Gemeinhaus* at Bethlehem, are full-dovetailed.[36] A Swedish or Finnish prototype for square and half notching seems much more likely.

The absence in Midland America of the hook notch, companion to dovetail-

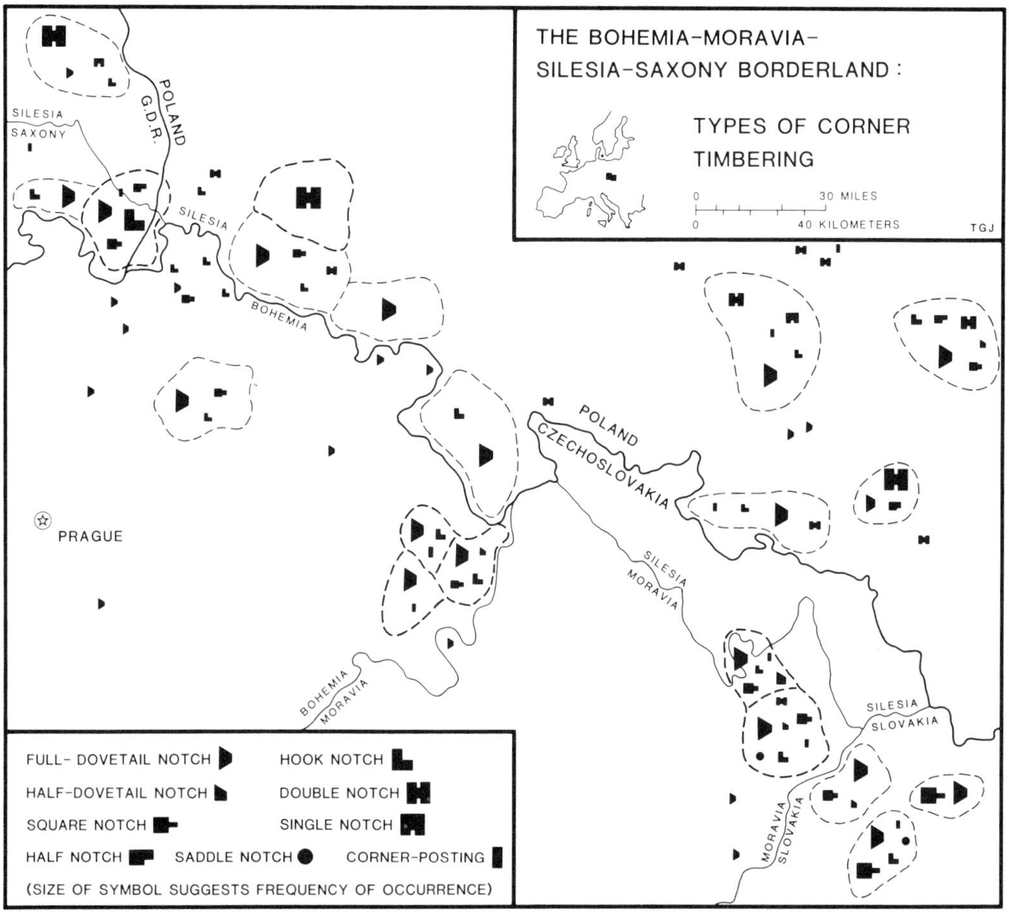

The German-Slavic Borderland

THE BOHEMIA-MORAVIA-SILESIA-SAXONY BORDERLAND:

TYPES OF CORNER TIMBERING

0   30 MILES
0   40 KILOMETERS

FULL-DOVETAIL NOTCH ▶
HALF-DOVETAIL NOTCH ◣
SQUARE NOTCH ▬
HALF NOTCH ■
SADDLE NOTCH ●
HOOK NOTCH ⌐
DOUBLE NOTCH ⋈
SINGLE NOTCH ■
CORNER-POSTING ▮
(SIZE OF SYMBOL SUGGESTS FREQUENCY OF OCCURRENCE)

Figure 5.19. Locations shown outside research districts indicate individual field observations and material drawn from published secondary sources.

Figure 5.20. Full-dovetailing and thick logs on a Moravian-built house in Nazareth, Pennsylvania, dating from the 1740s. These features closely resemble log construction in the eastern German source regions (compare to Figure 5.5). (Photo by T.G.J., 1980.)

Figure 5.21. Half-dovetail notching on the venerable log church at Koszęcin (Koschentin), located between Częstochowa and Katowice (Kattowitz) in Upper Silesia, Poland (field research district 17). Half-dovetailing, assumed by many to be an Americanism, occurs widely in the German-Slavic borderland. Note also the typical Upper Silesian chinkless construction. (Photo by T.G.J., 1982.)

Figure 5.22. Inverted half-dovetail notching on a chinked, whitewashed log house in Letohrad (Geiersberg), near Lanškroun in northeastern Bohemia (field research district 3). (Photo by T.G.J., 1982.)

ing through much of the eastern German lands, is perhaps noteworthy (Figure 5.13).[37] While somewhat similar to the square notch, the hook type contains a right-angle, locking offset, forming a complicated joint that would appeal to skilled craftsmen. It is particularly common in the Upper Lausitz source region. The failure of hook notching to take root in America could be interpreted as a sign of minimal eastern German influence, but it might also merely represent a simplification of European culture overseas.

The saddle notch, a primitive type applied mainly to logs left in the round, is rare and peripheral in the study area, almost certainly representing a remnant early Slavic type. The field study located saddle notching only in Moravian Valachia and western Slovakia, mostly in highland refuges (Figure

The German-Slavic Borderland 135

Figure 5.23. Slavic square notching on the 1770 town hall in Rožnov pod Radhoštěm, Moravian Valachia (field research district 6), now relocated to the open-air museum in the same town. The thick logs have been hewn on two sides, and false chinking can be seen. (Photo by T.G.J., 1982.)

Figure 5.24. Half notching on an *Umgebinde* log house in Hirschfelde, Saxon Upper Lausitz, German Democratic Republic (field research district 1). Similar half notching, without *Umgebinde*, appears as a minor type in America. (Photo by T.G.J., 1982.)

5.19). The abundance of saddle notching in Switzerland, Sweden, and Finland, and its rarity in the German-Slav borderland, suggests that the Midland form was not introduced by the Brethren.

Occasionally in the Midland tradition, log corners are secured by vertical slotted posts rather than notches, with the individual timbers tenoned to fit into the slot. Such corner-posting occurs widely, if infrequently, among the eastern Germans and is much more common in Alpine-Alemannic carpentry (Figures 5.19, 5.25).

The evidence for eastern German influence on Midland cornering techniques, while far from convincing, suggests some links. By virtue of their almost unanimous allegiance to dovetailing in America, the Brethren likely reinforced the use of similar notching

Figure 5.25. Corner-posting on a log house in Libchavy (Lichwe), near Litice nad Orlicí in northeastern Bohemia (field research district 4). This method of corner-timbering is relatively rare in the German-Slavic borderland and even more uncommon in America. (Photo by T.G.J., 1982.)

in the Midland culture area, assisting in the rise of dovetailing to prominence, and provided the prototype for half-dovetailing. Introduced toward the end of the period of diffusion of log carpentry to colonial America, Moravian dovetailing influenced the more refined log house stage of construction, as opposed to the earlier, cruder cabin phase, which bore a strong Fenno-Scandian imprint. The Delaware Swedes, to be sure, built some fine full-dovetailed structures before the arrival of the Moravians and also used square and half notching, but neither they nor the Alpine-Alemannic Germans relied on dovetailing as their major form in Europe.

Gable and Roof

The most common Midland American roof structure, a raftered type with boarded gables, occasional small pents sheltering the lower walls, and no ridgepole, lacks a satisfactory proto-

The German-Slavic Borderland

Figure 5.26. The Hans Yeakel House, a Schwenkfelder dwelling near Pennsburg, Pennsylvania. Note the pent roofs, central chimney, two-story "continental" plan, and board gable. The house, built about 1760, is no longer standing. (Photo provided by the Schwenkfelder Library, Pennsburg, Pennsylvania, and used with permission.)

type in Scandinavia and southern central Europe (Figures 5.10, 5.26).[38] However, each of these distinctive Midland roof form elements is prevalent in the log construction areas of Bohemia, Moravia, Silesia, and Saxony, lending additional support to the thesis of eastern German origin (Figures 5.1, 5.4, 5.18, 5.25, 5.27).[39]

Only a few of the very oldest structures, clearly Slavic in origin, have ridgepole-supported roofs, and in every field research district, Midland-style board gables prevail.[40] The similarities extend to the pitch of the roof and the style of the rafter support framework (Figure 5.28).[41]

The temptation then to assign major formative influence to the Brethren and Schwenkfelders is great. In most major respects, though, the eastern German roof represents Frankish practices that also occur in the Palatinate, a region lacking log construction that served as the principal source of the Pennsylvania "Dutch." Certain Brit-

Figure 5.27. House in Moravian Valachia (field research district 6), now in the open-air museum in Rožnov pod Radhoštěm (Roznau). Valachian chinking is often concealed beneath thin wood strips, presenting the outward appearance of chinkless walls. Note the board gable, pent roof, "bellcast" profile, and cellar. (Photo by T.G.J., 1982.)

ish forms are also very similar. The Midland raftered roof, with or without gable pent, is likely Rhenish and British in origin. Too, the very narrow wooden shingles, often rounded or grooved, found on eastern German and Slavic roofs differ in shape from those of America.[42] An Alpine Germanic origin of the Midland shingling tradition seems likely.

The only American roof features confined largely to the eastern German lands would seem to be the board gable cover and the simplest framing support for rafters (Figure 5.28C). These forms are so elementary that independent invention could explain their presence in America. In fact, board-covered gables appeared in Pennsylvania at least as early as 1686, a half-century before the arrival of the Brethren and Schwenkfelders.[43]

Another difficulty in accepting an eastern German model for the Midland roof form is the dominance in both Upper Lausitz and the Schwenkfelder source region of *Umgebinde* construction (Figure 5.12).[44] This term, meaning "bound up," describes a building in which the entire roof structure and, if present, upper story rest not upon the log walls but instead upon stiltlike vertical posts placed outside the logs (Figures 5.6, 5.7, 5.13–5.16, 5.24).[45] While it is true that *Umgebinde* structures are rare or absent in the northeastern Moravian, Upper Silesian, and eastern Bohemian source regions, the technique prevailed among the Schwenkfelders and was certainly observed by the Brethren during their stay in Saxon Lausitz. In any case, the complete absence of *Umgebinde* construction in America weakens the argument for eastern German influence in the Midland building tradition, as does the rar-

The German-Slavic Borderland

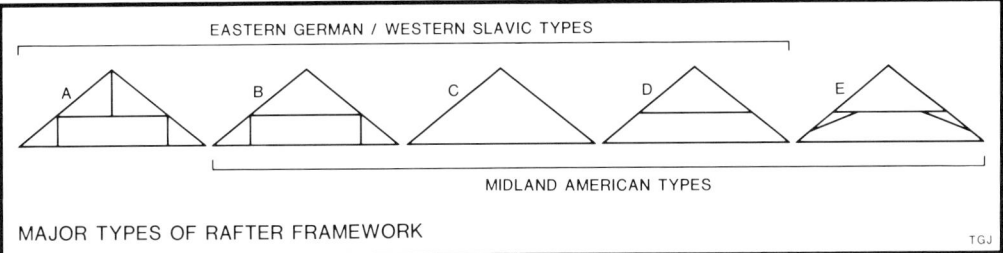

Figure 5.28. Type A occurs in Silesia and Lausitz; type B in Bohemia, Upper Silesia, and America; type C in Slovakia, eastern Moravia, and America; type D in Bohemia, Silesia, and America; type E only in America. (Sources: field research; Schier, *Hauslandschaften und Kulturbewegungen*, map 2; Chappell, "Acculturation in the Shenandoah Valley," p. 59.)

ity in the United States of the "saltbox" roof profile of the Silesian Schwenkfelders and the "bellcast" profile encountered widely in some of the Brethren source regions (Figure 5.27).[46] Still, the absence of all of these features in America could be explained by the process of overseas simplification of European culture, a process which typically eliminated more complex form elements.

House and Farmstead Types

No necessary connection exists between carpentry tradition and architectural style; log construction can be applied to a great variety of floor plans. Still, if eastern German houses and farmsteads could be proven ancestral to some Midland American types, then the case for a parallel diffusion of construction techniques would be strengthened.

At first glance, the Bohemian, Moravian, and Silesian source regions of the Brethren seem to offer viable prototypes for the central-chimney, side-gabled "continental" houses so common among the Pennsylvania Germans (Figures 5.1, 5.29).[47] Three- and four-room, story-and-a-half continental log houses similar to those prevalent among the colonial German-Americans occur widely in the Slavic-German borderland.[48] Closer analysis reveals, however, that the houses in question represent a basic Frankish or Middle German type found in half-timbered construction in the Rhenish lands.[49] Too, the continental plan was being employed in Pennsylvania long before the arrival of the Brethren and Schwenkfelders.[50] In addition, the continental log house of the Czech–Polish–East German borderland, following Frankish custom, often has the stall attached to the dwelling, an extremely rare arrangement in Midland America (Figure 5.29).[51] Indeed, the first house erected by the Moravian Brethren in Bethlehem, Pennsylvania, is one of

Figure 5.29. A "continental," story-and-a-half log house in Koburk (Koburg), near Výprachtice (Weinersdorf) in the region north of Lanškroun, northeastern Bohemia (field research district 3). Note the attached stall, a Frankish influence, and the false chinking—nicely illustrated toward the top of the wall, where the logs project beyond the notch. The house is painted blue. (Photo by T.G.J., 1982.)

very few in America to combine stalls and human quarters under one roof (Figure 5.10).[52] In the Schwenkfelder source region in Lower Silesia, as well as in Upper Lausitz, a massive two-story continental house with attached barn is the dominant type (Figure 5.30).[53] Compounding these dissimilarities is the prevalence of the Frankish courtyard farmstead in most eastern German source areas, including the Kineland, Loučná headwaters, Upper Lausitz, and Schwenkfelder source area.[54] In America the Frankish courtyard plan, with structures tightly clustered to enclose three sides of a central farmyard, never occurs.

The story-and-a-half continental log house without attached stall and lacking the Frankish courtyard is most common in purely Slavic areas such as Moravian Valachia, and German ethnographers recognize it as distinctively non-Teutonic.[55] It also occurs in the Lanškroun source region in eastern Bohemia and in Wendish Lower Lau-

Figure 5.30. A two-story "continental" house with attached stall in the Schwenkfelder source village of Czaple (Hainwald) in Lower Silesia, Poland (field research district 7). This is the typical farmhouse of the region; if the stall were removed, it would resemble certain Schwenkfelder dwellings in Pennsylvania (see Figure 5.26). (Photo by T.G.J., 1982.)

sitz. While it is tempting to declare the Midland continental log house a successor to this Slavic type, chronology dictates otherwise.

Barn Form Elements

Several features of eastern German barns and sheds are reminiscent of Midland forms. The double-crib plan, in which two log cribs flank a central threshing floor, occurs widely through the Czech–Polish–East German borderland, in a variety of sizes and subtypes (Figures 5.31, 5.32).[56] The oldest forms, quite different from American plans and presumably Slavic in origin, are of hexagonal or octagonal shape, with recessed doors and hipped roofs (Figure 5.33A, B).[57] More typical are low, rectangular double-crib barns, generally built in stone or half-timbering rather than log, that are derived from the basic Frankish *Grundscheuer*, or "ground-level barn" (Figure 5.31).[58] Such Frankish barns occur in nearly

Figure 5.31. The simplest of the western Slavic double-crib log barns, in the village of Čičmany, Rajčanka Valley, Slovakia (field research district 19). The board gable has a "hex-sign" opening cut into it. (Photo by T.G.J., 1982.)

all the eastern German source regions, and generally have asymmetrical floor plans (Figure 5.33). Some of these Frankish plans were introduced into Pennsylvania by Rhenish Germans decades before the Brethren and Schwenkfelders arrived, and there is no reason to attribute any formative influence to the eastern Germans. Moreover, log double-crib barns more closely akin to Midland American forms are found in both the Alpine and Fenno-Scandian areas. Certain Midland types, such as the doorless double-crib barn of the American South, do not occur among the eastern Germans.

Much less common in the eastern lands are banked entrances to multi-level storage structures. In Moravia, Slovakia, and Upper Silesia, the most Slavicized portions of the borderland, bank barns are absent altogether, and they are relatively rare even in more

The German-Slavic Borderland

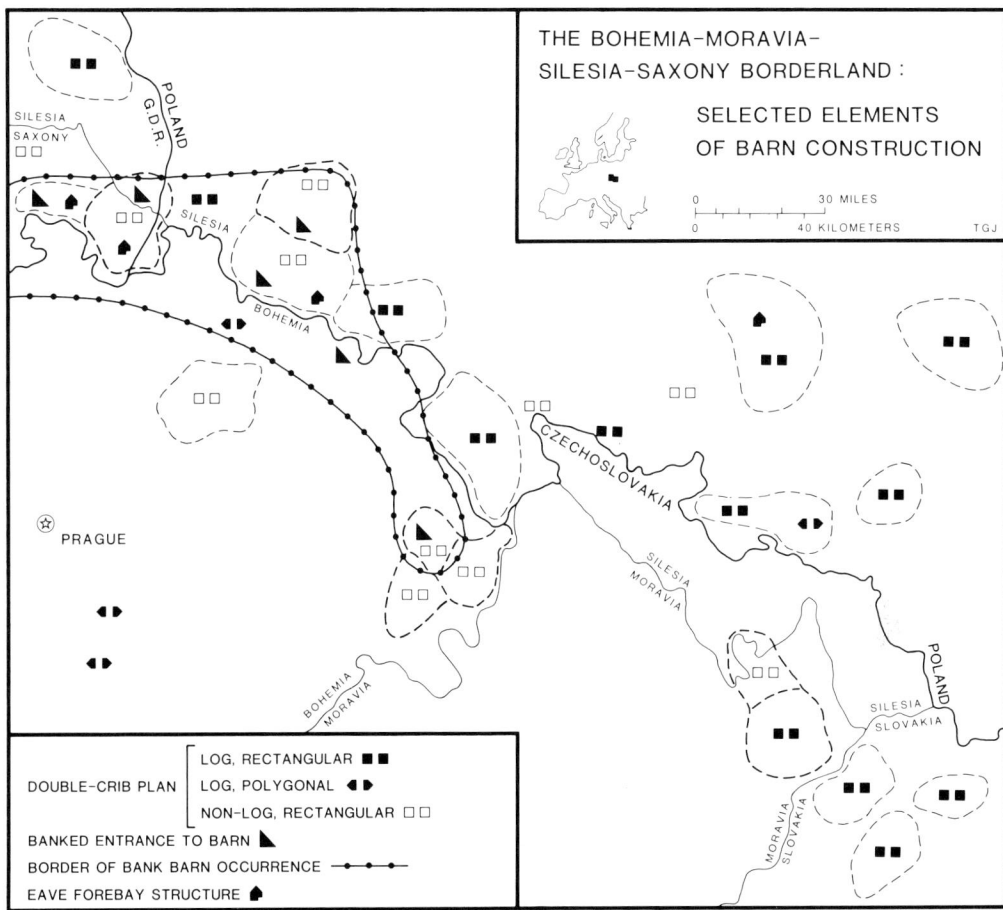

Figure 5.32. Locations shown outside research districts indicate individual field observations and material drawn from published secondary sources.

Germanized areas, such as Upper Lausitz, Lower Silesia, and the northern Bohemian mountain fringe (Figure 5.32).[59] In almost every example observed, the banked structures contain house and barn under one roof, presenting a fundamental contrast to Midland American tradition.[60]

A small minority of eastern European barns, particularly in Upper Lausitz, display cantilevered projections similar to American forebays (Figure 5.34). Close inspection revealed most of these to be "false" forebays, built to accommodate an enclosed walkway, called a *Galerie*, rather than to provide extra storage space as in America.[61] One of the few genuine forebays, in the Silesian Karkonosze (Riesengebirge), turned out to be an Alpine type, built in the early nineteenth century by immigrants from Austrian Tirol.[62] In view of the Alpine material presented in chapter 4,

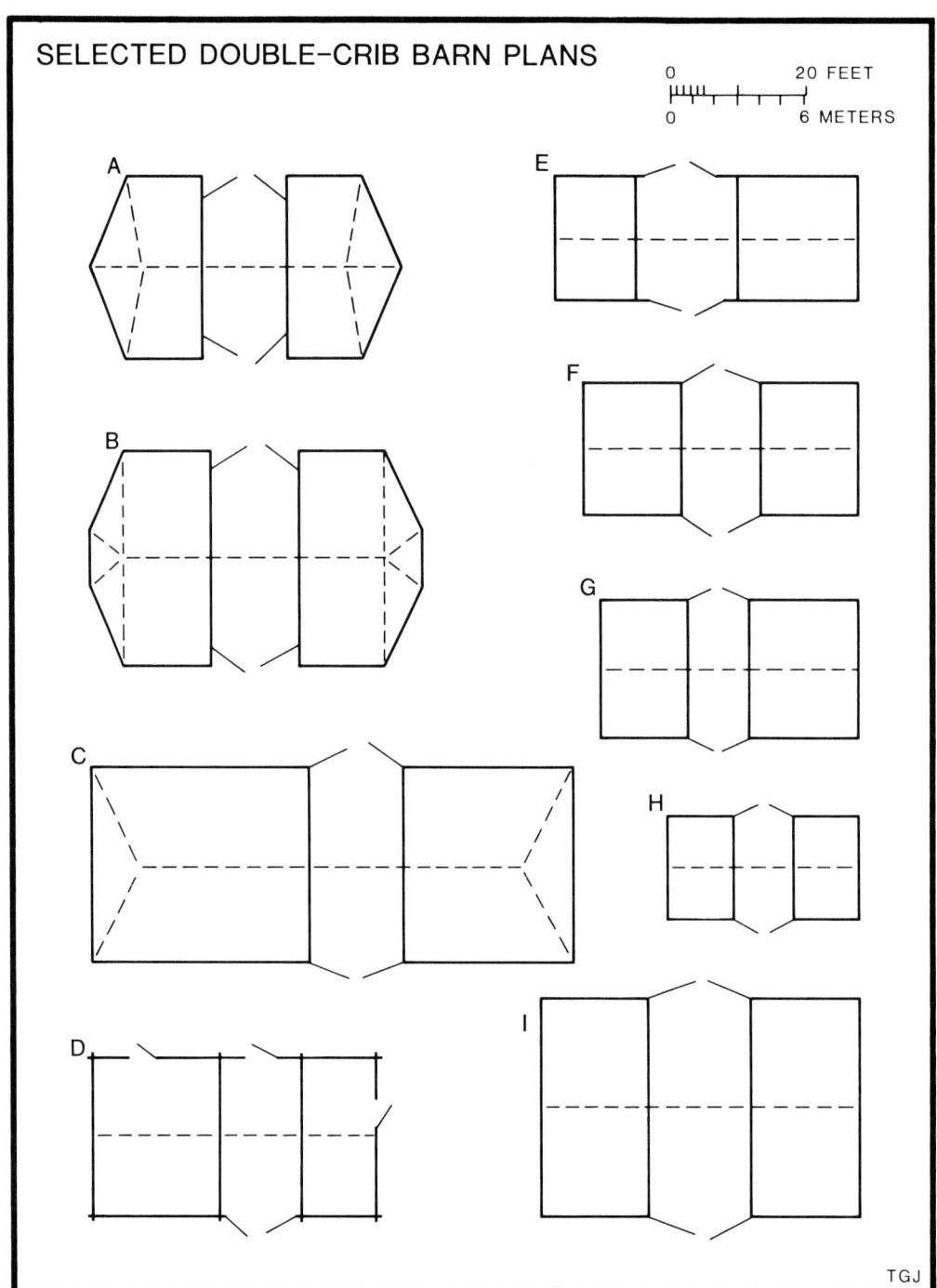

The German-Slavic Borderland

(Opposite)
Figure 5.33. The examples are A and B, district of Votice (Wotitz), southern Bohemia; C, near Racibórz, Upper Silesia; D, Spreewald, Lower Lausitz; E, Vsetín (Wsetin) in Moravian Valachia; F, Gliwice area, Upper Silesia; G, Opole district, Upper Silesia; H, Čičmany, western Slovakia; and I, Wałbrzych district, Lower Silesia. Several of these barns are now in outdoor folk museums, including example D, at the Lehde/Lĕdy Wendish Freiland Museum near Lübbenau, German Democratic Republic; example E in the Valašské Muzeum v Přírodĕ at Rožnov pod Radhoštĕm, Moravia; and example G at Muzeum wsi Opolskiej at Bierkowice near Opole, Poland. (Sources: field measurements and Palm, *Haus und Hof in Oberschlesien*, p. 59; Deutschmann, *Lausitzer Holzbaukunst*, p. 67 and Figure 42; Härtel, *Ländliche Baukultur*, p. 21; and Baláš and Klíma, "Vesnické Stavby v Okrese Votickém," p. 164.)

Figure 5.34. *Galerie* forebay on a storage barn in the Opole district of Upper Silesia (field research district 14). The structure, now in the open-air Muzeum wsi Opolskiej at Opole-Bierkowice, is somewhat similar to the forebay barns of Pennsylvania, but fundamental differences can also be detected. (Photo by T.G.J., 1982.)

Glassie's suggestion that some American forebays derive from the overhang inherent in eastern German *Umgebinde* construction must be rejected.[63] The barns of the eastern Germans and western Slavs, then, while revealing some similarities to American forms, offer no satisfactory, or even needed, prototypes for Midland structures. The earlier immigrations of Swiss, Palatines, Britons, Swedes, and Finns brought the basic American log barns.

Six
Conclusion

Northern European Influence

A careful analysis of surviving log structures in northern Europe, the Alpine-Alemannic region, and the German-Slavic borderland leaves little doubt that the greatest shaping influence on Midland American log construction was exerted by settlers from the Fenno-Scandian area. Many elements of the American style are northern European in origin, and the discarded, much-maligned thesis of Swedish and Finnish antecedence is, in great measure, valid after all. Numerous architectural features and techniques linked to the Midland culture area find their closest European equivalents in the Baltic lands and should, therefore, be considered probable introductions from Sweden and Finland (Tables 6.1, 6.2). In this category we would place V, diamond, square, half, and saddle notching; chink construction; the corncrib and single-crib barn; the use of round logs and two-sided ax-and-adze hewing; the ridgepole and purlin roof with board covering; and the dogtrot and gable-entrance single-pen dwelling plans. Midland rural folk who retain a knowledge of log structures and still use them recognize photographs of these Fenno-Scandian features as familiar things. This familiarity reflects a folk architectural continuity stretching from East Texas to central Sweden, a continuity based in part on widespread blood kinship to the Delaware Finns and Swedes.

For still other features, northern European origin is certainly possible. Forms similar or identical to shed porches, forebays, double-crib barns, military blockhouses, rail fences, the saddlebag and Cumberland house plans, the bank barn, vertical siding

Conclusion

Table 6.1. Origin of Midland American Carpentry Features

Midland Feature	Fenno-Scandian Source Region	Alpine-Alemannic Source Region	German-Slavic Borderland	British Isles	Probable Source(s)
Use of round logs	◉	◉	○	×	Sweden, reinforced by Alpine Germans
Half-round logs	○	◎	○	×	Canton Bern or Central Sweden
Planking	◉	◉	○	●	Sweden, Switzerland
Tall, thin planking	●	◉	○	●	Black Forest, Swiss Jura, Britain
Two-sided hewing	◎	×	◉	×	Sweden, Bohemia
Chinks	◎	●	◉	×	Sweden
Chinking	○	○	◉	×	Sweden, Bohemia
Full-dovetail notch	●	●	◉	×	Sweden, reinforced from eastern Germany
Half-dovetail notch	○	×	◎	×	Americanism, or Silesia or Moravia
Saddle notch	◉	◉	○	×	Central Sweden, Alps
Semilunate notch	○	◎	×	×	Canton Bern
Diamond notch	◎	×	×	×	Götland province
Square notch	●	○	●	×	Central Sweden
Half notch	○	×	○	×	Central Sweden
V notch	◎	×	×	×	Värmland or Dalsland provinces
Ridgepole and purlin roof	◉	◉	○	●	Central Sweden, reinforced by British
Raftered roof	×	×	◉	◉	Britain or Rhenish Germany
Shingled roof	○	◉	●	×	Alps
Board roof	◉	×	×	×	Central Sweden
Board-covered gable	○	×	◉	○	Sweden and Britain, reinforced by eastern Germans

Key: ◉ = very common   ● = common   ◎ = occasional   ○ = rare   × = absent over logs, red-painted barns, and I houses occur in Sweden and Finland. At the very least, the familiarity of the Delaware Swedes and Finns with these forms could have reinforced similar forms known to other immigrant groups.

The strongest Fenno-Scandian influence occurs in the most primitive Midland American forms—those associated with pioneering and the frontier. The log cabin, with its round timbers, saddle or crude V notching, log gable, and gently pitched ridgepole and purlin roof covered with boards, is largely Fenno-Scandian, as are the more crudely constructed outbuildings. To find these forms today, one must seek out remote, poverty-stricken districts of Midland America and the hinter portions of northern Europe where vestiges of woodland pioneering remain. From the sixteenth century to the twentieth, backcountry Finns have borne the brunt of forest colonization, both in Finland and Sweden, and they were likely the principal agents of diffusion in introducing the Fenno-Scandian form elements that survived in Midland America. Indeed, the Finns who came to New Sweden constituted the only immigrant group to arrive in colonial America already in possession of a tested and successful woodland pioneering culture. As they had few adjustments to make to the new environment, they were free to demonstrate their considerable skill as backwoodsmen. Later immigrants entering Midland America by way of Philadelphia had to run a gauntlet of Finnish and Swedish log buildings and pioneer farms lining both banks of the Delaware.

The Fenno-Scandian carpentry techniques and architectural styles were simple and well suited to frontier conditions, easily learned and adopted by the English, Welsh, and Scotch-Irish, who had no previous log carpentry experience. The large majority of the Germans who came to Pennsylvania were unfamiliar with log construction and were, therefore, as likely as the Britishers to adopt the expedient Fenno-Scandian construction techniques. In this manner, Fenno-Scandian methods penetrated the German-speaking population perhaps a decade or more before the first Teutonic log carpenters arrived from the Alps and Black Forest about 1710. Upon arrival, the German log craftsmen thus encountered a primitive log carpentry tradition among their ethnic kin, a tradition they modified and refined but did not eliminate.

Or, better put, they encountered two traditions. In the few surviving log structures of New Sweden, one can see two carpentry styles, Finnish and Swedish, side by side. The former, characterized by chink construction, saddle notching, V notching, round logs, and two-sided hewing, is by far the cruder; good representations of this style may be found in the upper and lower "Swedish cabins" on Upper Darby Creek in Clifton Heights, Pennsylvania, and in the New Castle County, Delaware, house on display at the National Museum of American History in Washington, D.C. (Figure 3.17). The Swedish type, displaying chinkless walls, carefully shaped timbers hewn on four sides, and notching of the full-dovetail and square varieties, can be seen in the Morton house at Prospect Park, Pennsylvania, and in a house in Salem, New Jersey (Figures 3.12, 3.34). Of the two traditions, as previously suggested, the more primitive Finnish

Conclusion

Table 6.2. Origin of Midland American Dwellings, Barns, Fences, and Bridges

Midland Feature	Fenno-Scandian Source Region	Alpine-Alemannic Source Region	German-Slavic Borderland	British Isles	Probable Source(s)
Single-pen house, gable entrance	◎	○	×	○	Värmland
Single-pen house, square, front and rear eave entrance	×	×	×	●	England (non-log)
Single-pen house, rectangular, subdivided (hall and parlor)	●	×	×	○	Celtic Britain, Sweden
Continental house	×	○	●	×	Rhenish Germany
Dogtrot house	◎	×	×	×	Sweden
Central-hall house	◉	○	◎	●	Sweden, British Isles
Saddlebag house	◎	×	×	◎	Britain or Värmland & Dalsland
Cumberland house	○	×	×	◎	Sweden or Britain
I house	◉	×	×	●	Britain
Single-crib barn	◉	◎	×	×	Sweden, reinforced by Alpine Germans
Double-crib plan	◉	◎	◎	●	British Isles, Sweden, Rhenish lands, Alps
Open-passage double-crib barn	○	◎	×	×	Salzburg province
Bank barn	●	◉	◎	◎	Switzerland
Eave forebay	◉	◎	○	×	Canton Graubünden
Transverse-crib barn	×	○	×	×	Americanism
Four-crib barn	×	×	×	×	Americanism
Pennsylvania barn	○	◎	×	×	Canton Graubünden
Red color for barns	◉	×	×	○	Central Sweden or Americanism
Rail fences	◉	◎	×	×	Central Sweden or Austrian Alps
Blockhouse (fort)	●	×	×	×	Sweden, British army
Covered bridge	×	●	○	×	Canton Bern

Key: ◉ = very common ● = common ◎ = occasional ○ = rare × = absent

style exerted the greater influence on Midland American construction.

Putting aside for a moment the concepts of first effective settlement and cultural preadaptation, one must ask how a group as few in number as the Delaware Finns and Swedes could have exerted so significant an architectural influence. Even given their position along the "front sidewalk" of Penn's Woods and their status as successful forest pioneers, they would seem too few to bend other, larger groups to their cultural will. Finally, they subsequently vanished as a distinct people, to the extent that, by the time of the Revolution, few of their descendants would think of themselves as Swedish-Americans, much less Finnish-Americans. These are legitimate questions, questions which must be addressed if we are to reconcile the architectural evidence with the overall evolution of Midland colonial culture. The reply is threefold.

First, the final three decades of the seventeenth century constituted the crucial period during which elements of northern European folk architecture first spread from the Finns and Swedes to the incipient Midland American population at large, a diffusion begun on the very banks of the Delaware. Throughout this period, Scandinavians continued to form a substantial proportion of the local population, in rural areas perhaps a quarter or even more of the inhabitants. An early census of the New Castle area of Delaware, dated 1677, suggests as much.[1] The Scandinavians, in this view, remained proportionately important in the Delaware Valley through the initial decades of contact with other European colonists, facilitating diffusion of their culture.

Second, during that same period, the Finns and Swedes proved quite willing to mix, both by neighborhood and through marriage, with English, Germans, Hollanders, and others. In fact, a list of 139 "Swedish" families along the Delaware compiled in 1693 included Dutch, British, and German surnames such as Koenig, Talley, Stedham, Van der Weer, Meyer, and Dennis, implying ethnic mixing on a quite remarkable scale.[2] This willingness to mix, though endangering Finnish and Swedish ethnic survival, enhanced the ability of the northern Europeans to transfer elements of their culture to other groups and enlarged the potential number of their descendants. Even the adoption of log construction by certain eastern Amerindian groups may have begun during this period, or earlier, since contacts between the Scandinavians and local natives were both frequent and culturally significant.[3]

Finally, many persons wholly or, more commonly, partially of Finnish-Swedish blood left the Delaware Valley to penetrate the continental interior as pioneers. By the end of the seventeenth century, in possession of land grants from William Penn, Swedes and Finns led the advance westward, above the falls of the Schuylkill on a path that would lead to the main artery of Midland migration, the Great Valley of the Appalachians.[4] Delaware Scandinavian family names such as Rambo, Oleson, Yoakum, Paulson, Stalcup, Freeland, Holston, and Swanson appeared on the outer edge of the exploding Midland frontier through the remainder of the colonial period. We find them very early in the backcountry of Virginia, where, for example, Yoakums and Olesons reached Augusta County by 1750.[5] Nearby, Swain Paulson, resident

Conclusion

on the north fork of the Roanoke River, crossed Cumberland Gap with Boone to be numbered among the first settlers of Kentucky's Salt River country.[6] The Holston settlement in earliest northeastern Tennessee bore the name of a Delaware Scandinavian family, as did such outposts as Fort Freeland in Centre County, Pennsylvania, and Yokum Station in Lee County, Virginia.[7] Edward Swanson and George Freeland were two among a band of nine forming the initial expedition, in 1779, to Middle Tennessee, where Swanson became the first settler of Williamson County and Freeland's Station stood near the site of Nashville.[8] This list could be expanded almost indefinitely and carried even along the Oregon Trail, but the point should be clear: rather than cling to a seaboard ethnic enclave, many descendants of Delaware Finns and Swedes went west to be well represented even in the remotest backwoods of colonial Midland America. The price they paid for this diaspora was the loss of the last remnants of their ethnic identity; their reward, though they could not know it, lay in the incidental transferal of some part of their northern European culture to the Midland population at large, completing a diffusion begun before 1700 in the Delaware Valley cradle.

The Scandinavians in colonial Midland America, then, while few in number, remained proportionately important through a crucial early contact period, displayed a propensity to mix and marry with those not of their kind, and subsequently scattered to the frontier. These attributes, attitudes, and tendencies enabled them to spread some part of their culture to a much larger population.

Alpine-Alemannic Influence

The second most important contribution to Midland American log construction came from the Alpine-Alemannic Germans (Tables 6.1, 6.2). While their influence on dwelling types was minimal, these southern Teutonic immigrants should be credited with the introduction of many of the basic Midland barn types, including several double-crib plans, the bank entrance, the forebay, and the Pennsylvania barn. They probably should also be credited with tall, thin planking, semilunate notching, half-log construction, and shingling. Alpine-Alemannic Germans, in addition, reinforced certain features probably introduced earlier by the Finns and Swedes, in particular saddle notching, round-log construction, the use of chinks, the ridgepole and purlin roof, and the post-and-rail fence.

Why should Alpine-Alemannic influence have been confined so largely to barns? The answer likely lies in the perceptions and goals of the colonial immigrants. They were willing to discard certain aspects of their traditional culture for practical or social reasons, but as a rule they resisted changes perceived to endanger success in farming. The immigrants from southern central Europe may have discarded ancestral house types in a quest for social acceptance and acculturation, but barns are economic structures. The barn helped govern their prosperity and progress as New World farmers, and perhaps they recognized that traditional Alpine barns well fit the needs of American farming systems. Function may occasionally have changed—types 4 and 5 Alpine double-crib hay sheds, for example, proved to be excellent corncribs—but the barn form elements nonetheless proved viable in America. Unwilling to jeopardize their farming success, they clung to the European types. So well did their traditional forms serve New World agricultural purposes that the imported types and subtypes eventually spread to some non-Alpine and even non-German neighbors.

Too, the traditional Alpine and Alemannic houses were large, complex, and ornate, in contrast to the simplicity of the barns. To have built such dwellings in America would have drawn attention to these Germans at precisely the time when they sought acculturation. In addition, such complex forms were impractical in a frontier setting.

Influence of the German-Slavic Borderland

The case for eastern German–western Slavic influence in Midland American architecture has been overstated by its proponents. It is fundamentally inaccurate to describe the wooden architecture and carpentry of the German-Slavic borderland as being "exactly" like the Midland American type.[9] What appear at first glance to be striking similarities between designs and techniques of the two traditions prove, on close inspection, to be less compelling resemblances.

The Schwenkfelder influence can be discounted. Their Lower Silesian carpentry and floor plans, characterized by double notching, *Umgebinde* construction, false chinking, and massive two-story house-stall combinations, possess almost no features in common with the Midland tradition. The small numbers and late arrival of the Schwenkfelders, coupled with their reluctance to seek converts in America or to spread beyond their tiny enclave in eastern Pennsylvania, no doubt contributed to the failure of this group to exert architectural influence.

The more numerous Moravian Brethren, the last German sect to arrive in colonial America, helped modestly to shape the final, or house, stage of Midland log construction. Their contribution was apparently limited largely to refining, reinforcing, and encouraging certain form elements and practices that had been previously implanted by Fenno-Scandian and Alpine-Alemannic immigrants. We can see their influence in the reinforcement of two-sided hewing, chinking, board gables, and the raftered roof, all of which had been introduced earlier. Brethren craftsmen likely assisted the rise to dominance of dovetail notching, and it is possible, though unlikely, that they promoted the spread of square notching.

Even this limited claim for Brethren influence may be an exaggeration. At both Bethlehem in Pennsylvania and Wachovia in North Carolina, the Brethren found preexisting log structures, and to the present day one can distinguish Moravian buildings from those erected by other groups in the North Carolina Piedmont.[10] In spite of widespread missionary activity, the Brethren were singularly unsuccessful in winning converts to their faith in America, a failure that surely retarded diffusion of their carpentry traits.[11] Further weakening the likelihood of eastern German or western Slavic influence by way of the Brethren is the cosmopolitan nature of their membership. Tombstones at Herrnhut, Bethlehem, and Nazareth display an incredible diversity of eighteenth-century birthplaces, and only a minority of the

Conclusion

Brethren claimed Moravian, Bohemian, Silesian, or Saxon birth. Their epitaphs record natives of Norway, Sweden, Finland, Livonia, Denmark, England, Swabia, Russia, Alsace, Switzerland, and other lands far removed from the Czech–Polish–East German borderland. Also damaging the cause of Brethren influence was the weakness of their commitment to log construction. At Herrnhut, as in America, they quickly abandoned log carpentry to focus on stone and half-timbered structures.[12]

The Pennsylvania German culture and legacy have been interpreted by linguists and folklorists as basically Rhenish and Alpine-Alemannic, and this study has turned up relatively little to alter that view.[13] The eastern German pietists arrived late on the American colonial scene and exerted only a limited influence on the Midland tradition. The contribution of the Moravian Brethren was demonstrably less important than that of the Fenno-Scandian and Alpine-Alemannic immigrants (Tables 6.1, 6.2).

British Influence

Britishers, including large numbers of English and Scotch-Irish settlers, together with a smaller Welsh contingent, formed well over half of the Midland American population by the time of the Revolution. This presence, coupled with English rule during the last century of the colonial era, permitted the British to form the host culture in the Middle Atlantic region. It is not surprising, then, that even though the British did not accomplish the first effective settlement of the region and had no previous knowledge of log construction, they did exert an influence on Midland American folk architecture.

One sees their mark in such floor plans as the side-gable, square, "one-bay" type of single-pen; the elongated single-pen, including the hall-and-parlor house; the enclosed central hall; the three-bay barn; and the I house. Certain of these plans reinforced earlier types introduced from the Alps and northern Europe, assisting their rise to importance. Placement of chimneys and fireplaces centrally in exterior gable walls in a variety of house plans is without question a British influence, one that modified, in particular, several Fenno-Scandian dwelling types.

The raftered roof also has deep British roots, paralleling a Rhenish or Palatine German practice. Sawn planking, board gables, and the practice of covering houses with horizontal siding very likely also reveal British influence.

Even so, the English and Scotch-Irish shaped Midland American architecture to a lesser degree than their numbers and status as the host culture would lead one to expect. Perhaps they arrived too late on the scene, or maybe cultural preadaptation worked against them.

Four Concepts

The conclusions concerning European origin strongly support Zelinsky's doctrine of first effective settlement. The Finns and Swedes, though few in number, accomplished the first effective occupancy of the Delaware Valley and were successfully established there decades before British and German colonists appeared on the scene. We should not be surprised that, in many respects, their pioneer architecture and carpentry served as the model for the Midland frontier. Indeed, one must now wonder whether many other elements of the American backwoods culture, such as slash-and-burn farming, hunting techniques, and pathfinding, do not, in some measure, also have northern European antecedents. Zelinsky's doctrine is valid. His curious ancillary statement that it did not apply to the settlers of New Sweden must be disregarded.[14]

To carry his doctrine a step further, this study of log construction suggests that the later a group arrives in successive waves of immigration, the less cultural impact it has. The Moravians and Schwenkfelders, last to appear on the Midland American scene, exerted the least influence on log construction.

The findings of this study are also entirely consistent with the concept of simplification of European culture in overseas colonial areas. In the diffusion of log construction from each of the European source areas, only a minority of Old World styles and techniques was successfully introduced. American log construction never approached the complexity or sophistication displayed in the source regions. To a certain extent, this simplification seems to have reflected the specific origins of the immigrants. V notching, for example, is one of a great many local Scandinavian types, and it reached America because of the local importance of Värmland and Dalsland as emigration sources. Similarly, the open-passage double-crib barn is common in America probably because upper Salzburg Province sent hundreds of settlers to Georgia and other colonies.

At the same time, more diversity was implanted than survived. The demise in America of the Swiss bank house, the Moravian house-barn, Swedish chinkless construction, and Salzburger double notching provides convincing evidence that part of the simplification process occurred not at the point of departure but in the colonial areas. In this context, Dell Upton's conclusions concerning Virginia ring true. By and large, it was the simpler, more efficient forms and techniques that survived in America, suggesting the importance of frontier pressures.

A third process also helps explain simplification. Because of English rule, the British became the host culture in the middle colonies, and other ethnic groups desired acculturation. Architectural forms that appeared too alien, too un-British, fell aside. Partly for this reason, the spectacular, ornate Alemannic houses of the Bernese and Black Forest Germans or *Umgebinde* construction of lower Silesia never took root.

Simplification was, as Zelinsky proposed, accompanied by a lack of inventiveness on the part of the American colonists and their descendants. Not one of the forty features of architecture and carpentry listed in Tables 6.1 and 6.2 lacks a possible European prototype. Only a few features are probable Americanisms, including half-dovetail notching and two barn plans, the four-crib and transverse crib.

The architectural evidence that American colonial culture was syncretic is compelling. How else can one explain such Midland phenomena as a Graubünden barn with Swedish V notching, an English one-bay house built in logs, a Swedish meadow barn used as a container for Indian corn, or an Alpine shingled roof and British exterior gable chimney on a Finnish dog-

Conclusion

trot house? The features that survived the simplification process to become part of the syncretic architecture very often had been known to more than one of the immigrant groups in their European homelands. Both Swiss and Swedes knew the eave forebay on two-level outbuildings; double-crib log barns appear in the Alps, Scandinavia, and German-Slavic borderland; the I house is both British and Scandinavian; central-hall, side-gable dwellings occur widely in Europe north of the Alps; dovetail notching is found among Alemannic Germans, western Slavs, Swedes, Silesians, and Sudeten Germans; post-and-rail fences are both Alpine and Swedish; and bank barns are present in all three source areas for log construction, as well as England. A syncretic colonial culture, then, develops in part by a process of mutual reinforcement, involving the merging of similar traits from diverse sources. The dogtrot house provides a fine example. It derives from a merger of the British central-hall house, containing exterior chimneys centrally positioned in each gable wall, with the most primitive Fenno-Scandian log double-house, characterized by interior corner chimneys and an open passage rather than a hall.

The validity of the concept of cultural preadaptation is also suggested by this study of American log construction. Certainly the best example is the simple, crude backwoods Finnish carpentry, a type identified with woodland colonization in northern Europe and preadapted to success on the forested American frontier. A Finnish culture and technology held in contempt by seventeenth-century Swedish rulers, a culture of forest destroyers and cabin builders who were condemned, branded, and exiled to the Delaware, proved to be the ideal technology for the occupiers of the forests of Midland America.

Milton Newton seriously erred, however, in his demarcation of the zone and period where the preadapted traits meshed. He should look earlier than 1725 and not only to the backcountry but also to the Delaware Valley cradle of the Midland culture between 1670 and 1700, to the river corridor where Finn and Swede first met and mixed with Briton, Teuton, and Hollander. It was along that river, well before 1700, that a veritable marketplace of preadapted material culture first awaited inspection and exchange. Midland American log construction, then, is a reflection of a simplified, syncretic, uninventive, and preadapted culture. Northern, central, and western European in unequal measure shaped it. This is the most important message of the humble log cabin, icon and index to culture.

Notes

Chapter One

1. Kniffen, "Folk Housing."
2. Meitzen, *Das deutsche Haus*, p. 3.
3. Brumbaugh, "Colonial Architecture of Pennsylvania Germans," p. 6.
4. Gunderson, *Log-Cabin Campaign*; Thayer, *From Log-Cabin to White House*.
5. Lavender, *Dog Trots and Mud Cats*, p. 3.
6. Jordan, *Texas Log Buildings*, pp. 212–21; Kauffman, "Literature on Log Architecture," pp. 30–34.
7. Zelinsky, *Cultural Geography of the United States*, p. 13.
8. Kniffen, "Folk Housing," p. 551.
9. Harris, "Simplification of Europe Overseas," p. 469.
10. Foster, *Culture and Conquest*, p. 13.
11. Hartz, *Founding of New Societies*, p. 3.
12. Upton, "Vernacular Domestic Architecture," p. 96.
13. Zelinsky, *Cultural Geography of the United States*, p. 83.
14. Hartz, *Founding of New Societies*, p. 3; Harris, "Simplification of Europe Overseas," p. 474.
15. Jordan, *Texas Graveyards*, pp. 17, 39–40; Jordan, *Trails to Texas*, p. 156.
16. Harris, "Simplification of Europe Overseas," p. 474; Newton and Pulliam-DiNapoli, "Log Houses as Public Occasions," p. 378.
17. Zelinsky, *Cultural Geography of the United States*, p. 6.
18. Newton, "Cultural Preadaptation and the Upland South," p. 147.
19. Zelinsky, *Cultural Geography of the United States*, p. 6.
20. Newton, "Cultural Preadaptation and the Upland South," p. 147.
21. Turner, *Frontier in American History*.
22. Kniffen, "Folk Housing," p. 571; Kniffen and Glassie, "Building in Wood in Eastern United States," p. 60.
23. Winberry, "Log House in Mexico," pp. 66–68.
24. Gritzner, "Log Housing in New Mexico"; Winberry, "Log House in Mexico"; Wonders, "Log Dwellings in Canadian Folk Architecture"; Lehr, "Log Buildings of Ukrainian Settlers in Western Canada."

25. Candee, "Wooden Buildings in Early Maine and New Hampshire"; Kelly, "Seventeenth-Century Connecticut Log House."

26. Kaups, "Finnish Log Houses in Upper Middle West"; Kaups, "A Finnish *Savusauna*"; Brandt and Braatz, "Log Buildings in Portage County"; Kaups, "A Finnish *Riihi*."

27. See, as examples of this debate, Erixon, "Är den nordamerikanska timringstekniken överförd från Sverige?"; Roberts, "Comments on Log Construction in Scandinavia and the United States"; Mercer, "Origin of Log Houses"; and Glassie, "Types of Southern Mountain Cabin," pp. 345, 347.

28. Defenders of the Fenno-Scandian origin thesis include Mercer, "Origin of Log Houses," p. 63; Kimball, *Domestic Architecture of the American Colonies*, pp. 6–8; Waterman, *Dwellings of Colonial America*, pp. 118–23; Morrison, *Early American Architecture*, p. 506; Weslager, *Log Cabin in America*, chapter 7; and Wright, "Antecedents of the Double-Pen House."

29. Wright, "Log Cabin in the South," pp. 1, 6.

30. Mercer, "Origin of Log Houses," p. 55; Wright, "Log Culture in Hill Louisiana," p. 95; Wright, "Antecedents of the Double-Pen House."

31. Wertenbaker, *Founding of American Civilization*, pp. 298–303; Erixon, "Är den nordamerikanska timringstekniken överförd från Sverige?" pp. 56–68; Kniffen and Glassie, "Building in Wood in Eastern United States," pp. 58, 59, 63; and Bucher, "Continental Log House," p. 14.

32. Glassie, "Eighteenth-Century Cultural Process in Delaware Valley," p. 49.

33. Allen, "European Origins of Early Pennsylvania Architecture," p. 126.

34. Glassie, "Old Barns of Appalachia," pp. 28–29; Glassie, "Double-Crib Barn in South-Central Pennsylvania," pt. 4, p. 25.

35. Bucher, "Swiss Bank House in Pennsylvania"; Long, "Bank (Multi-Level) Structures," p. 31; Ensminger, "Search for Origin of Pennsylvania Barn," p. 67; Ludwig, *Influence of Pennsylvania Dutch in Midwest*, pp. 76–81; Jordan, "Alpine, Alemannic, and American Log Architecture."

36. Wertenbaker, *Founding of American Civilization*, p. 298.

37. Kniffen and Glassie, "Building in Wood in Eastern United States," p. 59.

38. Glassie, "Types of Southern Mountain Cabin," p. 345.

39. Kniffen and Glassie, "Building in Wood in Eastern United States," p. 59.

40. Glassie, "Types of Southern Mountain Cabin," p. 347.

41. Matuszczak, *Z Dziejów Architektury*, p. 159.

42. Härtel, *Ländliche Baukultur am Rande der Mittelsudeten*, p. 15.

43. Helmigk, *Oberschlesische Landbaukunst*, p. 19; Palm, *Haus und Hof in Oberschlesien*, pp. 9–10.

44. Roucek, "Moravian Brethren in America," pp. 60–61.

45. A notable exception to the previous neglect of European field research is Wright, "Antecedents of the Double-Pen House."

46. Zwingli Geburtshaus Museum, Wildhaus, Canton St. Gallen, Switzerland.

Chapter Two

1. General sources on American log architecture include Weslager, *Log Cabin in America*; Shurtleff, *Log Cabin Myth*; and Bealer and Ellis, *The Log Cabin*.

2. Some examples of regional and local studies of Midland log construction are Hutslar, *Log Architecture of Ohio*; Jordan, *Texas Log Buildings*; Weslager, "Log Houses in Pennsylvania"; Carlisle, *Architectural Study of Some Log Structures*; Marshall, *Folk Architecture in Little Dixie*; Taylor, *From Frontier to Factory*; and Yeager, *Log Structures in Warren County, Kentucky*.

3. Muir, *Texas in 1837*, p. 74.

4. Billingsley, "Trip to Texas," pp. 203–4.

5. A good general study is Kniffen and Glassie, "Building in Wood in Eastern United States."

6. Pillsbury, "Europeanization of Cherokee," pp. 65–66.

7. General sources are Kniffen, "On Corner Timbering"; Jordan, "Log Corner Notching in Texas"; and Jordan, "Log Corner-Timbering in Texas."

8. Roberts, "Some Comments on Log Construction."

9. Gritzner, "Log Housing in New Mexico," p. 60.

10. See, in particular, Kniffen, "Folk Housing"; and Pillsbury, "Patterns in Folk and Vernacular House Forms."

11. Wilson, "Single Pen Log House in the South"; Hughes-Jones and Gettys, "Single Pen Log Cabins in Oklahoma."

12. Kaups, "A Finnish *Riihi.*"

13. Bucher, "Continental Log House"; Glassie, "Central Chimney Continental Log House."

14. Vlach, "Canada Homestead."

15. Hulan, "Middle Tennessee and the Dogtrot House"; Hulan, "Dogtrot House and Its Pennsylvania Associations"; Price, "Dog-Trot Log Cabin."

16. O'Malley and Rehder, "Two-Story Log House in Upland South," pp. 904–15.

17. General sources on log barns include Arthur and Witney, *The Barn*; Ennals, "Nineteenth-Century Barns"; Glassie, "Old Barns of Appalachia"; and Noble and Seymour, "Distribution of Barn Types."

18. Glassie, "Double-Crib Barn in South-Central Pennsylvania"; Price, "Double-Crib Log Barns of Calhoun County."

19. Dornbusch and Heyl, *Pennsylvania German Barns*; Shoemaker, *Pennsylvania Barn*.

20. Ensminger, "Comparative Study of Pennsylvania and Wisconsin Barns"; Bastian, "Southeastern Pennsylvania and Central Wisconsin Barns"; Glassie, "Pennsylvania Barn in the South"; Wilhelm, "Pennsylvania-Dutch Barn in Southeastern Ohio."

21. Rehder, Morgan, and Medford, "Decline of Smokehouses."

22. Kniffen, "American Covered Bridge."

23. Raup, "Fence in the Cultural Landscape."

Chapter Three

1. This chapter incorporates material that originally appeared as "A Reappraisal of Fenno-Scandian Antecedents for Midland American Log Construction" (*Geographical Review* 73, no. 1 [Jan 1983]: 58–94). The most important secondary sources on northern European log construction are Alnaes, *Norwegian Architecture throughout the Ages*; Bartenev and Fyodorov, *North Russian Architecture*; Boëthius, *Studier i den nordiska timmerbyggnadskonsten*; Erixon, *Svensk byggnads kultur*; Kolehmainen and Laine, *Suomalainen Talonpoikaistalo*; Bielenstein, *Holzbauten und Holzgeräte der Letten*; Dethlefsen, *Bauernhäuser und Holzkirchen*; and Vreim, "Norsk byggekunst i middelalderen." For excellent examples of local studies, see Appelgren, "Om byformen och gårdstyperna i Åbolands," and Forsblom, "Allmogebyggnader i Esse."

2. Johnson, *Swedish Settlements on the Delaware*, vol. 2, pp. 674, 678, 688, 693, 697, 699, 706–14, 716, 720, 723–26; Dunlap and Moyne, "Finnish Language on the Delaware," p. 82; Nelson, *Swedes and the Swedish Settlements*, vol. 1, pp. 77–78, 91, 94; Wuorinen, *Finns on the Delaware*, pp. 51, 54–55, 79; Beck, "Moravian Graveyards of Lititz"; Kluge, "Moravian Graveyards at Nazareth"; Schultze, "Old Moravian Cemetery of Bethlehem"; Evjen, *Scandinavian Immigrants in New York*; Louhi, *Delaware Finns*; and Russell, "Swedish Settlement in Maryland."

3. Wuorinen, *Finns on the Delaware*, pp. 13–14; Sømme, *Geography of Norden*, p. 150.

4. Evjen, *Scandinavian Immigrants in New York*, p. 365.

5. Schultze, "Old Moravian Cemetery of Bethlehem"; Fries, *Records of the Moravians in North Carolina*, vol. 1, pp. 68–69, 73, 130.

6. J. Jordan, "Moravian Immigration to Pennsylvania, 1734–1765," p. 236; Fries, *Records of the Moravians in North Carolina*, vol. 1, pp. 73, 131; Schultze, "Old Mo-

ravian Cemetery of Bethlehem," pp. 111, 117.

7. Log construction on the eastern Baltic shore closely resembles the northern European type and extends as far south as a Gdansk-Kiev line; see Kaups, "Log Architecture in America," p. 135.

8. Dethlefsen, *Bauernhäuser und Holzkirchen*; Bielenstein, *Holzbauten und Holzgeräte der Letten*. The Nordiska Museet in Stockholm has a special display on the material culture of the Estonian Swedes.

9. Vuorela, *Suomalainen kansankulttuuri*, p. 408; Boëthius, *Nordiska timmerbyggnadskonsten*, pp. 29, 64, 65, 106, 108, 152, 284; Bartenev and Fyodorov, *North Russian Architecture*, pp. 64–65, 80, 82, 104, 251, 301; Erixon, "North-European Technique," pp. 14, 15, 19, 23, 35, 39; Kolehmainen and Laine, *Suomalainen Talonpoikaistalo*, pp. 33, 57, 60–65, 111.

10. Weslager, "Log Houses in Pennsylvania," pp. 257, 262–63, 266; Wacker and Trindell, "Log House in New Jersey," pp. 254–55; Weslager, *Log Cabin in America*, pp. 167–68, 189, 197; Waterman, *Dwellings of Colonial America*, p. 120.

11. Erixon, *Svensk byggnads kultur*, pp. 161–62; Erixon, "North-European Technique," p. 44.

12. Erixon, "North-European Technique," p. 41, plate 9; Kolehmainen and Laine, *Suomalainen Talonpoikaistalo*, pp. 49, 55; Bielenstein, *Holzbauten und Holzgeräte der Letten*, p. 12.

13. Erixon, "North-European Technique," pp. 43, 51, 53.

14. Arnstberg, *Datering av knuttimrade hus*, pp. 34–36, 304; Boëthius, *Nordiska timmerbyggnadskonsten*, p. 53.

15. Bielenstein, *Holzbauten und Holzgeräte der Letten*, pp. 15, 75; Dethlefsen, *Bauernhäuser und Holzkirchen*, p. 10.

16. Wacker and Trindell, "Log House in New Jersey," pp. 255, 265; Weslager, *Log Cabin in America*, pp. 166–67, 171–72, 188–89.

17. Kolehmainen and Laine, *Suomalainen Talonpoikaistalo*, pp. 60–65, 193, 238, 425; Norberg-Schulz et al., *Wooden Houses*, p. 237; Bartenev and Fyodorov, *North Russian Architecture*, pp. 173, 306; Alnaes, *Norwegian Architecture*, p. 154; Mercer, "Origin of Log Houses," p. 61 (quoting the director of Nordiska Museet); and structures on display at Skansen, Seurasaari, and the Norsk Folkemuseum.

18. Mercer, "Origin of Log Houses," p. 62; Erixon, "Schwedische Holzbautechnik," p. 71; Kaups, "Log Architecture in America," p. 137.

19. Kalm, *Travels into North America*, pp. 84, 260.

20. Weslager, *Log Cabin in America*, pp. 159, 167–68, 184, 191–97; Wacker and Trindell, "Log House in New Jersey," pp. 254–55; Delaware house on display in the National Museum for Science and History, Washington, D.C.

21. Kalm, *Travels into North America*, p. 298.

22. Kolehmainen and Laine, *Suomalainen Talonpoikaistalo*, pp. 60–65, 193, 238, 425.

23. Erixon, "North-European Technique," pp. 14, 20; Bartenev and Fyodorov, *North Russian Architecture*, pp. 64–65, 80, 82, 91, 104, 150, 251, 258; Bielenstein, *Holzbauten und Holzgeräte der Letten*, p. 11.

24. Arnstberg, *Datering av knuttimrade hus*, pp. 128–29; Erixon, "North-European Technique," p. 39; Boëthius, *Nordiska timmerbyggnadskonsten*, p. 284; Kolehmainen and Laine, *Suomalainen Talonpoikaistalo*, pp. 57, 111; Forsblom, "Allmogebyggnader i Esse," p. 61.

25. Wacker and Trindell, "Log House in New Jersey," p. 255; Weslager, "Log Houses in Pennsylvania," p. 257; Weslager, *Log Cabin in America*, pp. 165, 168, 189, 198; Bealer and Ellis, *Log Cabin*, pp. 150, 155–56.

26. Wacker and Trindell, "Log House in New Jersey," p. 263; Kniffen and Glassie, "Building in Wood in Eastern United States," p. 59.

27. Mercer, "Origin of Log Houses," p. 55; Kniffen and Glassie, "Building in Wood in Eastern United States," p. 56.

28. Bealer and Ellis, *Log Cabin*, pp. 147–49; Weslager, *Log Cabin in America*, pp. 164, 167–68, 190–98.

29. Kniffen and Glassie, "Building in Wood in Eastern United States," pp. 53, 54; Wright, "Log Culture in Hill Louisiana," p. 74.

30. Erixon, "North-European Technique," pp. 39, 40, 45; Boëthius, *Nordiska timmerbyggnadskonsten*, pp. 284, 298, 318, 319; and the outdoor collection of the Hallingdal Folkemuseum in Nesbyen, Buskerud province, Norway.

31. Erixon, "North-European Technique," p. 40.

32. Arnstberg, *Datering av knuttimrade hus*, pp. 99, 100, 121, 138; Boëthius, *Nordiska timmerbyggnadskonsten*, pp. 60, 106, 124, 204, 238, 284; Erixon, "North-European Technique," pp. 15, 19, 21, 38; Kaups, "Finnish Log Houses in Upper Middle West," p. 8.

33. Personal communication, with photo, from Professor Robert F. Ensminger, geographer at Kutztown State College, Kutztown, Pa., July 1981.

34. Arnstberg, *Datering av knuttimrade hus*, pp. 96, 99.

35. Kniffen and Glassie, "Building in Wood in Eastern United States," pp. 54, 56.

36. Arnstberg, *Datering av knuttimrade hus*, pp. 133, 135; Kniffen and Glassie, "Building in Wood in Eastern United States," p. 64.

37. Norberg-Schulz et al., *Wooden Houses*, p. 232; "Blockwand," *Wasmuths Lexikon der Baukunst*, p. 553; Arnstberg, *Datering av knuttimrade hus*, p. 133; Kolehmainen and Laine, *Suomalainen Talonpoikaistalo*, pp. 264, 341; Bartenev and Fyodorov, *North Russian Architecture*, p. 266. At the Seurasaari open-air museum in Helsinki, one of the structures in unit 7 has square notching covered by vertical boards.

38. Boëthius, *Nordiska timmerbyggnadskonsten*, pp. 318, 319.

39. Bielenstein, *Holzbauten und Holzgeräte der Letten*, pp. 12–13, regarded this corner-board shield in Latvia as a nineteenth-century development.

40. Wacker and Trindell, "Log House in New Jersey," p. 258; Kaups, "Finnish Log Houses in Upper Middle West," pp. 8, 11.

41. McWhorter, *Border Settlers of Northwestern Virginia*, p. 468.

42. Arnstberg, *Datering av knuttimrade hus*, p. 131.

43. Ibid., p. 133; Jordan, *Texas Log Buildings*, p. 68.

44. Hansen, *Architecture in Wood*, p. 68; Arnstberg, *Datering av knuttimrade hus*, pp. 131–33; Bartenev and Fyodorov, *North Russian Architecture*, pp. 35, 58, 258; Erixon, "North-European Technique," pp. 32, 56–57, plate 11; Kolehmainen and Laine, *Suomalainen Talonpoikaistalo*, pp. 57, 127, 205, 211, 242; Boëthius, *Nordiska timmerbyggnadskonsten*, pp. 320, 342; Bielenstein, *Holzbauten und Holzgeräte der Letten*, pp. 12, 13; Weslager, *Log Cabin in America*, p. 153; Forsblom, "Allmogebyggnader i Esse," p. 61.

45. Boëthius, *Nordiska timmerbyggnadskonsten*, p. 320.

46. Wacker and Trindell, "Log House in New Jersey," pp. 255, 258. See also the log house from New Castle County, Delaware, preserved in the National Museum for Science and History, Washington, D.C.

47. Johnson, *Swedish Settlements*, vol. 2, pp. 703, 706, 711, 713, 716, 720; Kalm, *Pehr Kalms Resa*, p. 219; among the other ethnic Germans listed as New Sweden settlers were Jürgen Schneeweiss, Gottfried Hermer, Lukas Krüger, and G. M. Hollsten (Holstein).

48. Roberts, "Some Comments on Log Construction," pp. 439–45.

49. Jeffers, *Photographic Documentary of the Blue Ridge Mountains*, p. 44; Jordan, *Texas Log Buildings*, pp. 94, 106; Bealer and Ellis, *Log Cabin*, pp. 10, 15, 53, 93, 160; Carter, *Ghost Towns of the West*, pp. 103, 114, 173; Attebury, "Log Construction in the Sawtooth Valley," pp. 40, 42; Hutslar, *Log Architecture of Ohio*, pp. 29, 35; Goins and Morris, *Oklahoma Homes*, p. 29; Hudson, "Frontier Housing in North Dakota," pp. 10–11; Clemson, *Living with Logs*, pp. 18, 24, 32.

50. Gritzner, "Log Housing in New Mexico," p. 60; Bealer and Ellis, *Log Cabin*, pp. 19, 20; Attebury, "Log Construction in the Sawtooth Valley," pp. 39–40; Jordan, *Texas Log Buildings*, pp. 85, 86; Clemson,

Living with Logs, pp. 18, 24, 32.

51. Phleps, *Holzbaukunst: Der Blockbau*, p. 94; Kolehmainen and Laine, *Suomalainen Talonpoikaistalo*, pp. 145, 457; Boëthius, *Nordiska timmerbyggnadskonsten*, pp. 81, 182, 183, 193, 206, 233; Erixon, *Svensk byggnads kultur*, pp. 137, 193; Norberg-Schulz et al., *Wooden Houses*, p. 217; Bielenstein, *Holzbau und Holzgeräte der Letten*, pp. 25, 65.

52. Bealer and Ellis, *Log Cabin*, pp. 155–56; Carter, *Ghost Towns*, pp. 103, 110, 163; Attebury, "Log Construction in the Sawtooth Valley," p. 42; Jordan, *Texas Log Buildings*, p. 94; Hutslar, *Log Architecture of Ohio*, p. 36; Gettys and Hughes-Jones, "Log Pens and Lifestyles," pp. 60–62.

53. Vuorela, *Suomalainen kansankulttuuri*, p. 411; Boëthius, *Nordiska timmerbyggnadskonsten*, p. 200; Norberg-Schulz et al., *Wooden Houses*, pp. 218–27, 238; Erixon, *Svensk byggnads kultur*, p. 209; Bielenstein, *Holzbau und Holzgeräte der Letten*, pp. 28–29; Jordan, *Texas Log Buildings*, p. 106.

54. Kolehmainen and Laine, *Suomalainen Talonpoikaistalo*, pp. 220, 223, 230, 232.

55. Boëthius, *Nordiska timmerbyggnadskonsten*, p. 64; Erixon, *Svensk byggnads kultur*, p. 711; Kolehmainen and Laine, *Suomalainen Talonpoikaistalo*, pp. 46, 48, 120, 121, 136, 247; Norberg-Schulz et al., *Wooden Houses*, p. 235; Mercer, "Origin of Log Houses," pp. 59, 60.

56. Dethlefsen, *Bauernhäuser und Holzkirchen*, pp. 1, 27, 40–41, 57.

57. Kolehmainen and Laine, *Suomalainen Talonpoikaistalo*, pp. 50–52, 217, 230, 234, 365; Vuorela, *Suomalainen kansankulttuuri*, p. 385; Erixon, *Svensk byggnads kultur*, p. 96; Norberg-Schulz et al., *Wooden Houses*, pp. 238–39; Boëthius, *Nordiska timmerbyggnadskonsten*, pp. 212, 214, 259; Erixon, "Byggnadsskicket hos svenska bönder," p. 338.

58. Pillsbury, "Patterns in Folk and Vernacular House Forms," pp. 14, 16–20, 29; Kniffen, "Folk Housing," p. 561.

59. For an earlier, and far overstated, argument supporting Swedish influence in Midland American floor plans, see Waterman, *Dwellings of Colonial America*, pp. 124–38.

60. Erixon, *Svensk byggnads kultur*, pp. 502, 543; Norberg-Schulz et al., *Wooden Houses*, pp. 228–29.

61. Pillsbury, "Patterns in Folk and Vernacular House Forms," p. 20.

62. Kniffen, "Folk Housing," p. 556.

63. Weslager, *Log Cabin in America*, pp. 178, 197; Johnson, *Swedish Settlements*, vol. 2, pp. 541–42.

64. Wright, "Double-Pen House," pp. 113, 115–17; Wright, "Log Culture in Hill Louisiana," p. 51; Erixon, *Svensk byggnads kultur*, pp. 212, 215, 625; Kaups, "Log Architecture in America," p. 141; Hulan, "Dogtrot House and Its Pennsylvania Associations," pp. 25–32; see also a photograph entitled "Tatar House" on display at the Museum of Soviet Ethnography in Leningrad.

65. Kolehmainen and Laine, *Suomalainen Talonpoikaistalo*, pp. 245, 388–92; Erixon, *Svensk byggnads kultur*, pp. 624, 626, 628, 631, 654, 662, 665, 682, 687, 690, 777, 778.

66. Kauffman, *American Farmhouse*, p. 68; Weslager, *Log Cabin in America*, pp. 166–67; Wright, "Double-Pen House," p. 109; Bealer and Ellis, *Log Cabin*, pp. 151–54.

67. Hulan, "Middle Tennessee and the Dogtrot House," pp. 44, 45; Glassie, *Pattern in Material Folk Culture*, pp. 88–89; Johnston and Waterman, *Early Architecture of North Carolina*, p. 7; Hutslar, *Log Architecture of Ohio*, pp. 28, 66, 67; Morrison, *Early American Architecture*, pp. 169–70; Kniffen, "Folk Housing," p. 561; Hulan, "Dogtrot House and Its Pennsylvania Associations," pp. 25–32; Johnston, *History of Middle New River Settlements*, follows p. 398; Whitwell and Winborne, *Architectural Heritage of the Roanoke Valley*, p. 42.

68. The idea presented here was first proposed in Hulan, "Delaware Valley Double-House and Its European Origin."

69. U.S. Bureau of the Census, *Heads of Families at the First Census, North Carolina*; Nelson, *Swedes and Swedish Settlements*, p. 90.

70. Kolehmainen and Laine, *Suomalainen Talonpoikaistalo*, pp. 20–21, 153, 226, 252–53; Neuenschwander, *Finnish Architecture and Alvar Aalto*, p. 10; Nylén, *Swedish Handcraft*, p. 35; Boëthius, *Nordiska timmerbyggnadskonsten*, p. 41; Erixon, *Svensk byggnads kultur*, pp. 286–346; Norberg-Schulz et al., *Wooden Houses*, p. 220; Bielenstein, *Holzbau und Holzgeräte der Letten*, p. 60; Kaups, "Log Architecture in America," pp. 141–43.

71. Vlach, "Canada Homestead," pp. 8–17; Jordan, *Texas Log Buildings*, pp. 116–19; Hutslar, *Log Architecture of Ohio*, pp. 66–67; Kniffen, "Folk Housing," p. 561.

72. Erixon, *Svensk byggnads kultur*, pp. 376, 383; Bielenstein, *Holzbau und Holzgeräte der Letten*, pp. 62, 77; Dethlefsen, *Bauernhäuser und Holzkirchen*, p. 18; Kaups, "Finnish Log Houses in Upper Middle West," p. 18.

73. Erixon, *Svensk byggnads kultur*, p. 383.

74. MSS Texas Log Cabin Register, Jack County No. 1.

75. Kaups, "Log Architecture in America," pp. 141, 143; Johnson, *Swedish Settlements*, vol. 1, pp. 345–46.

76. Jordan, *Texas Log Buildings*, pp. 111, 113; Clemson, *Living with Logs*, pp. 16, 32.

77. Glassie, "Types of Southern Mountain Cabin," pp. 353–55; Waterman, *Dwellings of Colonial America*, p. 124.

78. Marshall, *Folk Architecture in Little Dixie*, pp. 48, 51; Pillsbury, "Patterns in Folk and Vernacular House Forms," pp. 14, 16.

79. Erixon, *Svensk byggnads kultur*, pp. 370, 383; Bielenstein, *Holzbau und Holzgeräte der Letten*, pp. 60–75; Waterman, *Dwellings of Colonial America*, p. 124.

80. Kolehmainen and Laine, *Suomalainen Talonpoikaistalo*, p. 19; Erixon, *Svensk byggnads kultur*, pp. 348–400; Nylén, *Swedish Handcraft*, p. 36; Waterman, *Dwellings of Colonial America*, p. 125.

81. Kauffman, *American Farmhouse*, p. 67; Bealer and Ellis, *Log Cabin*, pp. 147–50; Johnson, *Swedish Settlements*, vol. 2, p. 541; Waterman, *Dwellings of Colonial America*, pp. 118–19, 123.

82. Erixon, *Svensk byggnads kultur*, pp. 147, 168; Bielenstein, *Holzbau und Holzgeräte der Letten*, pp. 62, 159–60.

83. Nylén, *Swedish Handcraft*, p. 93.

84. Erixon, *Svensk byggnads kultur*, p. 435.

85. Boëthius, *Nordiska timmerbyggnadskonsten*, pp. 321–22; Söderberg and Erixon, "Svenska herrgårdar," p. 241; a replica of such a structure in Östergötland is on exhibit at Skansen in Stockholm.

86. Kolehmainen and Laine, *Suomalainen Talonpoikaistalo*, pp. 48, 145, 253; Erixon, *Svensk byggnads kultur*, p. 677; Bartenev and Fyodorov, *North Russian Architecture*, p. 80; Hansen, *Architecture in Wood*, p. 78; Norberg-Schulz et al., *Wooden Houses*, pp. 256–57. See also exhibit 19 at the Seurasaari museum, Helsinki.

87. Boëthius, *Nordiska timmerbyggnadskonsten*, pp. 65, 190, 193, 196, 271, 276; Vuorela, *Suomalainen kansankulttuuri*, p. 362; Hansen, *Architecture in Wood*, p. 74; Erixon, *Svensk byggnads kultur*, pp. 137, 602, 606, 615, 621, 628, 631, 632, 638; Norberg-Schulz et al., *Wooden Houses*, pp. 234, 247, 256, 257; Erixon, "Byggnadsskicket hos svenska bönder," p. 337.

88. Calkins and Perkins, "Pomeranian Barn of Southeastern Wisconsin."

89. Erixon, *Svensk byggnads kultur*, pp. 201, 212, 221, 622; Boëthius, *Nordiska timmerbyggnadskonsten*, p. 43; Kolehmainen and Laine, *Suomalainen Talonpoikaistalo*, pp. 282, 322; Wright, "Log Culture in Hill Louisiana," p. 95.

90. Forsblom, "Allmogebyggnader i Esse," p. 33.

91. Leighly, "Towns of Mälardalen in Sweden," p. 32; Erixon, *Svensk byggnads kultur*, pp. 89, 94, 110; Boëthius, *Nordiska timmerbyggnadskonsten*, p. 223; Kolehmainen and Laine, *Suomalainen Talonpoikaistalo*, p. 322; field observations near Lahti, Häme, Finland.

92. Norberg-Schulz et al., *Wooden Houses*, pp. 250–51, 256–57; the Norsk Folkemuseum in Oslo contains two such barns.

93. Jordan, "Alpine, Alemannic, and American Log Architecture," pp. 168, 170, 171; Ensminger, "Search for the Origin," p. 66.

94. Glassie, "Old Barns of Appalachia," p. 22; Jordan, *Texas Log Buildings*, pp. 161–64.

95. Erixon, *Svensk byggnads kultur*, p. 146; Kolehmainen and Laine, *Suomalainen Talonpoikaistalo*, pp. 133, 167, 229, 272, 367; Phleps, *Holzbaukunst: Der Blockbau*, p. 170; Johnson, *Swedish Settlements*, vol. 1, pp. 362–63; Forsblom, "Allmogebyggnader i Esse," p. 31; see also exhibit 7 in the Seurasaari, Helsinki.

96. Interview with T. E. Mason of Indian Creek community, Cooke County, Tex., 14 March 1983.

97. Erixon, *Svensk byggnads kultur*, pp. 146, 162, 170; Boëthius, *Nordiska timmerbyggnadskonsten*, pp. 31, 73; Norberg-Schulz et al., *Wooden Houses*, p. 216; Jordan, *Texas Log Buildings*, pp. 177–78; exhibit 7 in the Seurasaari, Helsinki.

98. Comment by Riitta Ailonen, Curator, Museovirasto, National Board of Antiquities and Historical Monuments, Helsinki, January 1981. See also exhibit 4 in the Seurasaari museum, Helsinki.

99. *Skansen, Stockholm: A Short Guide*, p. 9; Hahr, *Architecture in Sweden*, p. 6.

100. Raup, "Fence in the Cultural Landscape," pp. 4–5.

101. Zelinsky, "Walls and Fences," p. 15.

102. Erixon, *Svensk byggnads kultur*, pp. 70, 89, 177, 201, 204, 318, 329, 528, 645, 704; Vuorela, *Suomalainen kansankulttuuri*, pp. 55, 172–74, 203, 379, 406; Boëthius, *Nordiska timmerbyggnadskonsten*, pp. 25, 92; Kolehmainen and Laine, *Suomalainen Talonpoikaistalo*, pp. 68–70, 113, 145, 174, 279, 287, 293, 363; Bielenstein, *Holzbau und Holzgeräte der Letten*, p. 172.

103. "Värmland," *Svensk Upplagsbok*, figures 2 and 8 following p. 1136.

104. Larsen, "Pehr Kalm's Observations on the Fences of North America," p. 77; Kalm, *Travels into North America*, pp. 228–29.

105. Johnson, "Sweden Gave America the Rail Fence," pp. 7, 29.

Chapter Four

1. A preliminary version of this chapter appeared as "Alpine, Alemannic, and American Log Architecture," *Annals of the Association of American Geographers* 70, no. 2 (June 1980): 154–80.

2. Information on the specific origins of Alpine and Alemannic German immigration to colonial America can be found in Faust and Brumbaugh, *Lists of Swiss Emigrants*; Yoder, "Emigrants from Wuerttemberg," pp. 132–237; Jones, *Henry Newman's Salzburger Letterbooks*; Kuhns, *German and Swiss Settlements*, pp. 10, 21, 31, 32, 45, 56, 64–66, 76, 235–36; Schultze, "Old Moravian Cemetery of Bethlehem"; Fries, *Records of the Moravians in North Carolina*, vol. 1, pp. 68–69, 131; Hopple, "Germanic European Origins," pp. 69–86; Voigt, "German and German-Swiss Element," pp. 8, 16, 17, 44, 46.

3. Phleps, *Holzbaukunst: Der Blockbau*, pp. 50–51; "Blockwand," *Wasmuths Lexikon*, pp. 552–53.

4. Weiss, *Häuser und Landschaften der Schweiz*, p. 54.

5. Phleps, *Holzbaukunst: Der Blockbau*, pp. 51–53; Gschwend, "Bäuerlicher Hausbau," sketch no. 6; in "Blockwand," *Wasmuths Lexikon*, p. 552, half-log construction is incorrectly described as a typical mountain type.

6. Swoboda, *Alte Holzbaukunst*, vol. 1, p. 44.

7. Sketches of nearly fifty European notching types are shown in Phleps, *Holzbaukunst: Der Blockbau*, pp. 57–60; see also "Holzbaukunst," *Wasmuths Lexikon*, p. 126. For comparative American types, see Kniffen, "On Corner Timbering." pp. 1–8.

8. Weiss, *Häuser und Landschaften der Schweiz*, p. 56.

9. Ibid., p. 56; Swoboda, *Alte Holzbaukunst*, vol. 1, p. 26.

10. Phleps, *Holzbaukunst: Der Blockbau*, pp. 59, 62, 78.

11. Ibid., p. 51, sketch no. 6; Kniffen and Glassie, "Building in Wood in Eastern United States," p. 64.

12. Kniffen and Glassie, "Building in

Wood in Eastern United States," pp. 48–53.

13. Kindig, *Architecture in York County*, p. 23.

14. Schilli, *Das Schwarzwaldhaus*; Weiss, *Häuser und Landschaften der Schweiz*, p. 43.

15. Matt, *Uri*, p. 77.

16. Schultze, "Old Moravian Cemetery of Bethlehem," p. 158.

17. Phleps, *Holzbaukunst: Der Blockbau*, pp. 85–125.

18. Swoboda, *Alte Holzbaukunst*, vol. 2, pp. 41, 49.

19. Moser, *Das Bauernhaus*, pp. 53, 59; Swoboda, *Alte Holzbaukunst*, vol. 1, p. 87.

20. Swoboda, *Alte Holzbaukunst*, vol. 1, pp. 43, 87, 122, vol. 2, pp. 76, 156.

21. Winberry, "Origin and Dispersal of the Shingle Roof," pp. 95–113.

22. Schröder, *Geographische Hausforschung*, pp. 6–8; Gschwend, *Schwyzer Bauernhäuser*; Weiss, *Häuser und Landschaften der Schweiz*.

23. Bucher, "Continental Log House," pp. 14–19; Glassie, "Central Chimney Continental Log House," pp. 32–39.

24. Stevens, "Swiss Bank House Revisited," pp. 78–86; Bucher, "Swiss Bank House in Pennsylvania," pp. 2–11.

25. Buffington, "Pennsylvania German," pp. 276–86.

26. Moser, *Das Bauernhaus*, p. 80; Swoboda, *Alte Holzbaukunst*, vol. 2, pp. 64, 71; Geramb, "Kulturgeschichte der Rauchstuben," pp. 8, 56; Geramb, "Geographische Verbreitung und Dichte," pp. 70–123.

27. Shoemaker, *Pennsylvania Barn*; Dornbusch and Heyl, *Pennsylvania German Barns*, pp. 1–299; Arthur and Witney, *The Barn*, pp. 84–113; Ensminger, "Comparative Study of Pennsylvania and Wisconsin Barns." The Pennsylvania Dutch use the terms *forbau* or *overshot* for the forebay, and the bank-ramp is called a *foddergang*.

28. Glassie, "Double-Crib Barn in South-Central Pennsylvania," pt. 4, p. 25; Shoemaker, *Pennsylvania Barn*, p. 29; in 1798 fully 52 percent of all barns in Pennsylvania were log or partially log.

29. Glassie, "Old Barns of Appalachia," p. 28.

30. Glassie, "Double-Crib Barn in South-Central Pennsylvania," pt. 4, p. 25.

31. Dornbusch and Heyl, *Pennsylvania German Barns*, p. x.

32. Glassie, "Old Barns of Appalachia," pp. 28, 29.

33. Glassie, "Double-Crib Barn in South-Central Pennsylvania," pt. 4, p. 25.

34. Glassie, "Old Barns of Appalachia," pp. 21, 23, 25, 26, 28–29; Glassie, "Double-Crib Barn in South-Central Pennsylvania," pt. 4, pp. 29–30; Glassie, "Pennsylvania Barn in the South," pt. 1, pp. 8–19, and pt. 2, pp. 12–25.

35. Wilhelm, "Pennsylvania-Dutch Barn in Southeastern Ohio," pp. 155–62; Ennals, "Nineteenth-Century Barns in Southern Ontario," pp. 256–70; Glassie, "Pennsylvania Barn in the South."

36. Ridlen, "Bank Barns in Cass County," pp. 25–43; Schreiber, "Pennsylvania Dutch Bank Barns in Ohio," pp. 15–28; Arthur and Witney, *The Barn*, pp. 53, 124–25, 138–39; see also the sources cited in note 35.

37. Wilhelm, "Amish-Mennonite Barns," p. 7.

38. Ensminger, "Search for the Origin of the Pennsylvania Barn," pp. 61, 62, 67; Gschwend, "Bäuerliche Haus- und Hofformen," examples 15–17; Simonett, *Bauernhäuser des Kantons Graubünden*, vol. 2, pp. 20–21; Swoboda, *Alte Holzbaukunst*, vol. 1, pp. 45, 50, 51, 94, 130, vol. 2, pp. 68, 149; Phleps, *Holzbaukunst: Der Blockbau*, p. 171; Moser, *Das Bauernhaus*, pp. 103, 108; Norberg-Schulz et al., *Wooden Houses*, pp. 85–86.

39. Voigt, "German and German-Swiss Element," pp. 8, 16, 44.

40. Long, "Bank (Multi-Level) Structures," p. 31.

41. Glassie, "Double-Crib Barn in South-Central Pennsylvania," pt. 4, p. 25; Bastian, "Indiana Folk Architecture," p. 129; Vesey-Fitzgerald, *British Countryside in Pictures*, p. 234.

42. Gschwend, "Bäuerliche Haus- und Hofformen," examples 16, 17; Weiss, "Stallbauten und Heutraggeräte," pp. 38–39; Ensminger, "Search for the Origin of the Pennsylvania Barn," p. 66.

43. Moser, *Das Bauernhaus*, p. 108.
44. Jordan, "Alpine, Alemannic, and American," p. 173; Ensminger, "Search for the Origin of the Pennsylvania Barn," p. 67; Parsons, "Postscript," p. 71.
45. Weiss, "Stallbauten und Heutraggeräte," pp. 38–39, map 1.
46. Ibid.; Faust and Brumbaugh, *Lists of Swiss Emigrants*, vol. 1, pp. 9, 12, 24; Kluge, "Moravian Graveyards at Nazareth," p. 143.
47. Fries, *Records of the Moravians in North Carolina*, vol. 1, pp. 68–69.
48. Hutslar, *Log Architecture of Ohio*, pp. 49–50; Shoemaker, *Pennsylvania Barn*, pp. 28, 31, 32; Dornbusch and Heyl, *Pennsylvania German Barns*, pp. 79–95.
49. Carter and Glossbrenner, *History of York County*, pp. 176–77. Siebenbürgen in Transylvania is a log construction area.
50. Loewe, *Schlesische Holzbauten*, p. 60.
51. Noble and Geib, "Sweitzer Barn," pp. 11–12; Noble, "Barns as Elements of the Settlement Landscape," pp. 65, 68, 70–71; Dornbusch and Heyl, *Pennsylvania German Barns*, p. 80; Shoemaker, *Pennsylvania Barn*, pp. 6–7. Pennsylvania variations of the term include "Switzer," "Swisser," "Sweisser," and "Swiss."
52. Ensminger, "Search for the Origin of the Pennsylvania Barn," pp. 65, 67.
53. Simonett, *Bauernhäuser des Kantons Graubünden*, vol. 2, p. 20.
54. Glassie, "Old Barns of Appalachia," pp. 22–23.
55. Brantley, "Salzburgers in Georgia," pp. 214–24; Hofer, "Georgia Salzburgers," pp. 99–117; Jones and Lacher, *Detailed Reports on the Salzburger Emigrants*, vol. 1. Some Effingham County Salzburgers moved to Pennsylvania; Jones, *Dead Towns of Georgia*, p. 42.
56. Schultze, "Old Moravian Cemetery of Bethlehem," p. 151; Kluge, "Moravian Graveyards at Nazareth," p. 102.
57. Wilson, "Salzburger Long-Lots of Colonial Georgia," pp. 134–38; Newton, "Industrial and Social Influences of the Salzburgers," pp. 335–53; LeBon, "Catahoula Hog Dog," pp. 43–44.
58. Pillsbury, personal communication; Glassie, "Double-Crib Barn in South-Central Pennsylvania," pt. 4, p. 29.
59. Callaway, *Early Settlement of Georgia*, p. 58.
60. Jones, *Dead Towns of Georgia*, p. 42; Gnann, *Georgia Salzburger Families*.
61. Candler, *Colonial Records of Georgia*, vol. 1, p. 201.
62. Zelinsky, "Log House in Georgia," pp. 184, 186; Bolzius, "Johann Martin Bolzius Answers," pt. 2, p. 251.
63. Hurst, "Salzburger Exiles in Georgia," p. 397.
64. Bolzius, "Johann Martin Bolzius Answers," pt. 2, p. 252.
65. Moser, *Das Bauernhaus*, p. 100; Weiss, "Stallbauten und Heutraggeräte," figures 1 and 2 following p. 32; Simonett, *Bauernhäuser des Kantons Graubünden*, vol. 2, pp. 18, 23.
66. Moser, *Das Bauernhaus*, p. 112.
67. Swoboda, *Alte Holzbaukunst*, vol. 1, pp. 155, 193–98, vol. 2, pp. 17, 198–202.
68. Kniffen, "American Covered Bridge," pp. 119–21.
69. Ludwig, *Influence of Pennsylvania Dutch in Middle West*, pp. 76–81.
70. Sloane, "First Covered Bridge in America," p. 319.
71. Swoboda, *Alte Holzbaukunst*, vol. 1, pp. 36, 179; Moser, *Das Bauernhaus*, pp. 152, 155; Simonett, *Bauernhäuser des Kantons Graubünden*, vol. 2, p. 328.
72. Swoboda, *Alte Holzbaukunst*, vol. 1, p. 55.

Chapter Five

1. This chapter is derived from my article "Moravian, Schwenkfelder, and American Log Construction," *Pennsylvania Folklife* 33, no. 3 (Spring 1984): 98–124.
2. Helmigk, *Oberschlesische Landbaukunst*, p. 17.
3. Härtel, *Ländliche Baukultur*, p. 20.
4. Deutschmann, *Lausitzer Holzbaukunst*, p. 74.
5. Richter, "Die Wand des Bauernhauses in Böhmen," p. 61.
6. For each Polish and Czechoslovak village or town name used, the present Slavic version will be given preference, followed

in parentheses at the first reference by the German version.

7. Hrejsa, "Sborové jednoty bratrské," 1935 and 1937; Zeman, *Anabaptists and the Czech Brethren*, pp. 72, 292–93; Hamilton, *History of the Church*, pp. 10–14; Eller, *Houses of Peace*, p. 47; Schweinitz, *History of the Church*, pp. 636–38.

8. Langton, *History of the Moravian Church*, p. 53; Hrejsa, "Sborové jednoty bratrské," 1939.

9. Hamilton and Hamilton, *History of the Moravian Church*, pp. 13–14.

10. Beck, "Moravian Graveyards of Lititz"; Kluge, "Moravian Graveyards at Nazareth"; Schultze, "Old Moravian Cemetery of Bethlehem"; Fries, *Records of the Moravians*; Reichel, *Moravians in North Carolina*.

11. Buzek and Langer, *Valachische Freilichtmuseum*.

12. Brecht, *Genealogical Record of the Schwenkfelder Families*; Hopple, "Spatial History of the Schwenkfelders"; Kriebel, *Schwenkfelders in Pennsylvania*.

13. Evjen, *Scandinavian Immigrants in New York*, p. 329.

14. Kriebel, *Schwenkfelders in Pennsylvania*, pp. 47–48; Schünzel, "Deutsche Auswanderung nach Nordamerika," p. 130; Durnbaugh, *Brethren in Colonial America*, p. 269; Hopple, "Spatial Organization of the Southeastern Pennsylvania Plain Dutch," p. 17.

15. J. Jordan, "Moravian Immigration to Pennsylvania," p. 228; Murtagh, *Moravian Architecture*, p. 6.

16. Murtagh, *Moravian Architecture*, pp. 6–9, 106, 108.

17. Wust, *Virginia Germans*, p. 46; Smith, Stewart, and Kyger, *Pennsylvania Germans of the Shenandoah Valley*, p. 72.

18. Reichel, *Moravians in North Carolina*; Fries, "Moravian Contribution to Colonial North Carolina."

19. Murtagh, *Moravian Architecture*, pp. 23–26, 46–47, 109, 122; J. Jordan, "Note on the Moravian Church," p. 113; Anonymous, "Forgotten Moravian Settlement," p. 249.

20. J. Jordan, "Moravian Immigration to Pennsylvania," pp. 237, 241, 243; Murtagh, *Moravian Architecture*, p. 132; Schultze, "Old Moravian Cemetery of Bethlehem," pp. 100, 112, 119, 124, 127; Kluge, "Moravian Graveyards at Nazareth," pp. 101, 119.

21. Murtagh, *Moravian Architecture*, p. 130.

22. Holder, "Social Life of the Early Moravians," p. 168.

23. Deutschmann, *Lausitzer Holzbaukunst*, pp. 143–44; Palm, *Haus und Hof in Oberschlesien*, p. 16.

24. Glassie, "Types of Southern Mountain Cabin," p. 345.

25. Pekař, *Kniha o kosti*, vol. 1, plates 37, 40; Hasalová and Vajdiš, *Folk Art of Czechoslovakia*, pp. 18, 19, 41, 42; Mrlian, *Slowakische Volkskunst*, pp. 18–19; Melicherčík, *Československá vlastivěda*, pp. 114, 117; Deutschmann, *Lausitzer Holzbaukunst*, p. 179.

26. Deutschmann, *Lausitzer Holzbaukunst*, pp. 74, 133, 147, 148.

27. Franke, *Ostgermanische Holzbaukultur*, pp. 35–37; Palm, *Haus und Hof in Oberschlesien*, p. 16; Phleps, *Holzbaukunst: Der Blockbau*, p. 51.

28. Kalm, *Travels into North America*, pp. 84, 260.

29. Phleps, *Holzbaukunst: Der Blockbau*, pp. 57–59.

30. T. Jordan, *Texas Log Buildings*, p. 65.

31. Kniffen and Glassie, "Building in Wood in Eastern United States," p. 59.

32. Palm, *Haus und Hof in Oberschlesien*, p. 16; Franke, *Ostgermanische Holzbaukultur*, p. 205; Loewe, *Schlesische Holzbauten*, p. 10; Hansen, *Architecture in Wood*, p. 75.

33. Evans, "Cultural Geographer and Folklife Research," p. 525; Štika, "Bádání o karpatském salašnictví," p. 522.

34. Hasalová and Vajdiš, *Folk Art of Czechoslovakia*, pp. 59, 69; Mrlian, *Slowakische Volkskunst*, pp. 18–19; Pražák, "Valašský dům pod Makytou," plates 3, 8, 17.

35. Helmigk, *Oberschlesische Landbaukunst*, p. 84; Matuszczak, *Z Dziejów Architektury*, plate 77.

36. Howland, "Reconstructional Problems," p. 183.

37. Helmigk, *Oberschlesische Landbaukunst*, p. 85; Schier, *Hauslandschaften und Kulturbewegungen*, p. 118; Franke, *Ostgermanische Holzbaukultur*, pp. 113, 116; Loewe, *Schlesische Holzbauten*, p. 158; Phleps, *Holzbaukunst: Der Blockbau*, p. 58.

38. Raymond, *Early Domestic Architecture*, p. 14; Kindig, *Architecture in York County*, p. 14; Kocher, "Early Architecture of Pennsylvania," pp. 38, 516.

39. Schier, *Hauslandschaften und Kulturbewegungen*, pp. 26–102; Franke, *Ostgermanische Holzbaukultur*, pp. 42–44; Palm, *Haus und Hof in Oberschlesien*, p. 14; Loewe, *Schlesische Holzbauten*, pp. 8, 63; Deutschmann, *Lausitzer Holzbaukunst*, pp. 43, 57, 163, 171; Chotek, "Staré Typy Valašského Domu," pp. 135–43.

40. Schier, *Hauslandschaften und Kulturbewegungen*, pp. 28, 37–38; Palm, *Haus und Hof in Oberschlesien*, p. 11; Deutschmann, *Lausitzer Holzbaukunst*, p. 13; Pražák, "Valašský dům pod Makytou," plates 9, 11.

41. Schier, *Hauslandschaften und Kulturbewegungen*, map 2.

42. Apáthy, "Šindliarstvo v okolí Bardejova," pp. 65–93; Loewe, *Schlesische Holzbauten*, p. 9.

43. Webb, "Detailed Information and Account," p. 129.

44. Härtel, *Ländliche Baukultur*, pp. 12–13; Matuszczak, *Z Dziejów Architektury*, p. 159.

45. Franke, *Ostgermanische Holzbaukultur*, pp. 36–37; Schier, *Hauslandschaften und Kulturbewegungen*, map 7; Richter, "Die Wand des Bauernhauses in Böhmen," p. 61; Deutschmann, *Lausitzer Holzbaukunst*, pp. 59, 62, 80–81.

46. Loewe, *Schlesische Holzbauten*, pp. 8, 112, 120, 128; Franke, *Ostgermanische Holzbaukultur*, pp. 88–89.

47. Milner, "Germanic Architecture in the New World," p. 299; Bucher, "Continental Log House," pp. 14–19; Glassie, "Central Chimney Continental Log House," pp. 32–39.

48. Chotek, "Staré Typy Valašského Domu," pp. 134–35; Pražák, "Valašský dům pod Makytou," pp. 108–9; Palm, *Haus und Hof in Oberschlesien*, p. 33.

49. Härtel, *Ländliche Baukultur*, p. 16.

50. Webb, "Detailed Information and Account," p. 128; Kauffman, *American Farmhouse*, p. 79.

51. Palm, *Haus und Hof in Oberschlesien*, pp. 22, 70; Grundmann and Hahm, *Schlesien*, p. 15.

52. Kauffman, *American Farmhouse*, p. 73; Murtagh, *Moravian Architecture*, pp. 23–24.

53. Loewe, *Schlesische Holzbauten*, pp. 136–38; Grundmann and Hahm, *Schlesien*, p. 14.

54. Palm, *Haus und Hof in Oberschlesien*, p. 20.

55. Härtel, *Ländliche Baukultur*, pp. 34–35; Palm, *Haus und Hof in Oberschlesien*, p. 17.

56. Deutschmann, *Lausitzer Holzbaukunst*, pp. 66–67; Helmigk, *Oberschlesische Baukultur*, pp. 28, 187, 197; Palm, *Haus und Hof in Oberschlesien*, pp. 59, 76; Loewe, *Schlesische Holzbauten*, p. 13; Vydra, *Lidové stavitelství na Slovensku*, p. 59.

57. Baláš and Klíma, "Vesnické stavby v okrese votickém," pp. 164–65; Kuhn, *Siedlungsgeschichte Oberschlesiens*, p. 332; Richter, "Die Wand des Bauernhauses in Böhmen," p. 39; Grundmann and Hahm, *Schlesien*, plate 14.

58. Palm, *Haus und Hof in Oberschlesien*, p. 90; Härtel, *Ländliche Baukultur*, p. 20; Loewe, *Schlesische Holzbauten*, p. 115.

59. Deutschmann, *Lausitzer Holzbaukunst*, p. 164; Loewe, *Schlesische Holzbauten*, pp. 90, 110, 111; Grundmann and Hahm, *Schlesien*, pp. 15, 18.

60. Deutschmann, *Lausitzer Holzbaukunst*, p. 164.

61. Ibid., pp. 42, 43, 164; Grundmann and Hahm, *Schlesien*, p. 14.

62. Loewe, *Schlesische Holzbauten*, p. 90.

63. Glassie, "Old Barns of Appalachia," p. 28.

Chapter Six

1. "Taxables Living within the Jurisdiction," pp. 352–54.

2. Clay, *Annals of the Swedes*, pp. 167–68.

3. Jessee, "Culture Contact and Accul-

turation in New Sweden," pp. 33–38, 42–44.

4. Rambo, "First Pioneers," pp. 8, 10.

5. Kegley, *Virginia Frontier*, pp. 96, 145.

6. Kegley, *Virginia Frontier*, p. 615; Collins, *History of Kentucky*, vol. 2, p. 606.

7. Williams, "Stephen Holston," pp. 26–34; Meginness, *Otzinachson*, fold map at end.

8. Clayton, *History of Davidson County*, map facing p. 32; McRaven, *Life and Times of Edward Swanson*, pp. 17, 18, 19.

9. Glassie, "Types of Southern Mountain Cabin," p. 345.

10. Rau, MSS album, p. 4, plate 181; Fries, "Moravian Contribution to Colonial North Carolina," p. 4; Taylor, *From Frontier to Factory*.

11. Langton, *History of Moravian Church*, p. 115; Smith, Stewart, and Kyger, *Pennsylvania Germans of Shenandoah Valley*, p. 72.

12. Uttendörfer, *Alt-Herrnhut*, p. 80; Snyder, "Moravian Architecture of Bethlehem"; Murtagh, *Moravian Architecture and Town Planning*; Kauffman, "Moravian Architecture in Bethlehem"; Howland, "Reconstructional Problems."

13. Buffington, "Pennsylvania German," p. 276.

14. Zelinsky, *Cultural Geography of the United States*, p. 20.

Bibliography

Archives and Museums

Archives of the Moravian Church, Bethlehem, Pennsylvania. (Visited 30 July 1980).

Äskhults By farm museum, near Kungsbacka in Halland, Sweden. (Visited 2 July 1981).

Bunratty Folk Park, near Limerick in County Clare, Republic of Ireland. (Visited 20 July 1974).

Chüechlihus Museum, Langnau, Emmental, Canton Bern, Switzerland. (Visited 5 July 1978).

Disagården open-air museum, Gamla Uppsala, Uppland, Sweden. (Visited 11 June 1981).

Ekeby village museum, Uppland, Sweden. (Visited 12 June 1981).

Eskilstuna open-air museum, Eskilstuna, Södermanland, Sweden. (Visited 8 June 1981).

Finneloftet dwelling museum, Voss, Hordaland, Norway. (Visited 21 June 1981).

Fyresdal bygdetun open-air museum, Fyresdal on the Fyresvatn, Telemark, Norway. (Visited 26 June 1981).

Gemein Haus Moravian Museum of Bethlehem, Bethlehem, Pennsylvania. (Visited 29 July 1980).

Hallingdal Folkemuseum, Nesbyen, Buskerud, Norway. (Visited 24 June 1981).

Hol Bygdemuseum, Hol, Hallingdal, Buskerud, Norway. (Visited 24 June 1981).

Jönköpings Läns Museum (an open-air collection), Jönköping, Småland, Sweden. (Visited 6–7 June 1981).

Julita Gård open-air museum, Julita, Södermanland, Sweden. (Visited 8 June 1981).

Kviteseid Bygetunet open-air museum near Kviteseid, Telemark, Norway. (Visited 26 June 1981).

Lehde Freiland-Museum, Lehde/Lědy, near Lübbenau in the Spreewald, Niederlausitz, German Democratic Republic. (Visited 22 July 1982).

Moravian Museum, Bethlehem, Pennsylvania. (Visited 29 July 1980).

Museum of Soviet Ethnography, Leningrad, U.S.S.R. (Visited 6 January 1981).

Muzeum wsi Opolskiej, Opole-Bierkowice, Opole district, Silesia, Poland. (Visited 10 July 1982).

Národopisné Muzeum, Petřinské Sady, Praha, Czechoslovakia. (Visited 20 June 1982).

National Museum of American History, Washington, D.C. (Visited 27 July 1980).

Nordiska Museet, Djurgården, Stockholm, Sweden. (Visited 10 June 1981).

Norsk Folkemuseum (an open-air collection), Oslo-Bygdöy, Norway. (Visited 28 June 1981).

Ransäter Hembygdsgård (an open-air museum), Ransäter, Värmland, Sweden. (Visited 14 June 1981).

Sandvig Maihaugen (an open-air museum), Lillehammer, Oppland, Norway. (Visited 15 June 1981).

Säter Hembygdsmuseum Åsgårdarna (an open-air collection), Säter, Dalarna, Sweden. (Visited 12 June 1981).

Schweizerisches Freilichtmuseum, Ballenberg, near Brienz, Canton Bern, Switzerland. (Visited 10 July 1978).

Schwenkfelder Library, Pennsburg, Pennsylvania. (Visited 31 July 1980).

Seurasaari open-air museum, Seurasaari Island, Helsinki, Finland. (Visited 8 January 1981).

Skansen (an open-air museum), Djurgården Island, Stockholm, Sweden. (Visited 9 June 1981).

Södra Råda Ödekyrka, near Knekterud in Värmland, Sweden. (Visited 7 June 1981).

Sunnfjord Folkemuseum (an open-air collection), near Förde in Sogne og Fjordane, Norway. (Visited 20 June 1981).

Texas Log Cabin Register, MSS collection housed in the Archive of the North Texas State University Historical Collection, Denton, Texas.

Tiroler Volkskunstmuseum, Innsbruck, Tirol, Austria. (Visited 21 July 1978).

Tröndelag Folkemuseum (open-air collection), Trondheim, Sör-Tröndelag, Norway. (Visited 17 June 1981).

Trubschachen Heimatsmuseum, Trubschachen, Canton Bern, Switzerland. (Visited 6 July 1978).

Valašské Muzeum v Přírodě, Rožnov pod Radhoštěm, Moravia, Czechoslovakia. (Visited 25 June 1982).

Vallby open-air museum, Västerås, Västmanland, Sweden. (Visited 8 June 1981).

Viby By farmstead museum, near Sigtuna, Uppland, Sweden. (Visited 11 June 1981).

Vogtsbauernhof Freilichtmuseum, near Hornberg in the Gutach, Black Forest, Federal Republic of Germany. (Visited 3 July 1978).

Voss Folkemuseum (open-air collection), Voss, Hordaland, Norway. (Visited 21 June 1981).

Wadköping open-air museum, Örebro, Närke, Sweden. (Visited 7–8 June 1981).

Zorns Gammelgård (open air museum), Mora, Dalarna, Sweden. (Visited 13 June 1981).

Zwingli Geburtshaus Museum, Wildhaus, Canton St. Gallen, Switzerland. (Visited 14 July 1978).

Correspondence and Interviews

Ailonen, Riitta, Curator, Museovirasto, National Board of Antiquities and Historical Monuments, Helsinki, interview, January 1981.

Ensminger, Robert, Kutztown State College, personal communication, 31 January 1981 and July 1981.

Mason, T. E., Indian Creek, Cooke County, Texas, interview, 14 March 1983.

Pillsbury, Richard, Georgia State University, personal communication, 29 November 1978 and 3 January 1979.

Books and Articles

Allen, George H. "Some European Origins of Early Pennsylvania Architecture." *American Journal of Archaeology* 40 (1936): 126.

Alnaes, Eyvind. *Norwegian Architecture throughout the Ages.* Oslo: H. Aschehoug and Company, 1950.

Anonymous. "A Forgotten Moravian Settlement in New Jersey." *Pennsylvania Magazine of History and Biography* 37 (1913): 248–52.

Apáthy, Štefan. "Šindliarstvo v okolí Bardejova." *Slovenský Národopis* 2 (1954): 65–93.

Appelgren, Arne. "Om byformen och gårdstyperna i Åbolands västra skärgård." *Skrifter utgivna av Svenska Litteratursällskapet i Finland* 217 (1931): 153–224.

Arfwedson, Carolus David. *A Brief History of the Colony of New Sweden*. Lancaster, Pa.: New Era Printing, 1909.

Arnstberg, Karl-Olov. *Datering av knuttimrade hus i Sverige*. Stockholm: Nordiska Museet, 1976.

Arthur, Eric, and Witney, Dudley. *The Barn: A Vanishing Landmark in North America*. Toronto: M. F. Feheley Arts Company, 1972.

Attebury, Jennifer Eastman. "Log Construction in the Sawtooth Valley of Idaho." *Pioneer America* 8, no. 1 (January 1976): 36–46.

Baláš, Emanuel, and Klíma, Vladimir. "Vesnické stavby v okrese votickém." *Český Lid* 4 (1954): 156–68.

Bartenev, Igor A., and Fyodorov, B. *North Russian Architecture*. Translated by Kathleen Cook. Moscow: Progress Publishers, 1972.

Bastian, Robert W. "Indiana Folk Architecture: A Lower Midwestern Index." *Pioneer America* 9, no. 2 (December 1977): 115–36.

———. "Southeastern Pennsylvania and Central Wisconsin Barns: Examples of Independent Parallel Development?" *Professional Geographer* 27 (1975): 200–204.

Bealer, Alex W., and Ellis, John O. *The Log Cabin: Homes of the North American Wilderness*. Barre, Mass.: Barre Publishing, 1978.

Beck, Abraham Reinke. "The Moravian Graveyards of Lititz, Pennsylvania, 1744–1905." *Transactions of the Moravian Historical Society* 7 (1905): 215–336.

Bernert, Karl. *Denkmale in Kreis Löbau* (a series of 12-page pamphlets, including "Volksbaukunst, 1. Teil," 1978; "Volksbaukunst, 2. Teil," 1978; "Ober- und Niedercunnersdorf," 1980; "Eibau, Oberoderwitz, Ruppersdorf, Walddorf," 1981; "Friedersdorf, Neusalza-Spremberg,

Schönbach," 1981). Löbau, G.D.R.: Rat des Kreises Löbau, Abteilung Kultur, 1978, 1980, 1981.

Bernheim, G. D. *History of the German Settlements and of the Lutheran Church in North and South Carolina*. Philadelphia: Lutheran Book Store, Sherman and Company, Printers, 1872.

Bielenstein, August. *Die Holzbauten und Holzgeräte der Letten. Ein Beitrag zur Ethnographie, Culturgeschichte und Archaeologie der Völker Russlands im Westgebiet*, part 1. St. Petersburg, Russia: n.p., 1907.

Billingsley, John B. "A Trip to Texas." Edited by Robert L. and Pauline Jones. *Texana* 7 (1969): 201–19.

"Blockwand." *Wasmuths Lexikon der Baukunst*. Vol. 1. Berlin: Verlag Ernst Wasmuth, 1929. Pp. 552–54.

Boëthius, Gerda. *Studier i den nordiska timmerbyggnadskonsten från vikingatiden till 1800 talet*. Stockholm: Fritzes Hovbokhandel i Distribution (Studier från Zornska Institutet för Nordisk och Jämförande Konsthistoria vid Stockholms Högskola, V), 1927.

Bolzius, Johann M. "Johann Martin Bolzius Answers a Questionnaire on Carolina and Georgia." Translated and edited by Klaus G. Loewald, Beverly Starika, and Paul S. Taylor. *William and Mary Quarterly*, third series, vol. 14 (1957): 218–61; vol. 15 (1958): 228–52.

Brandt, Lawrence R., and Braatz, Ned E. "Log Buildings in Portage County, Wisconsin: Some Cultural Implications." *Pioneer America* 4, no. 1 (January 1972): 29–39.

Brantley, R. L. "The Salzburgers in Georgia." *Georgia Historical Quarterly* 14 (1930): 214–24.

Brecht, Samuel K., ed. *The Genealogical Record of the Schwenkfelder Families, Seekers of Religious Liberty Who Fled From Silesia to Saxony and Thence to Pennsylvania in the Years 1731 to 1737*. New York and Chicago: Rand McNally and Company, for the Board of Publication of the Schwenkfelder Church, 1923.

Brumbaugh, G. Edwin. "Colonial Architecture of the Pennsylvania Germans." *Pennsylvania German Society* 41 (1933): part 2, pp. 5–60 plus 105 plates.

———. "Continental Influence on Early American Architecture." *American-German Review* 9, no. 3 (February 1943): 7–9, 37.

Bucher, Robert C. "The Continental Log House." *Pennsylvania Folklife* 12, no. 4 (Summer 1962): 14–19.

———. "The Swiss Bank House in Pennsylvania." *Pennsylvania Folklife* 18, no. 2 (Winter 1968–69): 2–11.

Buffington, Albert F. "Pennsylvania German: Its Relation to Other German Dialects." *American Speech* 14 (1939): 276–86.

Buzek, Ladislav, and Langer, Jiří, eds. *Das Valachische Freilichtmuseum*. Translated by Jiří Vašenda. Published for the Valašské Muzeum v Přírodě, Rožnov pod Radhoštěm, Czechoslovakia. Ostrava, Czechoslovakia: Profil, 1976.

Callaway, James E. *The Early Settlement of Georgia*. Athens: University of Georgia Press, 1948.

Candler, Allen D., comp. and ed. *The Colonial Records of Georgia*. Vol. 1. Atlanta: Franklin Printing and Publishing Company, 1904.

Carlisle, Ronald C. *An Architectural Study of Some Log Structures in the Area of the Yatesville Lake Dam, Lawrence County, Kentucky*. N.p.: Department of the Army, Huntington District, Corps of Engineers, Huntington, West Virginia, 1978.

Carson, Cary; Barka, Norman F.; Kelso, William M.; Stone, Garry W.; and Upton, Dell. "Impermanent Architecture in the Southern American Colonies." *Winterthur Portfolio* 16 (1981): 135–96.

Carter, W. C., and Glossbrenner, A. J. *History of York County, from Its Erection to the Present Time*. Harrisburg, Pa.: Aurand Press, 1930.

Carter, William. *Ghost Towns of the West*. Menlo Park, Ca.: Lane Publishing Company, 1978.

Chappell, Edward A. "Acculturation in the Shenandoah Valley: Rhenish Houses of the Massanutten Settlement." *Proceedings of the American Philosophical Society* 124 (1980): 54–89.

Chotek, Karel. "Staré Typy Valašského Domu." *Národopisný Věstník* 11 (1916): 133–45.

Clay, Jehu C. *Annals of the Swedes on the Delaware*. Philadelphia: F. Foster, 1858.

Clayton, W. Woodford. *History of Davidson County, Tennessee*. Philadelphia: J. W. Lewis, 1880.

Clemson, Donovan. *Living with Logs: British Columbia's Log Buildings and Rail Fences*. Saanichton, B.C.: Hancock House Publishers, 1974.

Collins, Lewis. *History of Kentucky*. 2 vols. Covington, Ky.: Collins & Co., 1874.

Czajkowski, Jerzy, ed. *Open-Air Museums in Poland*. Translated by Elzbieta Goździak and Jolanta Rogalińska. Biblioteka Muzeum Narodowego Rolnictwa w Szreniawie. Poznań: Państwowe Wydawnictwo Rolnicze i Leśne, 1981.

Demek, Jaromír, and Střída, Miroslav. *Geography of Czechoslovakia*. Prague: Academia, 1971.

Dethlefsen, Richard. *Bauernhäuser und Holzkirchen in Ostpreussen*. Berlin: Ernst Wasmuth, 1911.

Deutschmann, Eberhard. *Lausitzer Holzbaukunst, unter besonderer Würdigung des sorbischen Anteils*. Bautzen: Domowina-Verlag (Schriftenreihe des Instituts für Sorbische Volksforschung, No. 11), 1959.

Dornbusch, Charles H., and Heyl, John K. *Pennsylvania German Barns*. Pennsylvania German Folklore Society Yearbook Vol. 21, 1956. Allentown, Pa.: Schlechter's, 1958. Pp. 1–299.

Dunlap, A. R., and Moyne, E. J. "The Finnish Language on the Delaware." *American Speech* 27 (1952): 81–90.

Durnbaugh, Donald F., ed. *The Brethren in Colonial America*. Elgin, Ill.: The Brethren Press, 1967.

Eller, E. M. *The Houses of Peace, Being a Historical, Legendary, and Contemporary Account of the Moravians and their Settlement of Salem in North Carolina*. London and Edinburgh: Fleming H. Revell Company, 1937.

Ennals, Peter M. "Nineteenth-Century Barns in Southern Ontario." *Canadian Geographer* 16 (1972): 256–70.

Ensminger, Robert F. "A Comparative Study of Pennsylvania and Wisconsin Forebay Barns." *Pennsylvania Folklife* 32, no. 3 (Spring 1983): 98–114.

———. "A Search for the Origin of the Pennsylvania Barn." *Pennsylvania Folklife* 30, no. 2 (Winter 1980–81): 50–69.

Erixon, Sigurd. "Är den nordamerikanska timringstekniken överförd från Sverige?" *Folkliv* 19 (1955–56): 56–68.

———. "Byggnadsskicket hos svenska bönder under medeltiden, huvudsakligen i belysning av nyare tidens material." *Nordisk Kultur* 17 (1952): 284–347.

———. "The North-European Technique of Corner Timbering." *Folkliv* 1 (1937): 13–61.

———. "Schwedische Holzbautechnik in vergleichender Beleuchtung." *Liv och Folkkultur* 8 (1957): 42–112.

———. *Svensk byggnads kultur: Studier och skildringar belysande den svenska byggnadskulturens historia*. Stockholm: Aktiebolaget Bokverk, 1947.

Euzebiusz gil Muzeum wsi Opolskiej w Opolu-Bierkowicach, Przewodnik. Opole-Bierkowice: n.p., 1981.

Evans, E. Estyn. "The Cultural Geographer and Folklife Research." In Richard M. Dorson, ed., *Folklore and Folklife: An Introduction*. Chicago: University of Chicago Press, 1972. Pp. 516–32.

———. "Culture and Land Use in the Old West of North America." *Heidelberger Geographische Arbeiten*, no. 15 (1966): 72–80.

———. "The Scotch-Irish: Their Cultural Adaptation and Heritage in the American Old West." In E. E. R. Green, ed., *Essays in Scotch-Irish History*. London: Routledge and Kegan Paul, 1969. Pp. 69–86.

Evjen, John O. *Scandinavian Immigrants in New York, 1630–1674*. Minneapolis: K. C. Holter Publishing Company, 1916.

Faust, Albert B., and Brumbaugh, Gaius M. *Lists of Swiss Emigrants in the Eighteenth Century to the American Colonies*. 2 volumes. Washington, D.C.: National Genealogical Society, 1920, 1925.

Forsblom, Valter W. "Allmogebyggnader i Esse." *Skrifter utgivna av Svenska Litteratursällskapet i Finland* 217 (1931): 1–73.

Foster, George M. *Culture and Conquest: America's Spanish Heritage*. New York: Wenner-Gren Foundation for Anthropological Research, 1960.

Franke, Heinrich. *Ostgermanische Holzbaukultur und ihre Bedeutung für das deutsche Siedlungswerk*. Breslau: Wilh. Gottl. Korn Verlag, 1936.

Fries, Adelaide L. "The Moravian Contribution to Colonial North Carolina." *North Carolina Historical Review* 7 (1930): 1–14.

———. *The Moravians in Georgia, 1735–1740*. Raleigh, N.C.: Edwards and Broughton, 1905.

———. *Records of the Moravians in North Carolina*. 11 volumes. Raleigh, N.C.: Edwards and Broughton, State Department of Archives and History, 1922–69.

———. *The Road to Salem*. Chapel Hill: University of North Carolina Press, 1944.

Geramb, Viktor. "Die geographische Verbreitung und Dichte der ostalpinen Rauchstuben." *Wiener Zeitschrift für Volkskunde* 30 (1925): 70–123.

———. "Die Kulturgeschichte der Rauchstuben: Ein Beitrag zur Hausforschung." *Wörter und Sachen* 9 (1924): 1–67.

Gettys, Marshall. "The Dogtrot Log Cabin in Oklahoma." *Outlook in Historic Conservation*, January/February, 1981, unpaginated.

———, and Hughes-Jones, Alicia. "Log Pens and Lifestyles: The Aylesworth Photographic Collection." *Bulletin of the Oklahoma Anthropological Society* 30 (1981): 51–66.

Gibson, James R., ed. *European Settlement and Development in North America: Essays on Geographical Change in Honour and Memory of Andrew Hill Clark*. Toronto and Buffalo: University of Toronto Press, 1978.

Glassie, Henry. "A Central Chimney Continental Log House." *Pennsylvania Folklife* 18, no. 2 (Winter 1968–69): 32–39.

———. "The Double-Crib Barn in South-Central Pennsylvania." *Pioneer America* 1, no. 1 (January 1969): 9–16; 1, no. 2 (July 1969): 40–45; 2, no. 1 (January 1970): 47–52; 2, no. 2 (July 1970): 23–34.

———. "Eighteenth-Century Cultural Process in Delaware Valley Folk Building." *Winterthur Portfolio* 7 (1972): 29–57.

———. "The Old Barns of Appalachia." *Mountain Life and Work* 41, no. 2 (Summer 1965): 21–30.

———. *Pattern in the Material Folk Culture of the Eastern United States*. Philadelphia: University of Pennsylvania Press, 1968.

———. "The Pennsylvania Barn in the South." *Pennsylvania Folklife* 15, no. 2 (Winter 1965–66): 8–19; 15, no. 4 (Summer 1966): 12–25.

———. "The Types of the Southern Mountain Cabin." In Jan H. Brunvand, ed., *The Study of American Folklore: An Introduction*. New York: W. W. Norton Company, 1968. Pp. 338–70.

Gnann, Pearl R. *Georgia Salzburger and Allied Families*. Easley, S.C.: Southern Historical Press, 1956.

Goins, Charles R., and Morris, John W. *Oklahoma Homes, Past and Present*. Norman: University of Oklahoma Press, 1980.

Gritzner, Charles F. "Log Housing in New Mexico." *Pioneer America* 3, no. 2 (July 1971): 54–62.

Grundmann, Günther, and Hahm, Konrad. *Schlesien: Text und Bildersammlung mit 241 Bildern* (vol. 8 of the series Deutsche Volkskunst). München: Delphin Verlag, 1926.

Gschwend, Max. "Bäuerlicher Hausbau." Section 37 in Eduard Imhof (director), *Atlas der Schweiz*. Wabern-Bern: Verlag der Eidgenössischen Landestopographie, 1966.

———. "Bäuerliche Haus- und Hofformen." Sections 36 and 36a in Eduard Imhof (director), *Atlas der Schweiz*. Wabern-Bern: Verlag der Eidgenössischen Landestopographie, 1965.

———. *Schwyzer Bauernhäuser*. Bern: Paul Haupt, 1957.

Gunderson, Robert G. *The Log Cabin Campaign*. Lexington: University of Kentucky Press, 1957.

Hagen, Ernest S. "Herrnhut as It Is Today." *The Pennsylvania-German* 10, no. 8 (August 1909): 391–93.

Hahr, August. *Architecture in Sweden*. Stockholm: Alb. Bonniers Boktryckeri, 1938.

Hamilton, J. Taylor. *A History of the Church Known as the Moravian Church or the Unitas Fratrum or the Unity of the Brethren During the Eighteenth and Nineteenth Centuries*. Bethlehem, Pa.: Times Publishing Company, 1900.

———, and Hamilton, Kenneth G. *History of the Moravian Church: The Renewed Unitas Fratrum, 1722–1957*. Bethlehem, Pa., and Winston-Salem, N.C.: Interprovincial Board of Christian Education, Moravian Church in America, 1967.

Hansen, Hans Jürgen, ed. *Architecture in Wood: A History of Wood Building and Its Techniques in Europe and North America*. Translated by Janet Seligman. New York: Viking Press, 1971.

Harris, R. Cole. "The Simplification of Europe Overseas." *Annals of the Association of American Geographers* 67 (1977): 467–83.

Hart, John F., and Mather, Eugene C. "The American Fence." *Landscape* 6, no. 3 (Spring 1957): 4–9.

Härtel, Hans. *Ländliche Baukultur am Rande der Mittelsudeten als Beitrag zur Landesbaupflege in Schlesien* (Jahrgang 6 of *Schlesische Heimat*). Breslau: Schlesien-Verlag, 1941.

Hartz, Louis. *The Founding of New Societies: Studies in the History of the United States, Latin America, South Africa, Canada, and Australia*. New York: Harcourt, Brace and World, 1964.

Hasalová, Věra, and Vajdiš, Jaroslav. *Folk Art of Czechoslovakia*. Translated by Ivo Dvořák. New York: Arco Publishing Company, 1974.

Helmigk, Hans Joachim. *Oberschlesische Landbaukunst um 1800*. Berlin: Verlag für Kunstwissenschaft, 1937.

Hofer, J. M. "The Georgia Salzburgers."

Georgia Historical Quarterly 18 (1934): 99–117.
Holder, Edward M. "Social Life of the Early Moravians in North Carolina." *North Carolina Historical Review* 11 (1934): 167–84.
"Holzbaukunst." *Wasmuths Lexikon der Baukunst*. Vol. 3. Berlin: Verlag Ernst Wasmuth, 1931. P. 126.
Hopple, Lee C. "European Religious and Spatial Origins of the Pennsylvania Dutch." *Pennsylvania Folklife* 28, no. 4 (Summer 1979): 2–11.
_____. "Germanic European Origins and Geographical History of the Southeastern Pennsylvania Amish." *Pennsylvania Folklife* 31, no. 2 (Winter 1981–82): 69–86.
_____. "Spatial Organization of the Southeastern Pennsylvania Plain Dutch Group Culture Region to 1975." *Pennsylvania Folklife* 29, no. 1 (Autumn 1979): 13–26.
_____. "Spatial History of the Schwenkfelders." *Pennsylvania Geographer* 13 (December 1975): 2–17.
Howland, Garth A. "Reconstructional Problems Associated with the Moravian Buildings in Bethlehem." *Transactions of the Moravian Historical Society* 13, parts 3 and 4 (1944): 174–280.
Hrejsa, Ferdinand. "Sborové jednoty bratrské." *Reformační Sborník* 5 (1935): 17–79; 6 (1937): 10–111; 7 (1939): 10–114.
Hudson, John. "Frontier Housing in North Dakota." *North Dakota History* 42 (Fall 1975): 4–15.
Hughes-Jones, Alicia, and Gettys, Marshall. "Single Pen Log Cabins in Oklahoma." *Outlook in Historic Conservation*, May/June, 1981, unpaginated.
Hulan, Richard H. "The Dogtrot House and Its Pennsylvania Associations." *Pennsylvania Folklife* 26 (Summer 1977): 25–32.
_____. "Middle Tennessee and the Dogtrot House." *Pioneer America* 7, no. 2 (July 1975): 37–46.
Hurst, John F. "The Salzburger Exiles in Georgia." *Harper's New Monthly Magazine* 85 (1892): 392–99.
Hutslar, Donald A. *The Log Architecture of Ohio*. Columbus: Ohio Historical Society, 1977.

Jeffers, Jack. *A Photographic Documentary of the Blue Ridge Mountains*. Waynesboro, Va.: McClung Printers, 1973.
Johnson, Amandus. "Sweden Gave America the Rail Fence." *American Swedish Monthly* 49, no. 6 (June 1955): 6–7, 29.
_____. *The Swedish Settlements on the Delaware, 1638–1664*. 2 volumes. Reprint, Baltimore: Genealogical Publishing Company, 1964 (original edition 1911).
Johnston, David E. *A History of Middle New River Settlements and Contiguous Territory*. Huntington, W.V.: Standard Printing and Publishing, 1906.
Johnston, Frances B., and Waterman, Thomas T. *The Early Architecture of North Carolina: A Pictorial Survey*. Chapel Hill: University of North Carolina Press, 1941.
Jones, Charles C., Jr. *The Dead Towns of Georgia*. Savannah: Morning News Steam Printing House, 1878.
Jones, George F., ed. *Henry Newman's Salzburger Letterbooks*. Athens: University of Georgia Press, 1966.
_____, ed., and Lacher, Hermann J., trans. *Detailed Reports on the Salzburger Emigrants Who Settled in America*. Vol. 1. Athens: University of Georgia Press, 1968.
Jordan, John W. "Moravian Immigration to Pennsylvania, 1734–1765." *Pennsylvania Magazine of History and Biography* 33 (1909): 228–48.
_____. "Moravian Immigration to Pennsylvania, 1734–1767, with Some Account of the Transport Vessels." *Transactions of the Moravian Historical Society* 5 (1895): 49–90.
_____. "Note on the Moravian Church in Lebanon County." *Pennsylvania Magazine of History and Biography* 9 (1885): 113–14.
Jordan, Terry G. "Alpine, Alemannic, and American Log Architecture." *Annals of the Association of American Geographers* 70 (1980): 154–80.
_____. "A Forebay Bank Barn in Texas." *Pennsylvania Folklife* 30, no. 2 (Winter 1980–81): 72–77.
_____. "Log Corner Notching in Texas." In Francis E. Abernethy, ed., *Built in Texas*.

Waco, Tex.: E-Heart Press, 1979. Pp. 78–83.

———. "Log Corner-Timbering in Texas." *Pioneer America* 8, no. 1 (January 1976): 8–18.

———. "Moravian, Schwenkfelder, and American Log Construction." *Pennsylvania Folklife* 33, no. 3 (Spring 1984): 98–124.

———. "A Reappraisal of Fenno-Scandian Antecedents for Midland American Log Construction." *Geographical Review* 73 (1983): 58–94.

———. *Texas Graveyards: A Cultural Legacy.* Austin: University of Texas Press, 1982.

———. *Texas Log Buildings: A Folk Architecture.* Austin: University of Texas Press, 1978.

———. *Trails to Texas: Southern Roots of Western Cattle Ranching.* Lincoln: University of Nebraska Press, 1981.

Kalm, Pehr. *Pehr Kalms Resa till Norra Amerika.* Helsinki: Mercators Tryckeri, 1929.

———. *Travels into North America.* Translated by John R. Forster. Barre, Mass.: The Imprint Society, 1972.

Kauffman, Henry J. *The American Farmhouse.* New York: Hawthorn Books, 1975.

———. "Literature on Log Architecture: A Survey." *Pennsylvania Dutchman* 7 (1955): 30–34.

———. "Moravian Architecture in Bethlehem." *Pennsylvania Dutchman* 6, no. 4 (1954): 12–19.

Kaups, Matti. "Finnish Log Houses in the Upper Middle West: 1890–1920." *Journal of Cultural Geography* 3, no. 2 (Spring/Summer 1983): 2–26.

———. "A Finnish *Riihi* in Minnesota." *Journal, Minnesota Academy of Science* 38 (1972): 66–71.

———. "A Finnish *Savusauna* in Minnesota." *Minnesota History* 45 (1976): 11–20.

———. "Log Architecture in America: European Antecedents in a Finnish Context." *Journal of Cultural Geography* 2 (1981): 131–53.

Kegley, F. B. *Kegley's Virginia Frontier.* Roanoke: Southwest Virginia Historical Society, 1938.

Keith, Charles P. *Chronicles of Pennsylvania from the English Revolution to the Peace of Aix-la-Chapelle.* 3 volumes. Reprint, Port Washington, N.Y.: Ira J. Friedman, 1969 (originally published 1917).

Kelly, J. Frederick. "A Seventeenth-Century Connecticut Log House." *Old-Time New England* 31, no. 2 (October 1940): 28–40.

Kiefer, Wayne E. "An Agricultural Settlement Complex in Indiana." *Annals of the Association of American Geographers* 62 (1972): 487–506.

Kimball, Fiske. *Domestic Architecture of the American Colonies.* New York: Scribner's, 1922.

Kindig, Joe K., III, et al. *Architecture in York County.* York, Pa.: Historical Society of York County, [ca. 1975].

Kluge, Edward T. "The Moravian Graveyards at Nazareth, Pennsylvania, 1744–1904." *Transactions of the Moravian Historical Society* 7 (1905): 85–207.

Knie, J. G. *Alphabetisch-statistisch-topographische Uebersicht der Dörfer, Flecken, Städte und andern Orte der königl. Preuss. Provinz Schlesien.* 2nd ed. Breslau: Grass, Barth und Comp., 1845.

Kniffen, Fred B. "The American Covered Bridge." *Geographical Review* 41 (1951): 114–23.

———. "Folk Housing: Key to Diffusion." *Annals of the Association of American Geographers* 55 (1965): 549–77.

———. "On Corner Timbering." *Pioneer America* 1, no. 1 (January 1969): 1–8.

———, and Glassie, Henry. "Building in Wood in the Eastern United States: A Time-Place Perspective." *Geographical Review* 56 (1966): 40–66.

Kocher, A. Lawrence. "The Early Architecture of Pennsylvania." *Architectural Record* 48 (1920): 513–30; 49 (1921): 31–47.

Kohnova, Marie J. "The Moravians and Their Missionaries: A Problem in Americanization." *Mississippi Valley Historical Review* 19 (1932): 348–61.

Kolehmainen, Alfred, and Laine, Veijo A. *Suomalainen Talonpoikaistalo.* Helsinki: Helsingissä Kustannusosakeyhtiö Otava, 1979.

Kriebel, Howard Wiegner. *The Schwenk-*

felders in Pennsylvania: A Historical Sketch. Proceedings of the Pennsylvania German Society, vol. 13. Lancaster: Pennsylvania German Society, 1904.

Kuhn, Walter. *Siedlungsgeschichte Oberschlesiens*. Würzburg, West Germany: Oberschlesischer Heimatverlag, 1954.

Kuhns, Oscar. *The German and Swiss Settlements of Colonial Pennsylvania: A Study of the So-Called Pennsylvania Dutch*. New York: Eaton and Mains; Cincinnati: Jennings and Graham, 1901.

Lachnit, Emil. *Deutsche Bauernhäuser aus Mähren und dem böhmisch-mährischen Grenzlande*. Olmütz (Olomouc), Czechoslovakia: L. Kullil, 1937.

Langton, Edward. *History of the Moravian Church: The Story of the First International Protestant Church*. London: George Allen and Unwin, 1956.

Larsen, Esther L. "Pehr Kalm's Observations on the Fences of North America." *Agricultural History* 21 (1947): 75–78.

Lavender, Linda. *Dog Trots and Mud Cats: The Texas Log House*. Fort Worth: Motheral Printing Company, for the North Texas State University Historical Collection, 1979.

Lay, K. Edward. "European Antecedents of Seventeenth and Eighteenth Century Germanic and Scots-Irish Architecture in America." *Pennsylvania Folklife* 32, no. 1 (Autumn 1982): 2–43.

LeBon, J. W., Jr. "The Catahoula Hog Dog: A Folk Breed." *Pioneer America* 3, no. 2 (July 1971): 35–45.

Lehr, John. "The Log Buildings of Ukrainian Settlers in Western Canada." *Prairie Forum* 2 (1980): 183–96.

Leighly, John B. "The Towns of Mälardalen in Sweden: A Study in Urban Morphology." *University of California Publications in Geography* 3 (1928–30): 1–134.

Loewe, Ludwig. *Schlesische Holzbauten*. Düsseldorf: Werner-Verlag, 1969.

Long, Amos, Jr. "Bank (Multi-Level) Structures in Rural Pennsylvania." *Pennsylvania Folklife* 20, no. 2 (Winter 1970–71): 31–39.

———. *The Pennsylvania German Family Farm: A Regional Architectural and Folk Cultural Study of an American Agricultural Community*. Breinigsville, Pa.: Publications of the Pennsylvania German Society, vol. 6, 1972.

Louhi, E. A. *The Delaware Finns; or, the First Permanent Settlements in Pennsylvania, Delaware, West New Jersey and Eastern Part of Maryland*. New York: The Humanity Press, 1925.

Ludwig, G. M. *The Influence of the Pennsylvania Dutch in the Middle West*. The Pennsylvania German Folklore Society, vol. 10 (1945), pp. 1–108. Allentown, Pa.: Schlechter's, 1947.

McRaven, William H. *Life and Times of Edward Swanson*. Nashville and Kingsport: Kingsport Press, 1937.

McWhorter, Lucullus V. *The Border Settlers of Northwestern Virginia from 1768 to 1795*. Hamilton, Ohio: Republican Publishing Company, 1915.

Marshall, Howard W. *Folk Architecture in Little Dixie: A Regional Culture in Missouri*. Columbia: University of Missouri Press, 1981.

Matt, Leonard von, ed. *Uri* (vol. 6 of the series Das Volkserbe der Schweiz). Basel: Urs Graf Verlag, 1946.

Matuszczak, Jósef. *Z Dziejów Architektury Drewnianej na Śląsku*. Bytom, Poland: Rocznik Muzeum Górnośląskiego w Bytomiu, Sztuka, Zeszyt Nr. 5, 1971.

Meginness, John F. *Otzinachson: A History of the West Branch Valley of the Susquehanna*. Philadelphia: B. B. Ashmead, 1857.

Meitzen, August. *Das deutsche Haus*. Berlin: Dietrich Reimer, 1882.

Melicherčík, Andrej, ed. *Československá vlastivěda díl III: Lidová kultura*. Praha: Orbis, 1968.

Mercer, Henry C. "The Origin of Log Houses in the United States." *Old-Time New England* 18, no. 1 (July 1927): 2–20; 18, no. 2 (October 1927): 51–63.

———. "The Origin of Log Houses in the United States." *Papers, Bucks County Historical Society* 5 (1926): 568–83.

Milner, John D. "Germanic Architecture in the New World." *Journal of the Society of Architectural Historians* 34 (1975): 299.

Mitchell, Robert D. "The Formation of Early American Cultural Regions: An Interpretation." In James R. Gibson, ed., *European Settlement and Development in North America: Essays on Geographical Change in Honour and Memory of Andrew Hill Clark.* Toronto: University of Toronto Press, 1978. Pp. 66–90.

Momatiuk, Yva, and Eastcott, John. "Poland's Mountain People." *National Geographic Magazine* 159 (January 1981), pp. 104–29.

Montell, William L., and Morse, Michael. *Kentucky Folk Architecture.* Lexington: University Press of Kentucky, 1976.

Morrison, Hugh. *Early American Architecture, from the First Colonial Settlements to the National Period.* New York: Oxford University Press, 1952.

Moser, Oskar. *Das Bauernhaus und seine landschaftliche und historische Entwicklung in Kärnten.* Klagenfurt, Austria: Verlag des Landesmuseums für Kärnten, 1974.

Mrlian, Rudolf, et al., eds. *Slowakische Volkskunst.* Bratislava: Verlagsanstalt "Tatran," 1953.

Muir, Andrew F., ed. *Texas in 1837: An Anonymous, Contemporary Narrative.* Austin: University of Texas Press, 1958.

Murtagh, William J. *Moravian Architecture and Town Planning: Bethlehem, Pennsylvania, and Other Eighteenth-Century American Settlements.* Chapel Hill: University of North Carolina Press, 1967.

Nelson, Helge. *The Swedes and the Swedish Settlements in North America.* Lund, Sweden: C. W. K. Gleerup, 1943.

Nelson, Vernon H., and Madeheim, Lothar. "The Moravian Settlements of Pennsylvania in 1757: The Nicholas Garrison Views." *Pennsylvania Folklife* 19, no. 1 (Autumn 1969): 2–13.

Neuenschwander, Ed., and Neuenschwander, Cl. *Finnish Architecture and Alvar Aalto.* New York: Praeger, 1954.

Newton, Hester W. "The Industrial and Social Influences of the Salzburgers in Colonial Georgia." *Georgia Historical Quarterly* 18 (1934): 335–53.

Newton, Milton. "Cultural Preadaptation and the Upland South." *Geoscience and Man (Man and Cultural Heritage,* edited by H. F. Walker and W. G. Haag) 5 (1974): 143–54.

———, and Pulliam-DiNapoli, Linda. "Log Houses as Public Occasions: A Historical Theory." *Annals of the Association of American Geographers* 67 (1977): 360–83.

Niederle, Lubor. "Starý selský dům na moravaském Slovensku." *Národopisný Věstník Českoslovanský* 7 (1912): 97–113.

Noble, Allen G. "Barns as Elements of the Settlement Landscape of Rural Ohio." *Pioneer America* 9, no. 1 (July 1977): 63–79.

———, and Geib, M. Margaret. "The Sweitzer Barn." *Places* 3 (November 1976): 11–12.

———, and Seymour, Gayle A. "Distribution of Barn Types in Northeastern United States." *Geographical Review* 72 (1982): 155–70.

Norberg-Schulz, Christian; Suzuki, Makoto; and Futagawa, Yukio. *Wooden Houses.* New York: Harry N. Abrams, 1978.

Nylén, Anna-Maja. *Swedish Handcraft.* Translated by Anne-Charlotte Hanes Harvey. New York: Van Nostrand Reinhold, 1977.

O'Malley, James R., and Rehder, John B. "The Two-Story Log House in the Upland South." *Journal of Popular Culture* 11, no. 4 (Spring 1978): 904–15.

Pacovský, Jaroslav. *Český Ráj.* Praha: Olympia, 1970.

Paddock, B. B., ed. *A Twentieth Century History and Biographical Record of North and West Texas.* 2 volumes. Chicago and New York: Lewis Publishing Company, 1906.

Palm, Hanns. *Haus und Hof in Oberschlesien.* Danzig: Verlag A. W. Kafemann, 1939.

Parsons, William T. "Postscript." *Pennsylvania Folklife* 30, no. 2 (Winter 1980–81): 71.

Paullin, Charles O., and Wright, John K. *Atlas of the Historical Geography of the United States.* Washington, D.C.: Carnegie Institution and the American Geographical Society, 1932.

Pekař, Josef. *Kniha o kosti, kus české historie*. Vol. 1. Praha: Československý Spisovatel, 1970.

Phleps, Hermann. *Alemannische Holzbaukunst*. Edited by Ernst Mix. Wiesbaden: Franz Steiner Verlag, 1967.

———. "Holzbaukunst." *Wasmuths Lexikon der Baukunst*. Vol. 3. Berlin: Verlag Ernst Wasmuth, 1931. Pp. 124–32.

———. *Holzbaukunst: Der Blockbau*. Karlsruhe: Fachblattverlag Dr. Albert Bruder, 1942.

Pillsbury, Richard. "The Europeanization of the Cherokee Settlement Landscape Prior to Removal: A Georgia Case Study." *Geoscience and Man* 23 (1983): 59–69.

———. "Patterns in the Folk and Vernacular House Forms of the Pennsylvania Culture Region." *Pioneer America* 9 (1977): 12–31.

Pražák, Vilém. "Valašský dům pod Makytou." *Národopisný Sborník* 8 (1947): 189–200; 9 (1950): 68–161.

Price, Beulah M. D'Olive. "The Dog-Trot Log Cabin: A Development in American Folk Architecture." *Mississippi Folklore Register* 4, no. 3 (1970): 84–89.

Price, H. Wayne. "The Double-Crib Log Barns of Calhoun County." *Journal of the Illinois State Historical Society* 73, no. 2 (Summer 1980): 140–60.

Prosěk, Josef. *Československo*. Praha: Orbis, 1965.

Radig, Werner. *Frühformen der Hausentwicklung in Deutschland*. Berlin: Henschelverlag, 1958.

Rambo, Ormond, Jr. "The First Pioneers: The Rambo Family." *American Swedish Historical Foundation Yearbook*, 1948, pp. 1–19.

Raup, H. F. "The Fence in the Cultural Landscape." *Western Folklore* 6 (1947): 1–12.

Raymond, Eleanor. *Early Domestic Architecture of Pennsylvania*. New York: William Helburn, 1931.

Rehder, John B.; Morgan, John; and Medford, Joy L. "The Decline of Smokehouses in Grainger County, Tennessee." *West Georgia College Studies in the Social Sciences* 18 (June 1979): 75–83.

Reichel, Levin T. *The Moravians in North Carolina: An Authentic History*. Reprint, Baltimore: Genealogical Publishing Company, 1968 (originally published at Philadelphia in 1857).

Richter, Helmut. "Die Wand des Bauernhauses in Böhmen, Sachsen, Schlesien in Beziehung zum angrenzenden Bayern." *Bayerische Hefte für Volkskunde* 13, no. 3 (1940): 38–42; 13, no. 4 (1940): 60–64.

Ridlen, Susanne S. "Bank Barns in Cass County, Indiana." *Pioneer America* 4, no. 2 (July 1972): 25–43.

Riedl, Norbert F.; Ball, Donald B.; and Cavender, Anthony P. *A Survey of Traditional Architecture and Related Material Folk Culture Patterns in the Normandy Reservoir, Coffee County, Tennessee*. Department of Anthropology Report of Investigations, No. 17. Knoxville: University of Tennessee and Tennessee Valley Authority, 1976.

Roberts, Warren E. "Some Comments on Log Construction in Scandinavia and the United States." In Linda Dégh, Felix Oinas, and Henry Glassie, eds., *Folklore Today: A Festschrift for Richard M. Dorson*. Bloomington: Indiana University Research Center for Language and Semiotic Studies, 1976. Pp. 437–50.

Roucek, Joseph S. "The Moravian Brethren in America." *Social Studies* 43 (1952): 58–61.

Russell, George E. "The Swedish Settlement in Maryland, 1654." *American Genealogist* 54, no. 4 (October 1978): 203–10.

Sauer, Carl O. "The Settlement of the Humid East." *Climate and Man* (1941 Yearbook of Agriculture, United States Department of Agriculture). Washington, D.C.: Government Printing Office, 1941. Pp. 157–66.

Schier, Bruno. *Hauslandschaften und Kulturbewegungen im östlichen Mitteleuropa*. Beitrage zur sudetendeutschen Volkskunde, vol. 21. Reichenberg, Czechoslovakia: Sudetendeutscher Verlag Franz Kraus, 1932.

Schilli, Hermann. *Das Schwarzwaldhaus*. Stuttgart: W. Kohlhammer, 1953.

Schreiber, William I. "The Pennsylvania Dutch Bank Barns in Ohio." *Journal of* the *Ohio Folklore Society* 2 (Spring 1967): 15–28.

Schröder, Karl H., ed. *Geographische Hausforschung im südwestlichen Mitteleuropa.* Tübingen: Tübinger Geographische Studien, Heft 54, im Selbstverlag des Geographischen Instituts der Universität Tübingen, 1974.

Schultze, Augustus. "The Old Moravian Cemetery of Bethlehem, Pennsylvania, 1742–1897." *Transactions of the Moravian Historical Society* 5 (1899): 97–294.

Schweinitz, Edmund de. *The History of the Church Known as the Unitas Fratrum or the Unity of the Brethren.* Bethlehem, Pa.: Moravian Publication Office, 1885.

Shoemaker, Alfred L. *The Pennsylvania Barn.* Lancaster: Pennsylvania Dutch Folklore Center, Franklin and Marshall College, 1955.

Shurtleff, Harold R. *The Log Cabin Myth: A Study of the Early Dwellings of the English Colonists in North America.* Cambridge: Harvard University Press, 1939.

Simonett, Christoph. *Die Bauernhäuser des Kantons Graubünden.* Volume 2: *Wirtschaftsbauten, Verzierung Brauchtum, Siedlungen.* Basel: Verlag Schweizerische Gesellschaft für Volkskunde, 1968.

Skansen, Stockholm: A Short Guide for Visitors. Norrköping, Sweden: AB Trycksaker, 1979.

Sloane, Eric. "The First Covered Bridge in America." *Geographical Review* 49 (1959): 315–21.

Śmiałowski, Rudolf. *Architektura i Budownictwo Pasterskie w Tatrach Polskich.* Krakow: Pánstwowe Wydawn, Naukowe, 1959.

Smith, Elmer L.; Stewart, John G.; and Kyger, M. Ellsworth. *The Pennsylvania Germans of the Shenandoah Valley.* Pennsylvania German Folklore Society, vol. 26, 1962. Allentown, Pa.: Schlechter's, 1964.

Snyder, Karl H. "Moravian Architecture of Bethlehem, Pennsylvania." The White Pine Series, vol. 13, no. 4. New York: R. F. Whitestead, 1927. Pp. 1–24.

Söderberg, Bengt, and Erixon, Sigurd. "Svenska herrgårdar under medeltiden jämte klostrens byggnadsskick." *Nordisk Kultur* 17 (1952): 216–45.

Sømme, Axel. *A Geography of Norden.* Oslo: J. W. Cappelens Forlag, 1960.

Stevens, Bryan J. "The Swiss Bank House Revisited: The Messerschmidt-Dietz Cabin." *Pennsylvania Folklife* 30, no. 2 (Winter 1980–81): 78–86.

Stewart, Janice S. *The Folk Arts of Norway.* Madison: University of Wisconsin Press, 1953.

Štika, Jaroslav. "Bádání o karpatském salašnictví a valašské kolonizaci na Moravě." *Slovenský Národopis* 9 (1961): 513–48.

Stoner, Paula. "Early Folk Architecture of Washington County." *Maryland Historical Magazine* 72 (1977): 512–22.

Swaim, Doug, ed. *Carolina Dwelling: Towards Preservation of Place, in Celebration of the North Carolina Vernacular Landscape.* Raleigh: Student Publications of the School of Design, North Carolina State University, vol. 26, 1978.

Swanton, John R. *The Indians of the Southeastern United States.* Bureau of American Ethnology, Bulletin No. 137. Washington, D.C.: Government Printing Office, 1946.

Swoboda, Otto. *Alte Holzbaukunst in Österreich.* 2 vols. Salzburg, Austria: Otto Müller Verlag, 1975 and 1978.

"Taxables Living within the Jurisdiction of New Castle Court in November, 1677." *Pennsylvania Magazine of History and Biography* 3 (1879): 352–54.

Taylor, Gwynne Stephens. *From Frontier to Factory: An Architectural History of Forsyth County.* Winston-Salem, N.C.: North Carolina Department of Cultural Resources, Division of Archives and History, with Winston Salem/Forsyth County Historic Properties Commission and City-County Planning Board of Forsyth County and Winston-Salem, 1981.

Thayer, William M. *From Log-Cabin to the White House: Life of James A. Garfield.* Boston: James H. Earle, 1881.

Thiede, Klaus. *Alte deutsche Bauernhäuser.* Stuttgart: J. F. Steinkopf, 1963.

Bibliography

Turner, Frederick Jackson. *The Frontier in American History.* New York: Henry Holt & Co., 1921.

United States Bureau of the Census. *Heads of Families at the First Census of the United States taken in the year 1790. North Carolina.* Washington, D.C.: Government Printing Office, 1908.

Upton, Dell. "Vernacular Domestic Architecture in Eighteenth-Century Virginia." *Winterthur Portfolio* 17 (1982): 95–119.

Uttendörfer, Otto. *Alt-Herrnhut.* Herrnhut, Germany: Verlag Missionsbuchhandlung, 1925.

"Värmland." In *Svensk Upplagsbok.* Vol. 31, pp. 1133–57. Malmö: Förlagshuset Norden, 1955.

Vesey-Fitzgerald, Brian. *The British Countryside in Pictures.* London: Odhams Press Ltd., n.d. (reprinted 1946).

Vlach, John M. "The Canada Homestead: A Saddlebag Log House in Monroe County, Indiana." *Pioneer America* 4, no. 2 (July 1972): 8–17.

———. "Form and House Types in American Folk Architecture." In Robert J. Adams, ed., *Introduction to Folklore.* Columbus, Ohio: Collegiate Publishing Company, 1972. Pp. 116–54.

Voigt, Gilbert P. "The German and German-Swiss Element in South Carolina, 1732–1752." Bulletin of the University of South Carolina, No. 113 (1922), pp. 1–60.

Vreim, Halvor. "Norsk byggekunst i middelalderen." *Nordisk Kultur* 17 (1952): 348–70.

Vuorela, Toivo. *Suomalainen kansankulttuuri.* Porvoo, Helsinki, and Juva: Werner Söderström, 1975.

Vydra, Josef. *Lidové stavitelství na Slovensku.* Praha: Jan Štenc, 1925.

Wacker, Peter O. "Relations between Cultural Origins, Relative Wealth, and the Size, Form and Materials of Construction of Rural Dwellings in New Jersey during the Eighteenth Century." In *Géographie historique du Village et de la Maison Rurale.* Pens: Centre National de la Recherche Scientifique, 1979. Pp. 201–30.

———. "Traditional House and Barn Types in New Jersey: Keys to Acculturation, Past Cultureographic Regions, and Settlement History." *Geoscience and Man* 5 (1974): 163–76.

———, and Trindell, Roger T. "The Log House in New Jersey: Origins and Diffusion." *Keystone Folklore Quarterly* 13 (1968): 248–68.

Waterman, Thomas Tileston. *The Dwellings of Colonial America.* Chapel Hill: University of North Carolina Press, 1950.

Webb, Robert. "Detailed Information and Account for those who are Inclined to America and are Interested in Settling in the Province of Pennsylvania." *Pennsylvania Magazine of History and Biography* 49 (1925): 115–40. (Originally published in Dutch at Amsterdam by Jacob Claus, 1686.)

Weiss, Richard. *Häuser und Landschaften der Schweiz.* Erlenbach-Zürich and Stuttgart: Eugen Rentsch Verlag, 1959.

———. "Stallbauten und Heutraggeräte Graubündens in sachgeographischer Betrachtung." In *Sache, Ort und Wort: Jakob Jud zum sechzigsten Geburtstag*, a special issue of *Romanica Helvetica* 20 (1943): 30–48.

Wertenbaker, Thomas J. *The Founding of American Civilization: The Middle Colonies.* New York: Charles Scribner's Sons, 1938.

Weslager, C. A. *The Log Cabin in America from Pioneer Days to the Present.* New Brunswick: Rutgers University Press, 1969.

———. "Log Houses in Virginia during the 17th Century." *Quarterly Bulletin, Archaeological Society of Virginia* 9, no. 2 (1954): 2–8.

———. "Log Houses in Pennsylvania during the Seventeenth Century." *Pennsylvania History* 22 (July 1955): 256–66.

———. "Log Structures in New Sweden during the Seventeenth Century." *Delaware History* 5 (1952): 77–95.

Whitwell, W. L., and Winborne, Lee W. *The Architectural Heritage of the Roanoke Valley.* Charlottesville: University Press of

Virginia, 1982.

Wilhelm, Hubert G. H. "Amish-Mennonite Barns in Madison County, Ohio: The Persistence of Traditional Form Elements." *Ohio Geographers: Recent Research Themes* 4 (1976): 1–8.

———. "The Pennsylvania-Dutch Barn in Southeastern Ohio." *Geoscience and Man* 5 (1974): 155–62.

Williams, Samuel C. "Stephen Holston and Holston River." *East Tennessee Historical Society's Publications*, no. 8 (1936), pp. 26–34.

Wilson, Charles W. "The Salzburger Long-Lots of Colonial Georgia." *Papers of the Twenty-Seventh Annual Meeting, Southeastern Division, Association of American Geographers, 1972.* Vol. 2, *Methodological, Cultural, and Physical*, pp. 134–38. Miami, Fla.: n.p., 1972.

Wilson, Eugene M. "The Single Pen Log House in the South." *Pioneer America* 2, no. 1 (January 1970): 21–28.

Winberry, John J. "The Log House in Mexico." *Annals of the Association of American Geographers* 64 (1974): 54–69.

———. "The Origin and Dispersal of the Shingle Roof: A Preliminary Consideration." In R. L. Singh et al., eds., *Geographic Dimensions of Rural Settlements*. Varanasi, India: National Geographical Society of India, Research Publication No. 16, 1976. Pp. 190–98.

Wonders, William C. "Log Dwellings in Canadian Folk Architecture." *Annals of the Association of American Geographers* 69 (1979): 187–207.

Wright, Martin. "The Antecedents of the Double-Pen House Type." *Annals of the Association of American Geographers* 48 (1958): 109–17.

Wuorinen, John H. *The Finns on the Delaware 1638–1655: An Essay in American Colonial History.* New York: Columbia University Press, 1938.

Wust, Klaus. *The Virginia Germans.* Charlottesville: University Press of Virginia, 1969.

Yates, W. Ross, ed. *Bethlehem of Pennsylvania: The First One Hundred Years, 1741 to 1841.* Bethlehem, Pa.: Bethlehem Chamber of Commerce, 1968.

Yeager, Lyn Allison. *Log Structures in Warren County, Kentucky.* Bowling Green, Ky: Citizens National Bank, 1977.

Yoder, Donald H., ed. "Emigrants from Wuerttemberg: The Adolf Gerber Lists." Pennsylvania German Folklore Society, vol. 10, 1945. Allentown, Pa.: Schlechter's, 1947. Pp. 111–237.

Zelinsky, Wilbur. *The Cultural Geography of the United States.* Englewood Cliffs, N.J.: Prentice-Hall, 1973.

———. "The Log House in Georgia." *Geographical Review* 43 (1953): 173–93.

———. "Walls and Fences." *Landscape* 8, no. 3 (Spring 1959): 14–20.

Zeman, Jarold Knox. *The Anabaptists and the Czech Brethren in Moravia, 1526–1628.* The Hague and Paris: Mouton, 1969.

Unpublished Materials

Calkins, Charles F., and Perkins, Martin C. "The Pomeranian Barn of Southeastern Wisconsin." Unpublished paper read at the annual meeting of the Pioneer America Society at Shakertown, Pleasant Hill, Ky. 4 November 1978.

Candee, Richard M. "Wooden Buildings in Early Maine and New Hampshire: A Technological and Cultural History, 1600–1720." Ph.D. dissertation, University of Pennsylvania, 1976.

Glass, Joseph W. "The Pennsylvania Culture Region: A Geographical Interpretation of Barns and Farmhouses." Ph.D. dissertation, Pennsylvania State University, 1971.

Gordon, Michael H. "The Upland Southern–Lowland Southern Culture Areas: A Field Study of Building Characteristics in Southern Virginia." Ph.D. dissertation, Rutgers University, 1968.

Hulan, Richard H. "The Delaware Valley Double-House and Its European Origin." Unpublished manuscript, 1980.

Jessee, Glenn J. "Culture Contact and Acculturation in New Sweden, 1638–1655." M.A. thesis, College of William and Mary, 1983.

Rau, H. B. Album of photographs. Archives of the Moravian Church, Bethlehem, Pa.

Schünzel, Eva. "Die deutsche Auswanderung nach Nordamerika im 17. und 18. Jahrhundert." Inaugural dissertation, Julius-Maximilians-Universität, Würzburg, West Germany, 1959.

Wright, Martin. "The Log Cabin in the South." M.A. thesis, Louisiana State University, 1950.

―――. "Log Culture in Hill Louisiana." Ph.D. dissertation, Louisiana State University, 1956.

Index

Abernethy, Francis E., x, 110, 111
Adze, 16, 17, 47, 48, 91, 126
Alps: as architectural source area, 147, 149, 151–52; barns in, 11, 101–13; carpentry in, 89, 91, 94, 95, 96; emigrants from, 86, 87, 95, 106, 112; house types in, 98, 99; log buildings in, 13; roofs in, 98
Alsace, 86, 87, 89, 101, 153
Amerindians, 17, 22
Amish, 89, 101, 121
Ångermanland, 42, 72
Appalachians: barns in, 112; diffusion into, 11, 150; houses in, 28, 66, 68
Architecture: American, 14–15, 23–38; barn, 30–38, 75–83, 99–114, 141–45, 149; Fenno-Scandian, 64–83, 149; folk, 3; German, 97–114, 139–45, 149; house, 14–15, 23–30, 64–75, 97–99, 139–41, 149. *See also* Blockhouses; Bridges; Churches
Arkansas, 38, 54
Austria: as architectural source area, 149; barn types in, 101, 103, 105–12; carpentry in, 88–89, 91–97; emigrants from, 86, 87, 95; house types in, 97. *See also* Kärnten; Salzburg; Tirol
Ax, 116; broad-, 47, 126; in hewing logs, 16, 47, 48, 91, 126

Bank barns: Alpine-Alemannic, 99–103, 105, 106, 108, 109; American, 31, 34, 36; British, 102; Fenno-Scandian, 76, 77, 79, 80, 81, 102; in German-Slav borderland, 142–43; source of, 149
Barns, 30–38, 75–83, 99–114, 141–45; Alpine, 99–114, 151; Frankish, 141, 142; tobacco, 21, 38. *See also* Bank barns; Double-crib barn; Drive-in corncrib; Forebays; Four-crib barn; Pennsylvania, barn type; Single-crib barn; Three-bay barn; Transverse-crib barn
Basel-Land (canton), 86, 87
Bavaria, 87, 92, 101, 103, 109
Bern (canton): as architectural source area, 147, 149; barns in, 99, 101, 103, 115; bridges in, 114; carpentry in, 89, 92, 96; emigrants from, 86, 87; location of, 87
Bethlehem, Pa., 43, 119, 122, 125, 132, 139, 152
Bishir, Catherine W., x, 21
Black Forest: as architectural source area, 147; barns in, 99, 101; carpentry in, 90,

92, 95; emigrants from, 86, 148; house type, 98, 99, 154
Blekinge, 42, 47
Blockhouses, 38–39, 75, 146, 149
Bohemia: as architectural source area, 11, 116, 147; barns in, 143, 144–45; carpenters from, 122, 124; carpentry in, 117, 120, 127, 131, 134, 136; emigration from, 116, 117; field research in, 118, 119, 121; house types in, 117, 140; location of, 118; log buildings in, 12; roofs in, 137
Bridges, covered, 39, 97, 114, 149
British. *See* British Isles; English; Scotch-Irish; Welsh
British Isles: as architectural source area, 12, 147, 149, 153; field research in, 12; house types in, 66, 70. *See also* English; Scotch-Irish; Welsh
Broad-ax. *See* Ax
Brumbaugh, Edwin, 3
Butting poles, 22, 59

Cabins, 14, 22
Cades Cove, Tenn., 15, 37, 40, 60–61
Canada. *See* French-Canadians; Ontario; Québec; Ukrainians
Carinthia. *See* Kärnten
Carpentry: Alpine-Alemannic, 89–96; American, 15–21; British, 50, 131, 147, 148, 153; Fenno-Scandian, 43–59, 128, 136, 148, 155; German, 50, 53, 57–58, 89–96, 125–36, 148; Slavic, 125–27, 131, 134, 135, 137
Central-hall house: Alpine, 99; American, 24, 29, 30; British, 155; Fenno-Scandian, 65, 66, 69, 70–71; origin of, 149
Chalet, 98
Cherokee Indians, 17
Chimneys, 22, 23, 28, 153
Chink construction: absence of, 48, 50, 94, 120–21, 129, 131, 132, 134; Alpine, 94–97, 106; American, 17–18; Fenno-Scandian, 47–51; German, 94–97, 126–31; Slavic, 119, 120–21, 126–31; source of, 147. *See also* Chinking
Chinking: Alpine, 95, 97; American, 17, 18, 21, 94; false, 121, 126–30, 140; Fenno-Scandian, 48–50; German, 95, 97, 126–31; Slavic, 120–21, 126–31; source of, 147. *See also* Chink construction
Churches, log, 38, 55, 56, 132, 134
"Continental" house type: in Alps, 99; in America, 24, 26–28, 98–99, 124, 125, 137; in German-Slav borderland, 117, 139–41; in Rhine Plain, 99, 139; origins of, 149
Corncrib. *See* Drive-in corncrib; Single-crib barn
Corner posting: Alpine-Alemannic, 92–95; American, 22, 95; Fenno-Scandian, 62; German, 92–95, 133–36; Slavic, 133–36
Corner timbering. *See* Corner posting; Notching
Creek Indians, 22
"Cumberland" house type: in America, 24, 28, 72–73; origin of, 146, 149; similar to Swedish type, 72–73
Czechoslovakia: field research in, 116, 118. *See also* Bohemia; Czechs; Kineland; Moravia; Slovakia
Czechs: as agents of diffusion, 12; carpentry of, 125; in colonial America, 12. *See also* Moravian Brethren

Dalarna: carpentry in, 45, 46, 47, 53, 54; house types in, 68, 69; location of, 42; log structures in, 10; porches in, 62; as source area, 41, 42
Dalsland: as architectural source area, 147, 149, 154; carpentry in, 51, 53; house types in, 71, 75; location of, 42; settlers from, 41, 42
Danes, 41, 42, 43, 153
Delaware, 50, 63, 148, 150
Delaware Valley: carpentry in, 20, 50, 57, 58; colonization of, 41, 153; diffusion to, 83; as hearth area, 7, 8, 17, 19, 68, 70, 155; house types in, 63–64, 67; sources of settlers in, 45, 71–72, 150
Diamond notch, 21, 53, 54, 146, 147
"Dogtrot" house type: in America, 24, 29, 154–55; origin of, 146, 149; similar Fenno-Scandian type, 67–70; similarity to barn, 112
Double-crib barn: Alpine, 99, 100, 102–6, 108–13; American, 30–32, 34–36, 111; Fenno-Scandian, 61, 76, 77, 78–81; German, 102–13, 141–44; Slavic, 141–44; source of, 146, 149. *See also* Pennsylvania, barn type
Double notch: Alpine-Alemannic, 91–93; American, 56, 154; Fenno-Scandian, 55, 57; German, 91–93, 129, 132; sketch of, 92; Slavic, 133
Double-pen house type, 24, 28–30, 63–73,

Index

99. *See also* Central-hall house; "Cumberland" house type; "Dogtrot" house type; I house type; "Saddlebag" house type
Dovetail notch. *See* Full-dovetail notch; Half-dovetail notch
Drawknife, 47
Drive-in corncrib, 30, 32, 36, 109, 112
Dutch, 150

English: barn types of, 108, 113; carpentry of, 148; as colonial settlers, 12, 68, 150; house types of, 23–25, 63, 70; influence of, 153; type of single-pen, 23–25
Ensminger, Robert F., x, 35, 53, 55, 103, 108
Erixon, Sigurd, 72
Europe: architecture in, 64–83, 97–114, 139–45; carpentry in, 43–59, 88–93, 125–36; central, 86–115; diffusion from, 4–7, 9–13, 146–53; eastern, 116–45; emigration from, 41–43, 86–87, 116, 118, 121–22; northern, 41–85. *See also* Austria; British Isles; Czechoslovakia; Finland; German Democratic Republic; German Federal Republic; Germany; Lithuania; Norway; Poland; Romania; Russia; Sweden; Switzerland

Fences: Alpine, 114; American, 39–40, 84, 85; Fenno-Scandian, 82, 83–84; origins of, 149; post-and-rail, 39, 66, 82–85, 114; worm, 39, 40, 84
Finland: barn types in, 76–83; carpentry in, 45–62; fence types in, 83–84; house types in, 65, 69, 71; porches in, 62; roofs in, 60–61; settlers from, 42, 153. *See also* Karelia; Pohjanmaa; Satakunta; Savo; Uusimaa
Finns: as agents of diffusion, 146–51, 153; in American Midwest, 7, 53, 56, 72; carpentry of, 50, 51, 128, 148, 155; in colonial America, 7, 10, 41, 54, 68, 81, 150–51; dispersal of, 150–51; house plans of, 24–28, 38, 73–74; sources of, 41, 42; in Sweden, 41
First effective settlement, doctrine of, 5, 6, 153–54
Forebays: Alpine, 98–101; American, 31, 35–37, 101; false, 143; Fenno-Scandian, 57, 61, 76–80; German, 98–101, 143, 145; Slavic, 145; source of, 149
Foster, George M., 5
Foundations, 63
Four-crib barn, 32, 36, 38, 101, 149
France. *See* Alsace
French-Canadians, 5, 7, 101, 114
Fribourg (canton), 87, 94
Full-dovetail notch: Alpine-Alemannic, 90–94; American, 19, 20, 131, 133; Fenno-Scandian, 47, 52, 56–58; flared, 92; German, 90–94, 117, 119, 121, 131, 133; sketch of, 20, 92; Slavic, 117, 119, 121, 131, 133

Gables, 147; Alpine-Alemannic, 96, 98; American, 22–23, 60, 137; Fenno-Scandian, 49, 59, 60, 62; German, 96, 98, 120–21, 128, 132, 136; Slavic, 120–21, 128, 136, 138, 142
Georgia: barns in, 112; carpentry in, 17; colonial records of, 113; Hussites in, 121; Salzburgers in, 86, 110, 112–13, 154
German Democratic Republic: barns in, 144–45; field research in, 116, 118, 121. *See also* Germany; Saxony
German Federal Republic: field research in, 87. *See also* Bavaria; Black Forest; Palatinate; Württemberg
Germans: Alpine-Alemannic, 10–11, 86–115, 151–52; barns of, 31, 34–38, 100, 101, 103, 109, 141, 142, 145; carpentry of, 50, 53, 57–58, 131, 132, 148; in colonial America, 7, 10–12, 41–43, 58, 68, 86–87, 121–24, 150–52; eastern, 116–45, 152–53; house types of, 24, 26–28, 97–99, 139–41, 154; northern, 41–43; Swiss-, 86, 87. *See also* "Continental" house type
Germany: as architectural source area, 147, 149; barn types in, 78, 99, 101, 103, 109, 141–45; carpenters from, 43, 124; carpentry in, 88–95, 97, 125–36; eastern, 116–45; emigrants from, 10–11, 42, 118–19, 121; field research in, 87, 118; house types in, 98–99, 139–41, 154; northern, 41, 43; southwestern, 86–114. *See also* Bavaria; Black Forest; German Democratic Republic; German Federal Republic; Palatinate; Saxony; Silesia; Württemberg
Glassie, Henry: and double-crib barn, 102; favors eastern German origin, 11, 12, 116, 125, 126, 130; opposes Fenno-Scandian origin, 10; and forebays, 145; and Pennsylvania barn type, 100, 106, 145
Graubünden: as architectural source area,

149; barn types in, 11, 81, 98, 101, 103–6, 108, 109, 113; carpentry in, 91; emigrants from, 86, 106; location of, 87
Great Plains, 7, 26
Great Valley, 66, 150. *See also* Shenandoah Valley
Gulf Coastal Plain: barn types in, 78; carpentry in, 20; house types in, 29, 67–68, 112

Half-dovetail notch: absence of, 91; American, 17, 18–20; Fenno-Scandian, 58; German, 131–34; hooked, 58; sketch of, 20, 92; Slavic, 131–34; source of, 147
Half-log construction: Alpine-Alemannic, 88–91; American, 16, 17, 46; Fenno-Scandian, 44–46; source of, 147
Half notch: American, 21; Fenno-Scandian, 52–53, 56; German, 132, 133, 135; origin of, 146, 147; sketch of, 21, 53; Slavic, 132, 133
Halland, 42, 46, 47, 62, 77
Hall-and-parlor house, 24, 25, 26, 69, 74
Härjedalen, 45, 50
Harris, R. C., 5
Hartz, Louis, 5
Hatchet, 126
Herrnhut, 117, 118, 119, 124, 152, 153
Herrnhuters. *See* Moravian Brethren
Hewing. *See* Logs, shaping of
Heyl, John K., 100, 106
Hispanic-Americans, 7
Hook notch, 120–21, 129, 132, 133, 134
House types: Alpine-Alemannic, 97, 98–99; American, 14–15, 23–30, 63; Fenno-Scandian, 64–75; of German-Slav borderland, 139–41. *See also* "Continental" house type; "Cumberland" house type; "Dogtrot" house type; Double-pen house type; English, house types of; Hall-and-parlor house; I house type; "Saddlebag" house type; Single-pen house type
Hulan, Richard, x, 67
Hussites. *See* Moravian Brethren

I house type: American, 30, 31; British, 63, 64, 66; Fenno-Scandian, 63–66; origins of, 149
Illinois, 29
Indiana, 19, 101
Iowa, 101

Johnson, Amandus, 43, 84
Jura, 87, 90, 147

Karelia, 42, 45, 50, 51
Kärnten: barns in, 101, 103, 113, 114; carpentry in, 95; emigrants from, 95; fences in, 114; field research in, 89
Kaups, Matti, 72
Kentucky, 19, 151
Kineland: carpenters from, 124; carpentry in, 131, 132; emigrants from, 117, 118, 121, 124; houses in, 120–21; location of, 118; as research area, 118, 119
Kitchens, 26, 38, 75
Knife, 47, 126
Kniffen, Fred B.: favors British origin, 63; favors German origin, 11, 12, 116, 125, 130; and first effective settlement, 5; and I house, 66

Lithuania, 72
Log construction: Alpine-Alemannic, 86–115, 147; American, 7, 8, 14–40, 146–53; as cultural index, 155; Fenno-Scandian, 41–85, 147; French-Canadian, 7; German, 86–145, 147; Hispanic, 7; Slavic, 7, 116–45, 147; as symbol, 3–4. *See also* Barns; Blockhouses; Chink construction; Churches; Corner posting; House types; Logs; Notching; Planking
Logs: notching of, 18–21, 51–59, 91–93, 130–36; shaping of, 15–18, 43–48, 88–91, 125–26
Long, Amos, 102
Luzern (canton): barns in, 101, 108; carpentry in, 89, 92; location of, 87

Meitzen, August, 3
Mercer, Henry, 51
Mexico, 7
Michigan, 7
Midland American culture area, 7, 51; links to Britain, 147, 149, 153; links to central Europe, 86–115, 147, 149, 151–52; links to eastern Europe, 147, 149, 152–53; links to Germany, 147, 149, 151–53; log construction in, 14–40; map of, 8; links to northern Europe, 146–51
Midwest, 19, 31, 80
Mills, 38, 50
Missouri, 19, 29, 69

Moravia: as architectural source area, 11, 116, 147; barns in, 142, 144–45; carpenters from, 124; carpentry in, 119, 127, 131, 132, 134; emigration from, 116, 117; field research in, 118, 119; house types in, 138; location of, 118; roofs in, 137, 139

Moravian Brethren: as agents of diffusion, 12, 116, 126, 135–36, 137, 152–53, 154; in America, 20, 43, 121, 122, 123; carpentry of, 20, 132; in Europe, 11; houses of, 125; source regions of, 117–19. *See also* Bethlehem; Herrnhut; Nazareth

Närke: carpentry in, 46, 55, 57; house types in, 75; location of, 42; settlers from, 41, 42
Nazareth, Pa., 119, 122, 133, 152
New Jersey, 56, 63, 122, 148
New Sweden, 41, 54, 64, 67, 77, 148
Newton, Milton, 6, 155
New York, 84, 86, 122
North Carolina: carpentry in, 19, 20, 21, 53–54, 90, 91, 126; craftsmen in, 124; house types in, 25, 26, 68, 69; settlers in, 20, 43, 113, 122, 152
Norway: barn types in, 61, 77, 78, 79; carpenters from, 41, 43; carpentry in, 50, 51, 54; house types in, 67; roofs in, 61; settlers from, 42, 153
Norwegians: as carpenters, 41, 43; in colonial America, 41, 43, 153; sources of, 42
Notching, 18–21, 51–59, 91–93. *See also* Diamond notch; Double notch; Full-dovetail notch; Half notch; Half-dovetail notch; Hook notch; Saddle notch; Semilunate notch; Single notch; Square notch; and V notch

Ohio, 29, 68, 122
Ohio Valley, 19, 29
Oklahoma, 17, 23, 29
Ontario, 7, 31, 101
Österbotten. *See* Pohjanmaa
Östergötland, 42, 51, 75
Ozark Mountains, 38

Paint, 82, 83, 149
Palatinate, 86, 137
Pennsylvania: barn type, 31, 34–37, 80–81, 100, 103, 104, 106–8, 149; carpentry in, 19, 22, 50, 51, 55, 56, 92, 95, 131, 132, 133, 148; as hearth area, 7, 113, 132; house types in, 26–27, 29, 63, 66–70, 75, 124; immigrants in, 43, 86, 107, 112, 121, 122, 151. *See also* Bethlehem; Delaware Valley; Nazareth
Pillsbury, Richard, 63, 64
Piney Woods, 21
Planking, 15, 44, 47, 88–91, 126; four-sided, 46, 88; source of, 147; two-sided, 15, 44, 45–47, 48, 88
Pohjanmaa (Österbotten), 42, 51
Poland: barns in, 144–45; field research in, 116, 118, 119. *See also* Silesia
Porches, 23, 30, 62–63
Preadaptation, cultural, 6, 153, 155

"Quaker" house. *See* Hall-and-parlor house
Québec, 101

Raup, H. F., 83
Rocky Mountains, 26
Romania, 107
Roofs: Alpine, 96, 98; American, 22–23, 59, 60, 139; bellcast, 138, 139; board, 22, 49, 59, 60, 146, 147; Fenno-Scandian, 59–62; German, 96, 98, 136–39; pent, 117, 120–21, 136, 137, 140; raftered, 23, 59, 96, 137–39, 147, 153; saltbox, 139; Slavic, 136–39; ridgepole and purlin, 22–23, 59–60, 96, 98, 137, 146, 147. *See also* Gables; Shingling
Russia, 50, 153
Russians, 7

"Saddlebag" house type: American, 24, 29, 69; British, 149; Fenno-Scandian, 64, 65, 69, 71–72; source of, 146, 149
Saddle notch: Alpine, 91–93; American, 15, 18–19, 45; Fenno-Scandian, 45, 51, 52; German, 91–93; sketches of, 19, 92; Slavic, 133–35; source of, 146, 147; subtypes of, 19
Salzburg (province): as architectural source area, 149; barns in, 101, 103, 105, 108, 109–13; emigrants from, 86, 87, 112, 154; fences in, 114; location of, 87; Protestants in, 86, 109–13
Sankt Gallen (canton): barns in, 101, 102; carpentry in, 92, 94; emigrants from, 86
Satakunta, 42, 47, 60–61
Savo (Savolax), 42, 45, 71
Saw, 90, 126, 153

Saxony, Kingdom of: as architectural source area, 11, 116; carpenter from, 124; carpentry in, 120–21, 126, 127, 130, 132, 135; field research in, 118; Hussites in, 117; location of, 118; roofs in, 137; Schwenkfelders in, 119. *See also* Herrnhut

Scandinavia. *See* Danes; Norway; Norwegians; Sweden; Swedes

Schaffhausen, 86, 114

Schwenkfelders: as agents of diffusion, 11, 116, 126, 130–31, 137, 152, 154; in America, 121, 123; carpentry of, 124, 138; houses of, 124, 137, 140, 141; migrations of, 119; roofs of, 139; source region of, 118, 119, 122, 129, 132, 140

Scotch-Irish: carpentry of, 50, 131, 148; houses of, 25, 70, 73, 74; influence of, 12, 153; mix with others, 68

Semilunate notch: American, 21, 46; European, 46, 52, 89, 93; sketch of, 92; source of, 147

Seurasaari museum, 47, 60–61, 71, 84

Shed rooms, 23, 30

Shenandoah Valley, 19, 31, 101, 122. *See also* Great Valley

Shingling: Alpine, 96, 110, 111; American, 23, 111; German, 96, 110, 111, 138; Slavic, 138; source of, 147. *See also* Roofs

Siding: American, 18; Fenno-Scandian, 49, 62; source of, 146, 148

Silesia: as architectural source area, 11, 116, 147; barns in, 142, 143, 144–45; carpenters from, 124; carpentry in, 116, 122, 126, 127, 129, 131, 134, 154; emigration from, 116; field research in, 118, 119; house types in, 122, 129; Hussites in, 117, 119; location of, 118; log buildings in, 11, 12, 116; roofs in, 137, 139; Schwenkfelders in, 118, 119; Tirolers in, 107, 143

Single-crib barn: Alpine, 113–15; American, 30, 32, 33; Fenno-Scandian, 80, 81, 83; source of, 146, 149

Single notch, 53, 133

Single-pen houses, 22, 149. *See also* "Continental" house type; English, type of single-pen; Finns, house plans of; Hall-and-parlor house

Skansen museum, 13, 45, 56, 75

Slavs: barns of, 141, 142, 144–45; carpentry of, 125, 126, 127, 131, 134, 135, 137;
houses of, 138, 140–41; influence of, 11–12, 152–53, 155. *See also* Czechs; Russians; Ukrainians; Wends

Slovakia: barns in, 142, 144–45; carpentry in, 126, 131, 132, 134; field research in, 118, 121; location of, 118

Småland, 42, 51, 54, 56, 57, 69

Smokehouses, 38

Södermanland, 41, 42, 74

Solothurn (canton), 86, 89

South Carolina, 113

Springhouses, 38

Square notch: Alpine-Alemannic, 92–94; American, 16, 20–21, 50; evolution of, 53; Fenno-Scandian, 50, 52–57; German, 92–94, 120–21, 132, 133; sketches of, 21, 53, 92; Slavic, 132, 133, 135; source of, 146, 147

Stairs, 98, 105, 106

Sweden: barn types in, 76–83; carpenters from, 41, 43; carpentry in, 45–62; chapter on, 41–85; emigration from, 41, 42, 153; fence types in, 83–84; as hearth area, 147, 149; house types in, 64–75; porches in, 62–63; roofs in, 62; storage sheds in, 10. *See also* Ångermanland; Blekinge; Dalarna; Dalsland; Halland; Härjedalen; Östergötland; Småland; Södermanland; Uppland; Värmland; Västergötland; Västmanland

Swedes: as agents of diffusion, 146–51, 153; carpenters, 41, 43; carpentry of, 43–59, 128, 136, 148; in colonial America, 7, 10, 41–43, 68, 150–51; sources of, 42

Swiss: bank house, 99, 154; carpentry of, 88–98; as emigrants, 86, 87, 101, 106. *See also* Germans; Pennsylvania, barn type; Switzerland

Switzerland: as architectural source area, 147, 149; barns in, 11, 101, 102–6, 108, 109, 113; carpentry in, 88–98; emigrants from, 86, 87, 101, 106, 153. *See also* Basel-Land; Bern; Fribourg; Graubünden; Jura; Luzern; Sankt Gallen; Schaffhausen; Solothurn; Valais; Zug; Zürich

Syncretism, 6, 154–55

Tennessee: barn types in, 37, 39; carpentry in, 15, 91; fence types in, 40; house types in, 28; roofs in, 60–61; Swedish surnames in, 151

Texas: barn types in, 33, 34, 111, 112; carpentry in, 15, 18, 19, 20, 45, 46, 54, 91; fence types in, 85; house types in, 4, 26–27, 29, 69, 72, 73

Three-bay barn, 108, 113

Tirol: barns in, 101, 106, 107, 112; bridges in, 114; carpentry in, 91, 94; emigrants from, 107, 143; fences in, 114; location of, 87

Tools. *See* Adze; Ax; Drawknife; Knife; Saw

Transverse-crib barn: resemblance to Alpine barns, 101, 113; in America, 32, 36; origin of, 149

Turner, Frederick J., 6, 7

Ukrainians, 7

Umgebinde construction, 120–21, 122, 128, 129, 130, 131, 135, 138, 145, 152, 154

United States. *See* Appalachians; Delaware Valley; Great Plains; Great Valley; Gulf Coastal Plain; Midland American Culture Area; Midwest; Ohio Valley; Shenandoah Valley; and individual state entries

Uppland: barn types in, 79; carpentry in, 48, 58; house types in, 66; location of, 42; settlers from, 41, 42

Upton, Dell, 5, 154

Uusimaa (Nyland), 42, 69

V notch: absence of, 91, 130; American, 16, 20, 54, 55; evolution of, 53; Scandinavian, 51–55; sketch of, 92; source of, 146, 147, 154

Valais (Wallis), 87, 93, 106

Värmland: as architectural source area, 147, 149, 154; carpentry in, 45, 46, 51, 53, 55, 58; fence types in, 83; house types in, 71, 73, 75; location of, 42; settlers from, 41, 42

Västergötland: carpentry in, 51, 54; house types in, 75; location of, 42; settlers from, 41, 42

Västmanland, 42, 69, 71, 72

Virginia: carpentry in, 19, 21, 53; dialect in, 70; house types in, 31, 68; Hussites in, 122; Swedes and Finns in, 150; worm fence, 39–40

Walser, 106
Weiss, Richard, 106
Welsh, 70, 148, 153
Wends, 140, 144–45
Wertenbaker, Thomas J., 11
West Virginia, 56, 68
Wright, Martin, 10, 67, 78
Württemberg, 86, 87, 90

Zelinsky, Wilbur, 5, 6, 153, 154
Zug (canton), 87, 101
Zürich (canton), 86, 87, 94, 101